Fighter For Freedom

"... he lives and will live in the memory and gratitude of the wise and good, as a luminary of Science, as a votary of liberty, as a model of patriotism, and as a benefactor of human kind."
—*James Madison on learning of Thomas Jefferson's death.*

This is a stirring portrait of an extraordinary American —Thomas Jefferson—third President of the United States, architect of freedom and democracy. He began his remarkable career as a lawyer, served in the Virginia House of Delegates and subsequently became Governor of Virginia, Ambassador to France, Secretary of State, and President. He wrote his own epitaph, because he hoped to be remembered for three of his contributions to the American nation—author of the Declaration of Independence and the Statute of Virginia for Religious Freedom—and Father of the University of Virginia. Yet curiously enough, most of Jefferson's life was a struggle between his desire for a quiet, scholarly life on his plantation at Monticello and the sacrifices he had to make in order to serve his country.

Professor Padover deftly reveals the personality of Jefferson, the devoted husband and father, the farmer and philosopher, as well as the crises and achievements of his brilliant career as a statesman, in this absorbing, highly readable book. Henry Steele Commager says, *"It is one of the best of the numerous biographies of Jefferson."* R. L. Duffus, in the *New York Times* says, *"A rather unusual combination of sound scholarship . . . with a style that will appeal to the general reader."*

SAUL K. PADOVER

JEFFERSON

Abridged by the author

A MENTOR BOOK

MENTOR
Published by the Penguin Group
Penguin Books USA Inc., 375 Hudson Street,
New York, New York 10014, U.S.A.
Penguin Books Ltd, 27 Wrights Lane,
London W8 5TZ, England
Penguin Books Australia Ltd, Ringwood,
Victoria, Australia
Penguin Books Canada Ltd, 10 Alcorn Avenue,
Toronto, Ontario, Canada M4V 3B2
Penguin Books (N.Z.) Ltd, 182–190 Wairau Road,
Auckland 10, New Zealand

Penguin Books Ltd, Registered Offices:
Harmondsworth, Middlesex, England

Published by Mentor, an imprint of Dutton Signet,
a division of Penguin Books USA Inc.

First Mentor Printing, February, 1952
31

Published as a Mentor Book by arrangement with Harcourt Brace
Jovanovich, Inc. who have authorized this softcover edition.

This edition of *Jefferson* has been especially abridged
by the author to make possible its publication in this form.

 REGISTERED TRADEMARK—MARCA REGISTRADA

Printed in the United States of America

CONTENTS

Introduction to the Mentor Edition
By SAUL K. PADOVER

THIS is the story of an extraordinary man. Today, one hundred and thirty-six years after his death, his stature is greater than ever. One of the marks of Jefferson's greatness is, indeed, the perennial appeal of his unique personality and the enduring freshness of his ideas.

Jefferson, the son of the Virginia frontier, personified the quintessence of American idealism and practicality, and at the same time he was unlike any other American in our history. No man in this or any other country in the Western world—excepting only Leonardo da Vinci—ever matched Jefferson in the range of his activities, in the fertility of his thinking, and in the multiplicity of his interests. The number of things Jefferson did, or knew how to do, still astonishes. He was a mathematician, surveyor, architect, paleontologist, prosodist, lawyer, philosopher, farmer, fiddler and inventor. He set up an educational system; he built a university; he founded a great political party; he helped design the national capital; he was instrumental in establishing America's coinage; he doubled the territory of the United States; he invented machines and gadgets; he collected scientific materials in the fields of zoology, geology and anthropology; he wrote a classic essay on poetry; he codified the legal system of his native State. Everything interested him; nothing was alien to his mind.

One of the principal builders of the American Republic, Jefferson held nearly every important public office and enriched them all with his wisdom, humanity and democratic spirit. He was a Member of Congress, Governor of his State, Ambassador, Secretary of State, Vice President and President twice. Author of the Declaration of Independence and of Virginia's famous statute for religious freedom, as well as founder of the Democratic Party, Jefferson may be considered as a kind of political poet in action.

But over and above his intellectual interests and political activities, Jefferson stands out as the philosopher and theorist of American democracy—probably the foremost this country has produced. In brilliant letters (his total correspondence runs into 18,000 pieces of mail), in essays, in addresses, in conversation, in conferences, Jefferson formulated his ideas of progress, of democratic government, and of human freedom, with a consistency, depth and beauty rarely excelled. Like Abraham Lincoln, who so much resembled him bodily and spiritually, Jefferson was a passionate champion of the rights, freedom and dignity of man. He devoted his whole life to the spread and realization of the democratic ideal. And today his words still glow and still inspire.

"I have sworn upon the altar of God," he said, "eternal hostility against every form of tyranny over the mind of man." And he lived up to his oath.

This book is based upon my biography, *Jefferson*, published exactly ten years ago. I have abbreviated it, eliminated footnotes and other paraphernalia of scholarship, and made certain changes. In this sense, therefore, it is a new book, fresh and timely, as Jefferson himself is fresh and timely. Apart from being the study of a great historic figure, Jefferson's biography also makes good reading as a dramatic story of an exciting life.

CHAPTER ONE

YOUTH

(April 13, 1743-1759)

WHEN Thomas Jefferson was seventy-seven years old he put down on paper, for the information of his family, a few autobiographical remarks:

> The tradition in my father's family was that their ancestor came to this country from Wales, and from near the mountain of Snowdon, the highest in Gr[eat] Br[itain]. I noted once a case from Wales, in the law reports where a person of our name was either pl[aintiff] or def[endant] and one of the same name was Secretary to the Virginia company. These are the only instances in which I have met with the name in that country. . . . The first particular information I have of any ancestor was my grandfather. . . . He had three sons, Thomas who died young, Field who settled on the waters of Roanoke and left numerous descendants, and Peter my father, who settled on the lands I still own called Shadwell adjoining my present residence. He was born Feb. 29, 1707/08, and intermarried 1739, with Jane Randolph, of the age of 19. . . . They [the Randolph family] trace their pedigree far back in England and Scotland, to which let every one ascribe the faith & merit he chooses.

Peter Jefferson, Thomas's father, was one of the mighty men who broke the wilderness. His physical strength was prodigious; he could "head up" (raise to an upright position) two 1,000-pound hogshead of tobacco at one time. Thomas Jefferson used to tell his children how when three strong slaves were trying vainly to tear down an old shed with a rope, his father seized the rope and pulled it apart with one mighty jerk.

Peter Jefferson was in the great American tradition, self-made and self-educated. Intellectually and physically he "improved himself" in the same way that his son, who was fortunate enough to inherit an estate, was to do all his life. Peter mastered the practical art of surveying and became deputy surveyor of Albemarle County. In 1751 Jefferson and Joshua Fry, a professor of mathematics in William and Mary College, compiled a "Map of Inhabited Parts of Virginia." By this time Peter Jefferson was the wealthiest and most respected squire in the county. He succeeded Fry as County Lieutenant and Burgess.

Wealth, which meant land and slaves, Thomas Jefferson' father acquired the hard way. He cleared fields, surveyed un broken land, felled trees. Land was cheap in frontier Virginia

Peter Jefferson achieved social position at thirty-one, b marrying into the Virginia aristocracy. He had met Jane daughter of Isham Randolph, when she was seventeen. Having obtained from Jane Randolph the promise to marry him, Peter Jefferson rode into the dense forest and cleared 1,000 acres o land on the River Anna (Rivanna). After two years he had his farm cleared and a house built. Then he returned to Dungeness, on the north bank of the James, and claimed his bride.

Jane Randolph, Thomas Jefferson's mother, came from a family whose tree was ponderous with pedigrees. Throughout his life Thomas Jefferson, who loved and admired his father. rarely mentioned his mother. She was an amiable lady who gave birth to ten children, many of whom died young.

2

On April 2 (13, New Style), 1743, Jane Randolph Jefferson, at the age of twenty-three, gave birth to Thomas. He was her third child in three years, the other two being girls. The exact spot where Thomas Jefferson was born is not known, although a stone is supposed to mark the site. Shadwell, Thomas's birthplace, was a large wooden farm structure one and a half stories high with a red outside chimney; it was located in Albemarle County, about five miles east of Charlottesville.

The Jefferson family was hard-working, God-fearing, and affectionate. Peter Jefferson was a tender and warmhearted man. His house was always open to friends and to the widely scattered neighbors who were in the habit of coming for advice and hospitality. Even the Indians, whose distrust for the white man was not without sufficient cause, found a friend in Peter Jefferson and stopped to visit Shadwell on their way to Williamsburg, the capital of the colony. In after years Thomas Jefferson, who inherited from his father his generosity and kindness, recalled how those visiting Indians made an indelible impression upon him as a youth.

. When not working or entertaining, Peter Jefferson devoted his hours to reading. In his library were well-worn sets of the *Spectator*, of Shakespeare, of Swift and Pope.

Peter applied himself to molding his only son, who came to resemble him in face and figure, in his own image. The father developed in young Thomas the spirit of discipline and hard work. Peter taught his son to read and write, to keep accounts, and to work systematically. "Never," Peter was in the habit of saying, "ask another to do for you what you can do for yourself."

The father also set his impressionable boy an example of vigorous physical out-of-doors life. Thomas learned to ride, to shoot, to paddle a canoe on the Rivanna, and to hunt deer and turkey. His lean young body grew to marvelous health and endurance.

Tom did not ride and shoot and canoe only; he also studied diligently. His education consisted of the typical classical curriculum of the period.

Tom mastered languages, both classical and modern, with great ease. He read Homer in his canoe trips down the Rivanna and Virgil while lying under an oak tree.

CHAPTER TWO

STUDENT

(1760-1767)

PETER JEFFERSON died when Thomas was fourteen, leaving him the only grown up male in a family consisting of an infant boy and seven women, his mother and six sisters.[1] Years afterward he recalled that, upon his father's death, the "whole care & direction of myself was thrown on myself entirely, without a relation or friend qualified to advise or guide me."

Young Thomas decided, in typical American fashion, that the best way to improve his mind and strengthen his character was to go away to college. To a Virginian of Thomas Jefferson's social position, college in those days meant William and Mary at Williamsburg.

In December, 1759, Thomas bade good-by to his family at Shadwell and took the long road to Williamsburg. The distance was about 120 miles. Midway between Shadwell and Williamsburg there was a little place on the Pamunkey River called Hanover. Today Hanover is a metropolis of 75 people. It was probably not much bigger in 1760, although it boasted a court house and a tavern (Shelton's, made famous by Patrick Henry who had married the tavern-keeper's daughter). At Hanover was the home of Colonel Nathan Dandridge, and there the young student from Shadwell stopped off for the Christmas holidays.

The festivities over, "Long Tom," as his friends called him affectionately, left gay Hanover for an even gayer Williamsburg. Tom had made, as usual, an excellent impression upon both men and women. He was not handsome. Standing well over six feet, the boy from the woods of western Virginia was lean, bony, roughhewn, and broad-shouldered, but surprisingly slender. His neck was long and thin, and his face, like his hair, had a reddish tint, not unlike the soil of his native county. The cheeks were lean and the jaw square and firm, but the

---

[1] Thomas Jefferson's younger brother Randolph was a child of two when their father died. Although Randolph Jefferson lived to be sixty (1755-1815), he seems not to have played a great role.

ride-winged nose was somewhat feminine and inquisitive.
Quizzical hazel eyes, set deep, were flanked by bushy temples.
He danced gracefully, and his walk had the lightness of one
seasoned in the forest. His voice, which he always kept on a
low conversational level—the perpetual charmer—was soft
like his eyes, and well modulated.

Williamsburg, sitting placidly on the tongue of land between
the York and James rivers, was only a few miles from where
the broad Chesapeake joins the Atlantic. The town was not
large, but to the boy from Shadwell it was something of a
metropolis. Named in honor of William III and made the
capital of Virginia in the last year of the seventeenth century,
Williamsburg, when young Jefferson got there, had about two
hundred one-story houses and a population of around 1,000
whites and blacks. The capital of the royal colony had not yet
achieved the dignity of sidewalks or the refinement of sewers.
Grass grew in the half-dozen streets.

Despite its miniature size, the town was the political, social,
and cultural center of the upper South. Life was gay and hos-
pitable. The main stem was the Duke of Gloucester Street.
Along this street were some fine houses, including those com-
binations of bar-hotel-restaurant known as taverns, a court-
house, and Bruton Parish Church, supposed now to be the oldest Espiscopal church in the country. At the head of the Duke
of Gloucester Street snuggled three or four buildings, collec-
tively known as William and Mary College. At the end, and
within view of the college, was the capitol. Off on the side stood
the Governor's Palace. College, capitol, and palace formed a
tight triangle, knit by social ties and enclosing an animated
world, as Tom soon learned.

2

The registers show that Thomas Jefferson entered William
and Mary on March 25, 1760.

The college, to quote one of its historians, was then "rife
with dissensions and discontent," probably because it mixed
politics with theology. The Reverend Thomas Dawson was a
case in point. For £200 sterling per annum, the Reverend Mr.
Dawson united in his person the offices of president of the
college, commissary, member of the Council, and rector of
Bruton Church. His colleagues accused him of being a stooge
for Fauquier, the genial Acting Governor of the colony, which
was very likely. Also the Reverend Mr. Dawson was not in-
frequently drunk, a failing which he freely admitted to the
college board. Governor Fauquier, however, neatly defended
the president's drinking, on the ground that the intrigues of his
faculty drove him to it.

The faculty was full of Reverends. The Reverend Emanuel Jones was master of the Indian school (in 1754 eight of the seventy-five students at the college were Indians). The Reverend Thomas Robinson was in charge of the grammar school. The Reverend William Preston professed moral philosophy. The Reverend John Camm taught theology. The Reverend Richard Graham preached natural philosophy. But fortunately for Jefferson there was one professor—of natural philosophy and mathematics—who was not a Reverend. This man, William Small, a Scot of great learning and a friend of Erasmus Darwin, arrived at the college about the same time that Jefferson came there as a student. Dr. Small found that the redheaded boy had a thirst for learning equal to his own, and a curiosity that knew no restraint. A warm friendship sprang up between the two, despite the discrepancy of age and position. Young Jefferson benefited immeasurably from the association with the older man. To the eager boy from the American back woods the European professor introduced the larger universe of science and scholarship, and set a pattern of liberal thinking stripped of orthodoxy. Dr. Small had a lasting influence on Jefferson. Years later Jefferson said that Small "probably fixed the destinies of my life."

Dr. Small did more than merely bring his protégé into contact with the exciting world of ideas. What was almost as important, he introduced him to his select circle of friends. Perhaps the greatest man among these friends was the thirty-five-year-old George Wythe, professor of law at the college and the foremost jurist in Virginia. Wythe was a man of classic mold, thoughtful, scrupulous, ethical, and above all a believer in a republican form of government. Contemporaries called him Aristides the Just. Young Jefferson spoke of him as "my faithful and beloved Mentor." Fourteen years after meeting the boy from Shadwell, Wythe was destined to sign his name to a document entitled "The Unanimous Declaration of the thirteen united States of America," composed by his red-haired student and friend.[2]

Wythe and Small were so impressed by their soft-spoken and brilliant young friend that they introduced him to a third man, the biggest person in the town and in the whole colony, Francis Fauquier, Acting Governor of Virginia. The two professors were the Governor's *"amici omnium horarum."* When they inducted the stripling of eighteen, they became an inseparable *"partie quarrée."* (These expressions are Jefferson's own.)

Governor Fauquier contributed to the education of young Jefferson. The Governor was both a man of the world and a

[2] George Wythe's name headed the list of the Virginia signers of the Declaration of Independence.

scholar. The son of a director of the Bank of England, he warned Pitt against England's oppressive colonial policy, foreseeing resistance on the part of the American colonies. London did not heed Fauquier, but Jefferson undoubtedly listened with growing interest to his conversation on the subject of colonial policy. For Fauquier was an open-minded eighteenth-century gentleman, interested in new ideas and good talk. He was also a bon vivant, devoted, among other things, to cards. Half a century later, the great democrat Jefferson recalled the gentlemanly royalist Governor Fauquier as "the ablest man who ever filled that office."

Small, Wythe, and Jefferson, together with Dr. Smith, a professor of mathematics who treated the young student "as a father," frequently dined with the Governor and often listened to chamber music at the Governor's Palace. The dinners were a joy and a sweet memory ever after. They meant genial companionship, fine food, worldly manners, and, above all, conversation that struck fire. Young Jefferson absorbed what he saw and heard. It was as if fate had brought together three or four brilliant men for the express purpose of enriching the mind of a young man born to do great things.

Years later Jefferson wrote: "At these dinners I have heard more good sense, more rational and philosophical conversations, than in all my life besides. They were truly Attic societies. The Governor was musical also, and a good performer, and associated me with two or three other amateurs at his weekly concerts."

3

College was not all music and conversation. Jefferson also studied with intense absorption. He was robust enough to study fifteen hours a day and then, for exercise, run a mile out of Williamsburg and back. Often he rose at dawn and plunged into books, books, books, until two in the morning. William and Mary had never seen such a student. Everything interested him, nothing was alien to him. His mind seized with equal avidity upon Greek grammar and Newtonian physics. He mastered calculus with the same ease as Spanish. He learned to read Plato in Greek, Cicero in Latin, Montesquieu in French. To get to the roots of the English common law he studied Anglo-Saxon. To read Ossian ("this rude bard of the North [is] the greatest poet that has ever existed") he learned Gaelic. Apart from the classics—he preferred Greek thought to Roman—he read the English novelists Sterne, Fielding, Smollett. He also read Marmontel, Le Sage, and Cervantes— Don Quixote twice. Among the poets, his favorites were Shakespeare, Milton, Dryden, and Pope.

Jefferson was a normal youth who loved exercise, riding, singing, dancing, and flirting with the girls. Everyone was attracted to him. Animation and kindliness lent a kind of beauty to that freckled, angular, plain face. For a time he affected a certain foppishness in dress. On social occasions he would put on a flowered waistcoat and silk stockings, and carry a laced hat under his arm. Such dress was an extravagance which pricked his conscience and when, in a burst of contrition, he asked his guardian to deduct the cost from his share of his father's property, he received the droll reply: "No, no; if you have sowed your wild oats in this manner, Tom, the estate can well afford to pay your expenses."

Although Jefferson was not addicted to humor, he enlivened gatherings with his laughter as well as his fiddle. His hazel eyes would light up at something ludicrous or incongruous, but he rarely told funny stories. One of his favorite anecdotes was about Arthur Lee, who had a passion for contradiction. Lee once heard a man say that it was a very cloudy day and retorted: "It is cloudy, sir; but not very cloudy." Jefferson thought that was funny.

Society in Williamsburg was "fast." The young blades (and the old ones too) liked cockfighting, gambling, drinking, racing, and wenching. Young Jefferson participated in these activities sparingly. He did, however, play the swain as well as "at ye billiard tables." His moral sense and distaste for loafing diminished the pleasure that a youth might find in dissipation. Once after a binge with other students he wrote from the melancholy depths of a hangover:

> Last night, as merry as agreeable company and dancing with Belinda in the Apollo could make me. I never could have thought the succeeding sun would have seen me so wretched as I now am! . . . Affairs at W. and M. are in the greatest confusion. Walker, M'Clurg, and Wat Jones are expelled *pro tempore*, or, as Horrox softens it, rusticated for a month. Lewis Burwell, Warner Lewis, and one Thompson, have fied to escape flagellation.

Although there never was any real danger that the intellectually vital son of Peter Jefferson would become just another racing and gambling Virginia gentleman, Tom's young company was admittedly "bad." Nevertheless, Jefferson in later years often wondered what had kept him from becoming a wastrel; with characteristic modesty he concluded that what saved him was not any innate virtue but the examples of his great friends Small and Wythe (the third, Governor Fauquier, was himself an inveterate gambler), whom he incessantly strove to imitate.

At the end of two years and one month Jefferson left college. In William and Mary's Book of the Bursar there is a notation by John Blair: "Jefferson tells me he left the College ab^t 25th April" (1762).

Leaving college meant no interruption in his studies, his routine, or his friendships. For Jefferson had decided to remain at Williamsburg and to study law. At the age of nineteen he entered the law office of his friend George Wythe, and despite his dislike for the law and its jargon, which he always ridiculed, he worked at it for five years.

That he studied thoroughly and read arduously is shown by his *Commonplace Book*, a notebook in which he jotted down and sometimes fully summarized the volumes he read and the ideas they stimulated in him.[3]

One day in the spring of 1764 he had his first real experience in patriotic inspiration. He was attending the session of the Virginia House of Burgesses during the debate on the British Parliament's act to tax the American colonies. Suddenly up stood one of the delegates, an old friend of Tom's, and burst into a torrent of eloquence that electrified the assembly. "Caesar," thundered Patrick Henry, "had his Brutus, Charles the First his Cromwell—and George the Third—" The House of Burgesses echoed with the words "Treason!" "Treason!" But Henry finished his sentence—"may profit by their example. If *this* be treason, make the most of it." Upon Jefferson, who had no gift of eloquence, Henry's speech made a powerful impression. Although he was rather inclined to look down upon Henry as an uncouth and uneducated backwoodsman, he admitted that on this occasion the orator was "splendid." Patrick Henry, he said, "appeared to me to speak as Homer wrote."

It was at this time that the young Jefferson adopted for his motto the words "Rebellion to tyrants is obedience to God."

5

Hard studies and youthful pleasures went hand in hand. Feudal law, Anglo-Saxon tenets, *curia regis* procedure, all these did not make Tom a dull boy. He continued his dancing and fiddling and courting the belles. He was extremely susceptible to the fluttering and flirtatious beauties.

---

[3] *The Commonplace Book of Thomas Jefferson: A Repertory of His Ideas on Government*, with an introduction and notes by Gilbert Chinard (1926). Out of the 905 entries in *The Commonplace Book*, no less than 550 were written when Jefferson was a student or a young lawyer. These entries deal with technical legal questions. The entries on feudal law, on political science, on Montesquieu and Beccaria, were written between 1774 and 1776, before the Declaration of Independence.

One of his early loves was Rebecca, daughter of Lewis Burwell, president of the Virginia Council. She was beautiful, impish, not very intellectual, and men were crazy about her. Tom carried her portrait—"my dear picture"—in his watch and no doubt looked at it worshipfully many times a day.

The infatuated boy struck no responsive chord in Belinda, as he called her poetically. On a flyleaf of a book Tom wrote:

> Jane Nelson is a sweet girl,
> Betsy Page is a neat girl,
> Rebecca Burwell is the devil;
> If not the devil she's one of his imps.

He was not a bold lover. Instead of offering his love to his Belinda, he mooned and moped and moaned, and, typical intellectual that he was, debated the problem in lengthy communications with his friend Page. He asked Page in a letter written from Shadwell in January, 1763:

> How does R.B. do? Had I better stay here and do nothing, or go down and do less? . . . Inclination tells me to go, receive my sentence, and be no longer in suspense: but reason says, if you go, and your attempt proves unsuccessful, you will be ten times more wretched than ever.

John Page told his moping friend to talk to the girl frankly and directly. Tom was frightened at such boldness:

> . . . you advise me to go immediately and lay siege *in form*. . . . No, no, Page; whatever assurances I may give her in private of my esteem for her . . . they must be kept in private. . . . because I never can bear to remain in suspense so long a time. . . . if Belinda will not accept of my services, it shall never be offered to another. . . . that she will, she never gave me reason to hope.

He wanted Page to do the talking for him, for Belinda had a devastating effect upon his poise. When he met her he became tongue-tied with emotion. One evening—this was in October, 1763—he danced with her in the Apollo Room of the Raleigh tavern and excitement choked his speech. All he could manage, he admitted to Page, was "a few broken sentences, uttered in great disorder." Stammeringly he hinted to her about his plans, but did not have the courage to propose to her. "I asked no question which would admit of a categorical answer."

But in the midst of these youthful bitter-sweet love torments, he was already seeking philosophic consolation. If Rebecca would not have him, he would make the best of it. "Perfect happiness, I believe," concluded the philosopher of twenty, "was never intended by the Deity to be the lot of one of his creatures in this world." Thus Tom overcame his first love with his usual good sense. When Belinda announced that she would marry one Jacquelin Ambler, Jefferson's reaction was one of polite coolness. "I have been so abominably indolent," he wrote a friend a few months after his trembling-shy dance at the Apollo, "as not to have seen her since last October. . . . Well, the Lord bless her I say! . . . Many and great are the comforts of a single state."

6

In 1767, three years after his love affair with Belinda, Jefferson was admitted to the bar. He had spent five years preparing himself under George Wythe, his "most affectionate friend," as he called him. It was Wythe who led him "into the practice of the law at the bar of the General court."

Jefferson was now twenty-four, and one of the richest bachelors in Virginia. He also had the reputation of being the most learned and the most inquisitive young man in the colony. He wanted to know everything. A woman writing from Williamsburg at this time tells that she "never knew any one to ask so many question as Thomas Jefferson."

CHAPTER THREE

LAWYER

(1767-1774)

WHEN Thomas Jefferson began to practice law at the age of twenty-four, he was brilliantly prepared and poorly equipped for his profession. It cannot be denied that he was not cut out to be a lawyer; a scholar, a scientist, an inventor, an architect, a botanist, yes—but not a lawyer. His mind was too inquisitive, too speculative, and, above all, too much given to ideas as such to be happy in jurisprudence.

The literary artist in Jefferson found legal language repugnant. A man with an innate sense of style, Jefferson was repelled by the dry, flatulent legal verbiage with its plethora of "whereases" and its underlying chicanery. He often jeered at "lawyerish."

Nothing Jefferson undertook could be mediocre, and it is no surprise to learn that he became a successful lawyer. It did not take him long to achieve a place among the leaders of the Virginia bar, and his erudition was put at the service of his peers. Famous clients—Burwells, Byrds, Lees, Nelsons, Pages, Randolphs—sought his services, and distinguished lawyers consulted him. Leaders of the bar like Wythe, Pendleton, Patrick Henry, and Robert Carter Nicholas paid young Jefferson the compliment of retaining him as associate counsel. He, in turn, retained Wythe and Pendleton when he needed assistance. The relationship among these lawyers was cordial.

Jefferson's practice grew rapidly. In 1767 he was engaged in sixty-eight cases before the General Court. Four years later, in 1771, he had four hundred and thirty cases. His practice was so great that when Robert Carter Nicholas retired from the bar and offered his business to Jefferson, the latter was "under the necessity of declining it." The account book of the young lawyer shows that his law work was lucrative, despite the unfavorable economic conditions in the colony. In 1767 Jefferson's "total profits" amounted to £293 4s. This rose to £421 5s. in 1770. During the eight years of his practice he averaged the equivalent of about $3,000 a year, which was a good income in those days.

Legal business did not occupy Jefferson exclusively. He still read voluminously and made meticulous observations on everything that fell within the range of his unquenchable curiosity. Between law cases and overseeing the plantation, he continued to lead the agreeable social life of an eligible bachelor, especially when visiting Williamsburg. "I was bred to the law," he once told John Bernard during his Presidency; "that gave me a view of the dark side of humanity. Then I read poetry to qualify it with a gaze upon its bright side."

In his third year as a lawyer Jefferson began to carry into effect a dream of his youth: to build a home for himself on the highest summit of his estate. In 1769 he commenced to level off the top of the hill known as Monticello (580 feet high) and to plant numerous varieties of fruit trees on the slope. He had never studied architecture, but he read all the books he could find on the subject, and presently he knew as much as there was to know. Several hundred of his architectural drawings are still in existence.

The home on Monticello grew like a tree, slowly, solidly, gracefully. Jefferson was the architect, the builder, the engineer, the construction foreman, the cabinetmaker, the landscape artist. All the materials except such things as hardware (excluding nails) and glass were made on the plantation. It was a quarter-century before the house on the hill was completely finished. A one-room red-brick building on the south end of the terrace was ready for occupancy in the fall of 1769.

Within a few months after completion, the little red-brick structure (today mellowed with age and smothered with ivy) was occupied by its owner. Shadwell, Jefferson's birthplace and the residence of his family, burned to the ground early in 1770, and all the books, papers, and records were reduced to ashes. Only the fiddle seems to have escaped the flames. Nothing was left for the family but to move to Monticello, which was still being built. Jefferson's mother and sisters found quarters with the overseer.

The fire destroyed Jefferson's most precious possession, his books, a loss that would have been staggering to any but a wealthy man. In a letter to Page, Jefferson estimated "the *cost* of the books burned to have been £200 sterling." He could not live or work without books. Within three years he possessed a new library of 1,254 volumes.

Collecting such a library—and it kept growing throughout Jefferson's lifetime—was a costly process. It was expensive even for a landowner like Jefferson, who had inherited 1,900 acres, but had to support a family of thirty-four persons and eighty-three slaves. The plantation, it should be remembered, was not making money. Slavery was becoming unproductive; slaves ate up what profits there were. Jefferson's cash crop, tobacco, probably brought him on an average no more than £200 or £300 a year. The sale of tobacco, together with his earnings as a lawyer, boosted his annual income to the equivalent of about $5,000. He bought approximately four hundred books a year, and if the average book cost only $3, it meant that Jefferson may have spent as much as one-fourth of his income on books.

3

Sometime in the year 1770, when he was twenty-seven, he met and fell quietly in love with a beautiful brunette widow of twenty-one. Martha Wayles Skelton, the object of his love, combined in her slender person a number of irresistible qualities. She was well-born, beautiful, finely educated, warm-hearted, a graceful dancer, a fine musician, full of high spirits, and wealthy.

Her father, John Wayles, was a rich Williamsburg lawyer whom Jefferson knew in a business and social way. Wayles owned a dozen plantations and four hundred slaves. His home, The Forest, on the edge of Williamsburg, was a center of gaiety and music. Jefferson was a frequent visitor there.

Martha did not discourage Jefferson's shy wooing, but for a long time apparently she played no favorites among the young swains who courted her. Jefferson did not give up hope. More than a year after he met Martha he confessed to a friend: "In every scheme of happiness she is placed in the foreground of the picture, as the principal figure. Take that away, and it is no picture for me."

Toward the end of 1771 Martha Skelton agreed to marry Jefferson. The wedding took place at The Forest on New Year's Day, 1772, and was one of the festive occasions of the season. Friends and relatives came from far and near, and there was much dancing and jollity. The bridegroom paid £5 to each of the officiating clergymen (of the Church of England), 40s. for the marriage license, and 10s. to the fiddler. Apparently he was short of cash, for on the same day that he paid £5 to the Reverend Mr. Coutts he borrowed 20s. from him. The servants had to wait more than two weeks to receive presents of 5s. each.

The month of the wedding saw a record snowfall in Virginia. In places the colony was blanketed with snow three feet deep. Despite the storm, the newlyweds set out for Monticello, more than a hundred miles from Williamsburg. The two young people traveled in a two-horse chaise, which broke down on the way and had to be mended at a cost of 50s. It was not a comfortable honeymoon journey, but Mrs. Jefferson took it in good spirit. Jefferson's oldest daughter Martha was to relate years later:

> They were finally obliged to quit the carriage, and proceed on horseback. Having stopped for a short time at Blenheim, where an overseer only resided, they left it at sunset to pursue their way through a mountain track rather than a road, in which the snow lay from eighteen inches to two feet deep, having eight miles to go before reaching Monticello.

Deep into the night and deeper through the snow their horses trudged up the steep path leading to the summit of the hill, where Jefferson's home was still in the skeletal stage, with only the one-room lodge prepared for occupancy. The night was cold and dreary, and Jefferson, with his usual consideration for others, would not disturb the servants. He stabled the horses himself and took his bride into their new "home." The bridegroom kindled a fire, and found a bottle of wine on the shelf; the two shared a toast and succumbed to laughter out of sheer happiness.

The young couple was exceedingly happy and exceedingly busy. Martha Jefferson, despite her youth, knew how to run a plantation and how to be a gay and loving companion. Her husband reciprocated her devotion. Their lives were rich and full. Six children were born to them—three died in infancy; three others were to survive their mother. The house on the hill was still in the process of building, hundreds of acres were being cultivated, slaves had to be cared for, law and politics had to be attended to. There was much entertainment and good living. In the midst of it all Jefferson found time for reading and study.

A little over a year after her marriage, Martha Jefferson's father died and left her one-third of a "handsome fortune," which, Jefferson tells, "doubled the ease of our circumstances." To be specific, Martha inherited from her parent 40,000 acres of land and one hundred and thirty-five slaves.[1] This put the Jeffersons in the class of the greatest landholders in Virginia and enabled them to buy luxuries, such as imported wines and liquors.[2]

---

[1] Most of this land, however, was sold. Jefferson retained a total of about 10,000 acres.

[2] Even before his wife's inheritance Jefferson kept a small stock of liquor in his cellar. His account book for 1772 shows that he had 3 gallons of rum, about 12 gallons of Madeira, and several bottles of port and beer. He drank wine with his meals, always in great moderation.

As yet Jefferson had no specific politics, except the general enlightened liberalism of a cultivated gentleman who was rich and tolerant. Few of his early letters show any great passion for social causes. His career was the reverse of that described in Lord Chesterfield's celebrated quip to his son: "He who is not a radical at sixteen has no heart; he who is a radical at sixty has no head." Jefferson was not a radical at sixteen, but was one at sixty; and he had both a heart and a head. No doubt, even at this early date he was stirred by injustice and indignant at persecution. Still, he lacked motivation for action, being serene in his philosophical beliefs and happy in his personal pursuits. It took years of growth, as well as revolutionary upheavals and a personal tragedy, to propel him into the arena where men fight and sometimes die for causes.

An educated eighteenth-century Virginia landholder could not escape politics altogether. As a matter of course, the squire of Monticello, who had inherited his father's office of justice of the peace, entered politics. It was usual for the squire to represent his county in the House of Burgesses. In 1769 Jefferson stood for that body, and was of course elected. His electioneering method was as simple as the dress of the neighbors whose votes he solicited. Colonel Peter Jefferson's young son visited the neighbors in the county and invited them to Shadwell for a bowl. They came, had their drinks, and afterward quietly voted for the late Colonel's educated lawyer son.

Such elections took place as a matter of course, and were neither arduous nor costly. In 1771 Jefferson was re-elected, having spent the munificent sum of £4 19s. 3d.—the equivalent of about $25—on his "burgessing." The cakes which the prospective voters washed down with punch cost Jefferson 45 shillings. In the campaign of 1774 he spent only 24 shillings on "6 dozen cakes." Cakes and rum kept him in the Virginia legislature until the outbreak of the Revolution.

Jefferson was not at first a very conspicuous member of the House of Burgesses. This was partly due to his lack of any program, and partly to the fact that, being sensitive, he hesitated long before thrusting himself forward. In 1773, during his fifth year in the legislature, Pendleton asked young Jefferson to draft a reply to the Governor's address. It was a courtesy request, designed to give the young man a chance to distinguish himself. Either from excitement or from inexperience, Jefferson bungled the draft and it had to be rewritten. He was mortified. Later he admitted candidly: "Being a young man as well as a young member, it made on me an impression proportioned to the sensibility of that time of life."

Reluctantly the American colonies were coming to grips with the royal government in London. As George the Third's Cabinet was becoming more arbitrary and violent, the Americans grew more stubborn in their resistance.

Throughout the American colonies battle lines were forming and opinion crystallizing. In 1773 a group of young members of the Virginia House of Burgesses took a long step in the direction of resistance to the mother country. With great political perspicacity the young Virginians forged a weapon of considerable striking power—the Committee of Correspondence, designed to act as a channel of communication, and ultimately perhaps of union, among the various colonies, North and South. Jefferson was one of the organizers of the committee.

After they established the committee the defiant Virginians left Williamsburg to spend the autumn and winter of 1773-74 at home, in peace. Participation in the Committee of Correspondence was Jefferson's first important political act.

To all intents and purposes the squire of Monticello was still a loyal subject of George the Third, a landowner holding property under the protection of British laws, a gentleman educated in the English tradition. He was not a social rebel nor an open religious dissenter. Nor, seemingly, did he see anything objectionable in the institution of monarchy. His political readings on the eve of the American Revolution showed a definite trend. It is certain that about this time he read Lord Kames's *Historical Law Tracts* and his *History of Property*, Sir John Dalrymple's *Essay towards a General History of Feudal Property in Great Britain*, James Wilson's remarkable pamphlet, *Considerations on the Nature and Extent of the Legislative Authority of the British Parliament*, as well as Locke, Voltaire, Helvetius, and a number of constitutional historians.

In the spring of 1774, the city of Boston, which neither Jefferson nor most of his fellow legislators in Virginia had ever seen, supplied the spark. A group of Massachusetts rebels had thrown a cargo of tea overboard and the British Government ordered that the port of Boston be closed beginning with June 1, 1774. Instantly the radical wing of the Virginia House of Burgesses decided to support the Northern sister colony against the Crown.

The leadership of the House of Burgesses fell into the hands of Patrick Henry, the two Lees, and Jefferson. They had the support of George Mason and George Wythe, although the

latter was inclined to be cautious. With Henry the inflam
matory orator and Jefferson the subtle logician, the radical
group became a political power of major importance. Wise in
political maneuver and experienced in parliamentary ways, the
younger men did not make the mistake of alienating the con
servatives. As Jefferson later explained: "We slackened our
pace, that our less ardent colleagues might keep up with us,
and they . . . quickened their gait somewhat . . . and thus
consolidated the phalanx which breasted the power of Britain."

To stir up public opinion, the young radicals hit upon the
propaganda stratagem of appointing a day of fasting and
prayer. This would alarm the people and focus their attention
on what was happening elsewhere in the colonies. Henry, the
two Lees, Jefferson, and a few other legislators met in private
and cleverly prepared for the day of fasting.

Governor Dunmore curtly dissolved the House of Burgesses.
Undaunted, the Virginians met in the Apollo Room of the
Raleigh tavern, about one hundred steps from the capitol. Under the chairmanship of Peyton Randolph, they reorganized
and agreed to propose to the Committees of Correspondence in
the other colonies to meet annually in a united congress at
some convenient place. They denounced the action of the British Government and, what was most significant, they declared
that "an attack on any one colony should be considered as an
attack on the whole." Then they called upon the counties to
elect deputies to meet on August 1 in Williamsburg, to select
representatives for the congress.

All over Virginia, during those hot July days, freemen were
busy voting for delegates to represent them at the convention
in Williamsburg. Albemarle County chose Jefferson. Hanover
County voted for Patrick Henry. Fairfax County elected
George Washington. On that August 1, 1774, Williamsburg
was to see one of the most distinguished political gatherings
in its history.

7

Before leaving Monticello for Williamsburg, Delegate Jefferson sorted out his ideas and put them down on paper. He was
moved by the conviction that since America was settled by
freemen, it should be ruled by American freemen, and not by
any foreign authority. He wrote fast, consulting no reference
books but drawing upon the ample storehouse of his memory.
In record time he had whipped into shape about sixty-five
hundred words that were destined to ring throughout the colonies and Great Britain. Modestly he hoped that his paper,

which he drew up tentatively, "with some uncertainties and inaccuracies," would serve as instructions to the delegates who would be chosen in Williamsburg for the Continental Congress. He made two copies.

Jefferson called his paper simply "Instructions." Ultimately it was printed under the title of *A Summary View of the Rights of British America*, and as such it is known to posterity. *A Summary View* is a landmark in American history, and a mirror of the mind of Thomas Jefferson in the summer of 1774. This pamphlet is the first link that bound Jefferson to the active destinies of his country. It is the matrix of the Declaration of Independence, two years older and five thousand words longer than the Declaration. In it the son of Peter Jefferson bluntly told the English King that he had no right to impose his will upon an America that was built by pioneers and not by peers. There are sentences in the *Summary* that scathe, others that purr, and throughout one senses a mind capable of indignant protest and of tactful appeal. This is the work of a master of English prose:

Can any one reason be assigned why 160,000 electors in the island of Great Britain should give law to four millions in the States of America, every individual of whom is equal to every individual of them in virtue, in understanding, and in bodily strength? Were this to be admitted, instead of being a free people, as we have hitherto supposed, and mean to continue ourselves, we should suddenly be found the slaves not of one but of 160,000 tyrants.

But can his majesty . . . put down all law under his feet? Can he erect a power superior to that which erected himself? He has done it indeed by force, but let him remember that force cannot give right.

. . . these are our grievances which we have thus laid before his majesty, with that freedom of language and sentiment which becomes a free people claiming their rights, as derived from the laws of nature, and not as the gift of their chief magistrate. Let those flatter who fear, it is not an American art. . . . They know . . . that kings are the servants, not the proprietors of the people.

It is neither our wish nor our interest to separate from her [Great Britain]. We are willing, on our part, to sacrifice everything which reason can ask to the restoration of . . . tranquillity. . . . On their part, let them be ready to establish union on a generous plan. . . . But let them not think to exclude us from . . . other markets. . . . Still less let it be proposed that our properties within our own territories shall be taxed or regulated by any power on earth but our own.

The God who gave us life gave us liberty at the same time: the hand of force may destroy, but cannot disjoin them. This, sire, is our last, our determined resolution.

Jefferson never got to the convention at Williamsburg; on the way he was seized with a severe attack of dysentery and had to turn back home. A messenger carried two copies of his "Instructions" to Williamsburg, one copy to Patrick Henry and another to Peyton Randolph, the chairman of the assembly. The copy to Henry disappeared, Virginia's Demosthenes either losing it or throwing it away carelessly. "Whether Mr. Henry disapproved the ground taken," Jefferson tells, "or was too lazy to read it (for he was the laziest man in reading I ever knew) I never learned: but he communicated it to nobody." Randolph scrupulously presented his copy to the convention where it was read with considerable astonishment and some trepidation. The majority thought it "too bold for the present state of things."

Jefferson's bold ideas were talked about in the convention, but someone else's "Instructions," mild as a "sucking dove," were adopted for the Virginia delegates. Jefferson's draft, however, was awarded the special honor of being printed in pamphlet form. The pamphlet fell upon the excitable political world like a bombshell. It soon reached London, where it was promptly seized upon by an eloquent Irishman named Edmund Burke, who used it as a club with which to beat the British Ministry. *A Summary View* ran rapidly through several editions, and caused the British Parliament to put Jefferson's name on a bill of attainder for proscription.

CHAPTER FOUR

REBEL

(1774-1776)

THE LAWYERS and the planters and the orators of the thirteen separate colonies met in Philadelphia on the fourth of September, 1774, to talk over the situation created by the various acts of the British Parliament. Jefferson was not among the delegates. He stayed at Monticello recuperating from his illness, knowing that Virginia was well represented by seven eminent sons. These were Richard Henry Lee; the dry, anticlerical John Bland; the massive Benjamin Harrison; the lean and eloquent Edmund Pendleton; the torrential Patrick Henry; the learned and aristocratic Peyton Randolph (who was elected president of the Congress); and finally a big man with a chilly exterior and a sensitive shyness—George Washington.

The delegates, representing views as diverse as the colonies they came from, were not yet ripe for union. They aired many problems and then adjourned until the following May. In England Lord Chatham praised their sagacity and moderation.

In the meantime Virginia was preparing to oppose the British Government by setting up independent administrative units, known as Committees of Safety. These committees in the various counties took over many of the functions of government, including the enlisting and arming of volunteers. Jefferson was chosen chairman of the Committee of Safety in his own Albemarle County.

2

In May, 1775, as prearranged, the Second Continental Congress assembled in the City of Brotherly Love. To the north, the Battle of Lexington had just been fought, and the consequences of this "accident" weighed heavily upon the minds of those who, like Jefferson, were as yet disinclined to surgery in the realm of politics. Jefferson had a horror of bloodshed and a gentleman's aversion to violence. The affair at Lexington disturbed him. "This accident," he groaned, "has cut off our last hope of reconciliation. . . . It is a lamentable circum-

29

stance, that the only mediatory power [the King] . . . shoul
pursue the incendiary purpose of still blowing up the flames.
To the Congress, Virginia sent the same delegates as in th
previous year, with one exception—Jefferson went as an alter
nate to Peyton Randolph, who was expected to become presi
dent of the assembly.

Jefferson traveled to Philadelphia in a light four-wheeled car
riage, open at the sides but covered at the top to protect hin
from rain and sun. Like any good traveler, he carried spares—
two extra horses. The going was slow. The rivers were difficul
to ford and the muddy roads were rutted. Jefferson took th
short route to Fredericksburg and then swung eastward, cross
ing the Potomac to Annapolis at a narrow point somewhere
near what is Washington today, paying a guide to take hin
over. Then he crossed the Chesapeake and drove straight north
to Wilmington. Between Wilmington and Philadelphia the roac
was bad, and Jefferson again employed a guide.

Traveling, he looked about him with his usual curiosity
making observations on flora, fauna, weather, and coinage. Ir
Maryland he jotted down in his pocket account book the bewil
dering kinds of coins in circulation—pistareens, shillings, dol
lars, guineas, half-jos. It was financial disorder, disconcerting
to a rational mind.

Ten days after leaving Williamsburg he arrived in Phila
delphia. The distance was approximately three hundred miles
which means that Jefferson traveled about thirty miles a day
If we assume that he rode from morning to sunset—with two
hours off for lunch—his average was hardly more than three
miles an hour.

When Jefferson got to the big city, he took lodgings with a
carpenter in a handsome house on Chestnut Street and went to
the City Tavern to dine.

On the morrow—June 21—Jefferson entered the hall of the
Congress, taking the seat of the distinguished Peyton Ran
dolph, president of the assembly. The appearance of the now
famous author of *A Summary View* created a little flurry. His
reputation as a "fine writer," the possessor of a "masterly pen,"
had preceded him and aroused curiosity about his person.

He was something to look at, this angular, muscular, lean
man, a long-legged horseman with tanned skin and brick-red
hair. A tall man, he stood out among the delegates—many o
whom were short and some paunchy—with his virile youth and
exuberance. The youngest but one in an assembly of mature
men, Jefferson's face shone with goodwill and intelligence
Neither aggressive nor oratorical, he easily attracted men and
won their confidence. The testy little John Adams, a man of

first-class intelligence, detected a like intelligence in the young delegate from Virginia and paid him the rare tribute of admiration and affection—"he was so prompt, frank, explicit and decisive upon committees and in conversation, not even Samuel Adams was more so," John Adams tells, "that he soon seized upon my heart."

Jefferson's reputation as the wielder of a smooth pen spread quickly, and within five days after taking his seat he was put on a committee to draw up a declaration of causes for taking up arms against Great Britain. The other member of the committee was John Dickinson, a conservative Philadelphia lawyer who favored conciliation and opposed revolution. Dickinson disliked Jefferson's draft, and Jefferson did not agree with Dickinson's. Jefferson good-naturedly yielded.

Dickinson's conciliatory draft, which the Congress reluctantly approved, retained four paragraphs written by Jefferson.

The fervent Jeffersonian phrases ended with a feeble Dickinsonian plea to Great Britain for "reconciliation on reasonable terms." But Congress disliked the idea of conciliation. Patrick Henry's words were still fresh in the minds of the delegates— "Gentlemen may cry peace, peace—but there is no peace. The war is actually begun! . . . Our brethren are already in the field! Why stand we idle here?"

Several days after the unsuccessful Dickinson-Jefferson collaboration, the Congress appointed another committee to report on Lord North's conciliation proposal. Members were chosen by ballot and, close behind Franklin, Jefferson led all other candidates, including John Adams and Richard Henry Lee. Once more Jefferson was asked by his colleagues to draft a reply; once more he composed sonorous phrases defying King and Parliament. At the end of July the Congress adopted the young Virginian's resolution and adjourned.

In August Jefferson returned home as he came, by phaeton. His feelings, strongly aroused by stimulating contact with distinguished fellow Americans from other colonies, were nevertheless mixed, and his thoughts disturbed. Despite his fiery sentiments, he wanted neither separation from nor war with England. He was, however, to the roots of his innermost being a child of the American frontier, and the thought of any arbitrary authority, particularly one exercised from a distance of three thousand miles, touched his pride and anger. The idea of a foreign Power claiming superiority over indigenous Americans—the very word "colonial" had an invidious sound— galled the sensitive strain of the aristocratic Randolph in Jefferson. Who was this German-descended princeling in London, or his corrupt hirelings, to try arbitrary rule on freeborn sons of freeborn pioneers?

3

In January, 1776, a fiery pamphlet appeared in America. It was forty-seven pages long, sold for 2s., and was entitled Common Sense. The author, it turned out, was an Englishman only one year in Philadelphia, a corsetmaker by trade, a journalist by profession, and a propagandist by inclination. His name was Thomas Paine. Within three months Common Sense sold 120,000 copies—in time it reached the best-seller heights with 500,000 copies.

Common Sense cried out boldly what many Americans had been feeling and not saying. Paine's words were clean and straight, like shot from a musket. A self-educated proletarian who had suffered much in England, Paine shared with many Americans contempt for monarchy and hatred for tyranny. His words burned themselves into the colonial American conscience.

Common Sense delighted nonaristocratic, free Americans with its attack on kings as "crowned ruffians" and George the Third as the "Royal Brute." The pamphlet urged Americans to break with the corrupt tyranny of the British Empire and establish here a great haven of freedom.

> Freedom hath been hunted round the globe. Asia, and Africa, have long expelled her.—Europe regards her like a stranger and England hath given her warning to depart. O, receive the fugitive, and prepare in time an asylum for mankind.

The pamphlet made converts by the thousands. Aristocrats like General Charles Lee were won over by its torrential eloquence, considering it a "masterly, irresistible performance." Cool heads like that of George Washington were swept along by the pamphlet; the General praised its "flaming arguments," its "sound doctrine," and its "unanswerable reasoning."

As for Jefferson, unlike many other patriots, he continued to cherish a high regard for Thomas Paine. "No writer," Jefferson said in later years, "has exceeded Paine in ease and familiarity of style, in perspicacity of expression, happiness of elucidation, and in simple and unassuming language."

4

Jefferson was in Monticello in January, 1776, when the irascible Lord Dunmore, the Royal Governor of Virginia, burned Norfolk and thereby drove the colony to armed revolt. Jefferson remained at home, staying away from the Congress in Philadelphia while his mother was ailing and the South was

eething with revolution. In March the neighboring colony of
Iorth Carolina decided to declare its independence from
Great Britain. In the same month Jefferson's mother died.
There is a terse sentence in his pocket notebook: "March 31,
776. My mother died about eight o'clock this morning in the
57th year of her age."

Early in May he hurried northward to Philadelphia, where
e took lodgings in a three-story brick house on Market
treet, between Seventh and Eighth. Jefferson occupied the
econd floor, consisting of a parlor and bedroom, and paid
5s. (about $8.50 today) rent a week. "In that parlor I wrote
abitually," he says.

On May 13 he took his seat in the Congress and was wel-
omed by those who were sharpening the scalpel with which
o cut the umbilical cord that tied them to the mother country.

Jefferson was not the leader of the Virginia delegation in
Congress, but he was probably its most learned member and
ertainly its best writer. At the age of thirty-two, to quote one
f his earliest biographers, he was a gentleman "who could
alculate an eclipse, survey an estate, tie an artery, plan an
difice, try a cause, break a horse, dance a minuet and play the
iolin."

Despite an abundance of other gifts, he lacked that of eloquence. John Adams recalled that "during the whole time I
at with him in Congress I never heard him utter three sen-
ences together." But his reputation for learning was as solid
as his diction was flawless. Everyone admired his "peculiar
elicity of expression." When it came to drawing up resolu-
ions or penning declarations, Jefferson was a natural choice.

On Friday, June 7, 1776, Jefferson's colleague Richard
Henry Lee rose on the floor of Congress and introduced a
tartling resolution:

> That these United Colonies are & of right ought to be free &
> independent states, that they are absolved from all allegiance to
> the British crown, and that all political connection between them
> & the state of Great Britain is & ought to be, totally dissolved.

The Congress burst into an uproarious torrent of debate,
vhich continued passionately through Saturday and Monday
nd Tuesday.

The final vote on Lee's resolution was postponed until July 1.
n the meantime a committee of five was appointed to work
n a Declaration of Independence.

The committee consisted of Thomas Jefferson of Virginia,
ohn Adams of Massachusetts, Dr. Benjamin Franklin of

Pennsylvania, Roger Sherman of Connecticut, and Robert
Livingston of New York—a shrewd selection of men repr
senting the Southern, Northern, and Middle colonies. The
were instructed to draw up a declaration giving reasons "whic
impelled us to this mighty resolution."

The committee met as a whole and unanimously insiste
that Jefferson draw up the declaration.

5

When Jefferson went to his parlor on the second floor
the bricklayer's house on Market Street to pen a draft, he d
not feel that he was doing anything extraordinary nor did h
suspect that he was toying with immortality. In his *Autobio,
raphy* he says laconically: "The committee for drawing th
Declaration of Independence desired me to do it. It was a
cordingly done."

Between June 11 and June 28 Jefferson sat at a little im
provised desk in the stuffy parlor, his quill scratching tirelessl
For seventeen days he labored at the document, carving an
polishing the words. He wrote fine, clear, meticulous scrip
revealing the neat precision of a scientific and poetic min
aware that each word counted, as indeed it did.

The inspiration behind his quill was not personal. Only th
composition was his; the sentiments belonged to mankine
He always insisted that the Declaration of Independenc
merely gave voice to what his compatriots felt. He was onl
the instrument, not the creator. Almost half a century afte
writing the Declaration he said: "Neither aiming at originalit
of principle or sentiment, nor yet copied from any particula
and previous writing, it was intended to be an expression c
the American mind."

But the words had wings and the phrases a haunting beauty

> When in the course of human events
> it becomes necessary for one people
> to dissolve the political bonds
> which have connected them with another,
> and to assume
> among the powers of the earth,
> the separate and equal station
> to which the laws of nature
> and of nature's God
> entitle them,
> a decent respect to the opinions of mankind requires
> that they should declare the causes
> which impel them to the separation.[1]

---

[1] The ampersand so often used by Jefferson is changed to "and" i
quotations from the Declaration of Independence.

Thus far Jefferson was on familiar ground. Those who knew their Locke and Milton—and what educated gentleman did not?—would not quarrel with the principle of voluntary dissolution of political bonds. Few lawyers in America at this time disbelieved in the theory of the social compact. It was the dominant doctrine of the middle class. Moreover, it was the experience of Americans on this new continent.

Jefferson's second sentence was dynamite.

> We hold these truths
> to be self-evident,
> that all men are created equal,
> that they are endowed by their Creator
> with inherent and [2] unalienable rights,
> that among these
> are life, liberty, and the pursuit of Happiness.

The last three words are a declaration of faith, Jefferson's undying contribution to American life. The assertion that the pursuit of happiness was one of the objects for which governments exist was something new in the history of political doctrine. Ordinarily the triplex of political values included life, liberty, and property. By substituting "the pursuit of happiness" for "property" [3] Jefferson broke with the traditional concept and laid the foundation for a unique commonwealth of justice and freedom and security.

And he concluded:

> We therefore,
> the representatives of the United States of America
> in General Congress assembled, [4]
> in the name and by the authority of
> the good people of these states
> reject and renounce

[2] Congress struck out "inherent and" and substituted "certain."

[3] A month earlier George Mason had also used the word "happiness" in the Virginia Bill of Rights.

[4] From this point on Congress changed Jefferson's draft to read: ", appealing to the Supreme Judge of the world for the rectitude of our intentions, do, in the Name and by the Authority of the good People of these Colonies, solemnly publish and declare, that these United Colonies are, and of Right ought to be Free and Independent States; that they are Absolved from all allegiance to the British Crown, and that all political connection between them and the State of Great Britain, is and ought to be totally dissolved; and that as Free and Independent states, they have full Power to levy War, conclude Peace, contract Alliances, establish commerce, and to do all other acts and things which Independent States may of right do.

"And for the support of this Declaration, with a firm reliance on the protection of divine Providence, we mutually pledge each other our Lives, our Fortunes, and our sacred Honor." It will be seen that Congress added many capital letters here, as they did throughout.

all allegiance and subjection
to the kings of Great Britain
and all others
who may hereafter claim by, through, or under them;
we utterly dissolve
all political connection
which may heretofore have subsisted
between us
and the people or parliament
of Great Britain;
and finally we do assert and declare
these colonies to be free
and independent states,
and that
as free and independent states,
they have full power
to levy war,
conclude peace,
contract alliances,
establish commerce,
and do all other acts
and things
which independent states may of right do.
And for the support
of this declaration,
we mutually pledge to each other
our lives,
our fortunes,
and our sacred honour.

6

When Jefferson finished the draft, he presented it separately
to Franklin and Adams, who made a few slight corrections.
"Their alterations," Jefferson says, "were two or three only
and merely verbal." Then Jefferson meticulously rewrote the
whole draft, including the Franklin-Adams insertions, and
presented it to the whole committee. They approved unanimously, and on June 28 "A Declaration by the Representatives of the United States of America, in General Congress
Assembled" [5] was thrown into the lap of the Congress.

The sharp-witted lawyers of the Congress fell upon Jefferson's creation with a zest that cut the sensitive author to the
quick. For three days they flayed the paper, slicing off words
and phrases as if they were offensive tissue. Out of more than
eighteen hundred words the members of the Congress ex-
punged four hundred and sixty, or about one-fourth of the
whole. They altered about two dozen words and made two
insertions in the peroration—references to a "supreme judge"

[5] This was Jefferson's original title. On July 19 an act of Congress changed it
to "The Unanimous Declaration of the thirteen united States of America."

and a "divine providence." Jefferson had neglected the Deity here, though he had mentioned Him twice before.

The debate was an agonizing ordeal for Jefferson. He sat still and silent, "a passive auditor," he said, suffering more than his dignity permitted him to show. Burden of the defense lay with the chunky, hard-hitting John Adams, who, in the words of the grateful Jefferson, was "fighting fearlessly for every word." Every word under attack was a ruthless depredation upon the author's creation, and made him wince. Despite his pride, he could not altogether control his emotions.

7

The Declaration of Independence was approved on July 2. On July 3 the Congress took up Richard Henry Lee's original resolution of June 7 and debated the crucial point that "these United Colonies are & of right ought to be free & independent states." On that day Jefferson noted that the temperature was 76° Fahrenheit—not a hot afternoon for Philadelphia in July. On that same day Jefferson spent one hundred and three shillings. He bought a thermometer for "£3.15" and "7 pr. women's gloves" for 27 shillings; "1/6" he gave "in charity."

On July 4 the Congress debated all day—a comparatively cool one. Jefferson said nothing; he quietly took notes. He was not so absorbed, however, as to neglect to record the temperature in his notebook. He took at least four readings on his new $19 thermometer. While the statesmen of the newly born nation were arguing heatedly, Jefferson coolly recorded: "July 4th, 6 A.M., 68°; 9 A.M., 72¼°; 1 P.M., 76°, 9 P.M., 73½°." In the evening the debate was closed, and all the members present except John Dickinson signed the Declaration of Independence.[6]

Jefferson waited until the Articles of Confederation were reported in the Congress and then resigned. Early in September he left Philadelphia and hurried home.

[6] Many were not present and signed later.

CHAPTER FIVE

LEGISLATOR

(1776-1779)

AFTER Jefferson had been home about a month, happy with his three young daughters and active in his fields, word reached him that the Congress in Philadelphia had appointed him and the great Doctor Franklin commissioners to negotiate treaties with the France of Louis Sixteenth. He declined the honor. Not only was his young wife ailing, and he would not dream of leaving her for a prolonged stay abroad, but there was urgent work to do in Virginia. "The laboring oar was really at home," he said.

For Jefferson had quietly matured a plan to bring democracy to his home State. Without heat or rhetoric, he had come to the conclusion that a democratic (he used the word "republican") society, as he conceived it, could not be built upon a monarchical foundation. It was not enough to cast out the king; it was necessary also to destroy the king's institutions. To Jefferson's logical mind it was unreasonable to reject monarchy —in the person of the British King—and at the same time retain its trappings. Virginia was still a royalist State in everything but name.

No one knew better than Jefferson that in any civilized society the whole complex of social relationships is held together, like intricate basketry, in a legal code. Change the law and you change the social system; alter the social system and the law must be adjusted. Property relationships and personal status were anchored in a body of laws that perpetuated ownership and sanctioned privilege in the hands of a tight little ruling class. That Jefferson, by inheritance and marriage and position, was a member of the controlling class did not alter the situation nor affect his attitude. He saw no contradiction in owning thousands of acres of slave-tilled land and at the same time believing in equality. To him the concept of democracy did not rest upon an equality of property but upon one of opportunity. The purpose of the law was to protect man not in special privilege, but in his various social freedoms—freedom of conscience, of speech, of assembly, of enterprise. Any

38

ode that perpetuated privilege and froze personal status was
bad code. Any law that granted citizens equal opportunities
nd protected them in all their "inherent" liberties was a good
aw.

Socially, and even economically, Virginia was run by an
ristocracy of birth. In his quietly unyielding way Jefferson
eld fast to his human faith, that men had inalienable rights
o life, liberty, and the pursuit of happiness. Liberty could not
oexist with privileged aristocracy, nor happiness be found
vhere excess wealth was permitted to be concentrated in a
ew hands.

Virginia was stippled with magnificent manors, some of
hem as large as 50,000 acres. Black men, permanently en-
laved, worked those acres and created the wealth which en-
bled the aristocracy to live in princely splendor. The Virginia
aronies were held by a few families in entail. By the law of
rimogeniture the estates passed from heir to heir, and could
e neither broken up nor divided. The result was as Jefferson
lescribed it:

> The transmission of this property from generation to genera-
> tion in the same name raised up a distinct set of families who,
> being privileged by law in the perpetuation of their wealth, were
> thus formed into a Patrician order, distinguished by the splendor
> and luxury of their establishments.

This permanent aristocracy was a constant threat to self-
overnment. To establish and perpetuate free government,
vhich was Jefferson's ideal, it was necessary to blast away the
oundations of the aristocracy. He explained:

> To annul this privilege, and instead of an aristocracy of
> wealth, of more harm and danger, than benefit, to society, to
> make an opening for the aristocracy of virtue and talent, which
> nature has wisely provided for the direction of the interests of
> society, & scattered with equal hand through all its conditions,
> was deemed essential to a well ordered republic.

2

Early in October, 1776, Jefferson was in Williamsburg for
he autumn session of the Virginia House of Delegates. As
oon as the various committees were organized and the House
got down to business, Jefferson sprang his revolution upon Virginia. It was to be, he hoped, a peaceful revolution, a revolution
y law. "No violence was necessary, no deprivation of natural
ight," he says.

This was Jefferson's first major political effort, and his
trategy is worth observing. He was the organizer behind the

scenes, the indefatigable planner in small committees. Withou
a political party, he knew how to instil his ideas into other
so subtly that they came to feel themselves the originators
Singularly sweet-natured and devoid of aggressiveness, th
thirty-three-year-old delegate from Monticello was followed
by men who did not always know they were doing so. Tha
was how it came about that the party of Patrick Henry, a
popular leader without a program, supported some of the bill
of Jefferson, who had only a program.

Jefferson's strength came also from another source. He had
a genius for friendship and a shy warmth, and men of quality
rarely failed to be attracted to him. As he was now preparing
to transform Virginia by law and facing the hardest fight of
his career, he was able to depend upon the loyalty and affection of three men, each one a host in himself. Without these
devoted friends his bills might have been beaten, for the House
of Delegates was sharply divided on basic social issues.

First in importance was Jefferson's friend and teacher
George Wythe. Jefferson always spoke of him in terms close
to adoration.

The second of Jefferson's "strenuous coadjutors in debate"
was George Mason, one of the stanchest democrats in America. His fame should be greater than it is.

Finally there was a mousy little man in his middle twenties,
of great legal learning and dry humor, with an inexhaustible
capacity for work. His name was James Madison, a man
whose homely features did not betray his powerful intelligence.

Jefferson stormed the trenches of the old oligarchy with
carefully aimed bills, each designed to transform the royal
colony into a democratic commonwealth. The "Spirit of Level-
ling," Virginians called it. It took years to achieve the leveling,
but it was finally accomplished by four factors: the abolition
of entail, the overthrow of primogeniture, free public education, and the disestablishment of the Church.

The first bill had an innocent title: "to enable tenants in
taille to convey their lands in fee-simple." Its intent, however,
was not innocent in the eyes of the oligarchy. The bill was a
blow at entail, permitting an owner to leave his landed property
to whomever he liked.

3

No sooner had Jefferson won his first important legislative
victory with the passing of the entail bill than he introduced
a motion for the revision of the whole legal code. The motion
was adopted, and a committee of five "Revisors" was appointed

carry on the work. The composition of the committee was victory for Jefferson, for he himself was made chairman and wo of his friends, Wythe and Mason, were members. On the ther side were Pendleton and Thomas L. Lee. Virginia's Jus-inians met at Fredericksburg in January, 1777, to agree upon plan of operation. As soon as they assembled they found, robably much to their own amusement, their traditional roles eversed. Pendleton, the conservative lawyer, argued in favor f a new and complete legal system; Jefferson, the radical ormer lawyer, favored merely an alteration of the existing ode.

The reasons for Jefferson's seeming conservatism were as ubtle as Pendleton's reasons for his apparent radicalism. Both rere men of farseeing adroitness, inclined to take the long iew. Jefferson easily saw through Pendleton's purpose. He ealized that a completely new code, with untried principles nd unaccustomed concepts, would not only take too much ime, but would be at the mercy of those who would be in harge of interpreting it, that is, the judges. And judges, Jeffer-on knew, were a conservative tribe, leaning heavily to the side f property, precedent, and class. Much better, Jefferson hought, to leave the old legal notions intact, so as to make ure that the precedent-bound judges would tread in the beaten ath and not be tempted to stray too far in their own preju-ices. In this instance, reform was wiser than revolution.

Mason and Wythe concurred with the chairman. When it ame to a division of the work, Mason and Lee excused them-elves as not being lawyers. The burden, therefore, fell on Jef-erson, helped by Wythe and Pendleton. Jefferson took over he common law and the statutes to the year 1607, Wythe the aws from 1607 to 1776, and Pendleton the laws of colonial Virginia.

For two years Jefferson worked on the legal code. It was a remendous job, exacting, as Madison said, "perhaps the most evere of his public labours." But it was a task to Jefferson's aste, for it enabled him to bring into play all those faculties with which he was endowed: disciplined thinking, immense earning, and limpid diction.

> In the execution of my part I thought it material not to vary the diction of the ancient statutes by modernizing it, nor to give rise to new questions by new expressions. The text of these statutes had been so fully explained and defined by numerous adjudications, as scarcely ever now to produce a question in our courts. I thought it would be useful also, in all new draughts, to reform the style of the later British statutes, and of our own acts of Assembly: which from their verbosity, their endless

tautologies, their involutions of case within case, and parenthes within parenthesis, and their multiplied efforts at certainty t *saids* and *aforesaids*, by *ors* and by *ands*, to make them mor plain, do really render more perplexed and incomprehensibl not only to common readers, but to the lawyers themselves.

After two years of pruning the dead twigs of the old law and streamlining the new statutes, Jefferson met the other tw Revisors at Williamsburg early in 1779. They compared thei work critically, "sentence by sentence, scrutinizing and amend ing," until they agreed upon the whole. Then they returne home and made clean copies. The whole revised code was re fined into one hundred and twenty-six bills, so concisely draw that they were printed in a mere ninety folio pages.

The revised code was more than "a Model of technical pre cision, and perspicuous brevity," as James Madison called i It contained the principles of the new democracy. One of th bills, drawn by Jefferson, provided for the abolition of primo geniture in order to make real estate descendible to all th heirs. This was another blow at the upper classes, and Pendle ton protested. Since his protest was unsupported by the othe Revisors, Pendleton suggested a compromise on the basis o the ancient Hebrew principle of giving the elder son a doubl portion. But Jefferson, determined to eradicate every fiber o inequality, set his face against any compromise. He told hi colleague dryly that "if the eldest son could eat twice as much or do double work, it might be a natural evidence of his righ to a double portion; but being on a par in his powers & wants with his brothers and sisters, he should be on a par also in th partition of the patrimony."

Another long stride in the direction of Jefferson's ideal o an enlightened commonwealth of free men was made by hi three education bills: "for the more general diffusion of knowl edge," "for amending the constitution of the College of Willian and Mary," and "for establishing a public library." Underlyin these bills was the democratic-revolutionary assumptio that it was the duty of the State to supply free educa tion to the poor. Such public schools were to teach reading writing, and arithmetic, as well as acquaint the young student "with Graecian, Roman, English, and American history." The preamble to the first bill is a classic statement of the reasons for education in a democracy:

> Whereas . . . experience hath shewn, that . . . those en-
> trusted with power have, in time, and by slow operations, per-
> verted it into tyranny; and it is believed that the most effectual
> means of preventing this, would be to illuminate, as far as
> practicable, the minds of the people at large. . . .

And whereas it is generally true that the people will be happiest whose laws are best, and are best administered, and that laws will be wisely formed, and honestly administered, in proportion as those who form and administer them are wise and honest; whence it becomes expedient . . . that those persons, whom nature hath endowed with genius and virtue, should be rendered by liberal education worthy to receive . . . the sacred deposit of the rights and liberties of their fellow citizens, and that they should be called to that charge without regard to wealth, birth or other accidental condition or circumstance; but the indigence of the greater number disabling them from so educating, at their own expence . . . their children . . . to become useful instruments for the public, it is better that such should be . . . educated at the common expence of all, than that the happiness of all should be confided to the weak or wicked.

In brief, Jefferson boldly asserted four basic principles: that democracy cannot long exist without enlightenment; that it cannot function without wise and honest officials; that talent and virtue, needed in a free society, should be educated regardless of "wealth, birth or other accidental condition"; and finally, that children of the poor must be thus educated at the common expence." This document is hardly less important than the Declaration of Independence as a milestone in the evolution of the democratic doctrine.

4

Of all the bills, however, the greatest sensation was to be caused by the one proposing religious freedom. In back of that bill lay Jefferson's whole intellectual development. To Jefferson, who believed in reason with passionate conviction, it was axiomatic that religion, or rather the institution of the Church, was the enemy of freedom and the ally of obscurantism.

Jefferson's critical attitude did not extend to the ethical teachings of religion, which he accepted, but to its political alignments and aspects, which he rejected. Religion was a menace to a free society when it was either an instrument of the State, as was the case with Lutheranism in Prussia, or when it used the State for its sanguinary purposes, as was the case in Inquisition-ridden Spain. There was sufficient historical evidence to prove that the partnership of Church and State had always led, and perforce must lead, to tyranny and oppression. In every country and in every age," Jefferson said, "the priest has been hostile to liberty. He is always in alliance with the despot, abetting his abuses in return for protection of his own." So long as the Church was woven into the same fabric as the State, a self-governing commonwealth based upon justice and freedom was a fool's illusion.

In few things was Jefferson more consistent than in his advo
cacy of religious liberty, or more resolute than in his hatred
of religious tyranny. He went farther than those who merely
believed in toleration. Mere toleration was a lazy man's creed;
it meant indifference toward the political problems involved in
the religious question. Toleration, therefore, was not enough.
What Jefferson wanted, and ultimately achieved, was liberty-
liberty, fully protected by the law, to believe or not to believe
whatever a man saw fit; liberty of the genuine Protestant variety, for a man and his conscience to care for his soul in his
own fashion.

The problem of religion and all its sociopolitical implications had troubled Jefferson for a long time. A few months
after writing the Declaration of Independence, in October
1776, he had jotted down a few searching "Notes on Religion":

> The care of every man's soul belongs to himself. But what if
> he neglect the care of it? Well what if he neglect the care of his
> health or estate, which more nearly relate to the state. Will the
> magistrate make a law that he shall not be poor or sick? Laws
> provide against injury from others; but not from ourselves. God
> himself will not save men against their wills. . . .
>
> If the magistrate command me to bring my commodity to a
> publick store house I bring it because he can indemnify me if he
> erred & I thereby lose it; but what indemnification can he give
> one for the k[ing]dom of heaven?
>
> I cannot give up my guidance to the magistrates, bec[ause] he
> knows no more of the way to heaven than I do, & is less con-
> cerned to direct me right than I am to go right.

The battle for religious liberty was unending. All the entrenched forces of religious institutions and vested clerical interests had to be challenged if a free self-governing society
were to exist. To Jefferson it was a struggle between science
and superstition, a conflict between reason and dogmatism. He
knew that the beliefs of a lifetime die hard, and that it takes
tireless hammering to open up cracks for the light of reason to
enter. There was no margin for compromise. In his *Notes on
Virginia* Jefferson raked the whole problem with subdued passion. The arguments are still mint-fresh:

> The rights of conscience we never submitted, we could not
> submit. We are answerable for them to our God. The legitimate
> powers of government extend to such acts only as are injurious
> to others. But it does me no injury for my neighbor to say there
> are twenty gods, or no god. It neither picks my pocket nor
> breaks my leg. . . .
>
> Subject opinion to coercion: whom will you make your in-
> quisitors? Fallible men; men governed by bad passions, by
> private as well as public reasons. And why subject it to coer-

cion? To produce uniformity. But is uniformity desirable? No more than of face and stature. Introduce the bed of Procrustes then, and as there is danger that the large men may beat the small, make us all of a size, by lopping the former and stretching the latter. . . .

Is uniformity attainable? Millions of innocent men, women, and children, since the introduction of Christianity have been burnt, tortured, fined, imprisoned: yet we have not advanced one inch towards uniformity.

What has been the effect of coercion? To make one half the world fools, and the other half hypocrites. To support roguery and error all over the earth. . . .

Such were some of the ideas in Jefferson's mind when he drafted his Bill for Establishing Religious Freedom. The bill, together with the rest of the revised code, was submitted by Jefferson and Wythe to the House of Delegates in June, 1779. It stunned the majority of the House and enraged the oligarchic interests in the State. The whole code was subjected to bitter attack—"the endless quibbles, chicaneries, perversions, vexations and delays of lawyers and demi-lawyers," as Jefferson described the procedure, resulted in a momentary shelving of the code.

But Jefferson and his followers, particularly James Madison, never relinquished the battle. Victory was in their hearts, and they could afford to be patient. They did not have to wait long. Within six years virtually the whole code was passed, largely as a result of Madison's "unwearied exertions," as Jefferson gratefully acknowledged.

The Bill for Establishing Religious Freedom and severing the Church from the State, passed with but minor changes, opened a new era of freedom and toleration in American history. Since Virginia was far the most populous, and probably the most influential, State in the Union, Jefferson's bill set a model for the rest of the country. Jefferson himself was prouder of that bill than of all the high offices he was to hold, including the Presidency.

We the General Assembly of Virginia do enact that no man shall be compelled to frequent or support any religious worship, place, or ministry whatsoever, nor shall be enforced, restrained, molested, or burthened in his body or goods, or shall otherwise suffer, on account of his religious opinions or belief; but that all men shall be free to profess, and by argument to maintain, their opinions in matters of religion, and that the same shall in no wise diminish, enlarge, or affect their civil capacities.

The bill was designed to protect all citizens, regardless of race or creed, in their freedom of conscience. It aimed, Jefferson explained, "to comprehend, within the mantle of it's protection, the Jew and the Gentile, the Christian and Mahometan, the Hindoo, and infidel of every denomination."

5

It took nine years of struggle for Jefferson and his followers to transform Virginia into a democratic commonwealth. It was a bloodless revolution, carefully planned and calmly executed by the young philosopher-planter who led his forces with cool brilliance, subtle and unrelenting. "I considered 4 of these bills passed or reported," he tells almost casually, "as forming a system by which every fibre would be eradicated of antient or future aristocracy; and a foundation laid for a government truly republican." [1]

The process of "leveling" begun by Jefferson could not be halted, and the ultimate result was as Jefferson had foreseen and planned: a breaking-up of the power and the estates of the aristocracy.

[1] The repeal of entail prevented the "accumulation and perpetuation of wealth." The abolition of primogeniture removed feudal distinctions which made "one member of every family rich, and all the rest poor." The establishment of religious freedom relieved the poor people from taxation in support of the "religion of the rich." Finally, the bill for a general education helped the poor to learn to maintain their rights, and enabled them "to exercise with intelligence their parts in self-government," Jefferson explained.

CHAPTER SIX

GOVERNOR

(1779-1781)

In the spring of 1779, when Jefferson had completed revising the code, the governorship of Virginia fell vacant.

The one hundred and thirty-odd planters and tobacco farmers who made up the legislature looked to three candidates. These were John Page, Jefferson's friend from Williamsburg student days; General Thomas Nelson, a signer of the Declaration of Independence whom John Adams described as "a fat man . . . alert and lively for his weight"; and finally Jefferson, who was thirty-six years old and was hoping to find leisure from politics in order the better "to indulge my fondness for philosophical studies."

The democratic forces looked upon Jefferson as the natural leader in the struggle for political liberty and social reform. Next to Patrick Henry, the author of the Declaration of Independence was the most commanding figure in Virginia's House of Delegates.

Jefferson accepted the candidacy for the governorship more from a desire to please his supporters than from a yearning for the emoluments and the burdens of office. He was in the delicate position of having to run against Page, his boyhood friend whom he had always considered as a brother. "It had given me much pain," he told Page, "that the zeal of our respective friends ever have placed you and me in the situation of competitors. I was comforted, however . . . that it was their competition, not ours." Page amiably assured his friend that he felt the same way about it.

On the first ballot Jefferson led with 55 votes, against 36 for Page and 32 for Nelson. On the second ballot, with Nelson dropping out, Jefferson won a clear though not impressive majority—67 votes against 61 for Page. Thus he had reached the first major stage in his political career.

2

It was a bad time for a philosopher to be king. The war with Britain—the American Revolution—was now in its fourth year, and still no end was in sight. Hitherto the fighting had

taken place in the North. But unfortunately for Jefferson, at
about the time he became Governor both the international outlook and the British strategy underwent a change. The France
of Louis XVI, who had made an alliance with the United
States in 1778, at last threw her forces into the conflict and
thus potentially tipped the scales in favor of the young American States. The British then changed their tactics and shifted
the war to the South, which, because of its open coastline and
sparsity of settlement, was vulnerable to attack. Virginia, the
heart of the South, was to bear the brunt of the new assault.

Virginia had no defensive forces. To defend its vulnerable
and wide-open coastline, Virginia possessed a flotilla of four
little vessels (with a total of five dozen guns) and three armed
boats. Nowhere was there a fortification strong enough to
resist a stout British frigate. What military forces there were
consisted of poorly armed, untrained, undisciplined militia.
In short, from a military standpoint Governor Jefferson's State
was what a later generation of Americans would call a "push-
over."

Economically the State was no better off. There was an
absence of specie, and paper money was hardly worth the stuff
on which it was printed.[1] The State, whose administrative
machinery was by no means a model of efficiency, in despera-
tion did what States have been doing since time immemorial:
it imposed more and more taxes. But the people were too poor
and too disorganized to pay. Of sixty-odd counties, in the
spring of 1780 less than half paid their taxes and nine did not
even return any assessments. The accounts, moreover, were
not kept satisfactorily. Army commissaries and recruiting
officers lived by "sheer plunder."

The problems that the young Governor faced in a war-
exhausted State that was threatened by invasion were novel
and unprecedented. Peace-loving, compromising, devoted to
orderly and constitutional procedure, Jefferson was psycho-
logically unprepared to cope with the violent reality of war.
He did not seem to realize the gravity of the situation. When
the legislature proposed drastic retrenchment and a reduction
in the military establishment of the State, the Governor tacitly
approved, and Virginia found herself less protected than ever.
Perhaps his inveterate optimism made him feel that Virginia
would somehow escape the scourge of invasion.

The Governor had to supply Washington's army in the
North and Gates's troops in the South. He had to keep in
touch with the various commanders in the field—Steuben

---

[1] Currency depreciated so that a physician received £300 for a call, a
chicken cost about £10, and a quart of brandy brought about £24.

Nelson, Greene, Muhlenberg, Lafayette—for Virginia was a key State. He had to take care of British and Hessian prisoners of war. He had to think of shoes and of uniforms, of victuals and of arms, in response to the appeals of the harassed generals. (General Washington wrote him: "It [is] essentially necessary that every measure should be taken to procure supplies of Cloathing for them [the troops], especially of Shoes, Stockings and linen.") Finally, having formally taken possession of an enormous territory extending to the Mississippi in the West and the Great Lakes in the North, the Governor had to defend his vast State against Indians, who were being incited by the British.

The Governor's chief headache, however, was the ancient sinews of war, money. And of money Virginia had none. Nor could Jefferson, for all his ingenuity, find a proper substitute for money. Confiscation of supplies was neither constitutionally permissible nor physically possible, since the State was poor and exhausted. Jefferson himself virtually denuded his own estate of horses and wagons for the army, and so did other patriotic farmers. But not only were these voluntary supplies insufficient, they also crippled the productivity of the farms. In the meantime the British were invading North Carolina and threatening to crush the country in a pincer movement. All eyes, and all desperate appeals, were directed toward centrally situated Virginia.

General Washington, worried for the safety of his native State and discouraged by the poverty of his troops, kept on writing at least twice a month to his fellow Virginian in Richmond, asking for urgent help, complaining, pleading. These letters throw a glaring and almost embarrassing light on the plight of the Commander in Chief, struggling against defeatism and despair.

The burden of Washington's complaint—not against Jefferson, but against the whole American system of waging the war—was lack of men and lack of supplies. The independent citizens of the young democracy could not be recruited and forced into uniform like so many Prussians or Hessians. The American yeomen had to be cajoled and attracted by bounties, and then they took up arms under contract, usually for short periods of time. As soon as their time was up—and often before that—they simply left everything and went home. These "deserters" (some were technically deserters and others were not) drove General Washington to fury.

General Washington kept on pleading for periods of enlistment of at least eighteen months' duration. If he could be sure of having an army for over a year, he could plan a campaign and try for victory. But what was the use of attempting anything when his soldiers melted away like snow in the sun? "Short inlistments," he wrote to Jefferson bitterly, "have subjected Us to such distresses, to such enormous expences, have so intimately hazarded our liberties that I never reflect upon them, but with a degree of horror."

The Governor, almost as hard-pressed as the General, could give him little more than sympathy.

3

Money was not all the Governor lacked. The State had no troops for land defense, no fortresses at the wide mouth of the rivers, and no armed ships to protect hundreds of miles of coast. There was one gun for every five militiamen, one militiaman to every square mile of territory to be defended, little powder, and no containers for cartridges. If the enemy came to Virginia, he could just walk in.

The enemy came. On December 30, 1780, a fleet of twenty-seven boats was sighted at the mouth of Chesapeake Bay, off the Virginia capes. Governor Jefferson, in Richmond, was immediately informed and he sent General Nelson down the river "to call on the Militia in that quarter."

In Richmond no one knew the origin or destination of the hostile fleet at the capes, since the Governor's intelligence service was virtually nonexistent. It took him three days to learn that the enemy fleet was sailing up the James River, that it carried several hundred armed British troops, and that it was commanded by an American turncoat, General Benedict Arnold. Distressed, Jefferson ordered out the militia and consulted with General Steuben, who commanded in Virginia. The legislature went home. The Governor was left to face the British music.

Not until Benedict Arnold was close to Richmond did Jefferson realize that the State capital was the enemy objective. Richmond had no defenses. Quickly Jefferson ordered that the public stores be removed. Men worked all night. At one o'clock in the morning of January 6 the Governor hurried from the capital to get his wife and young children, who were at Tuckahoe, out of reach of danger. He took them eight miles farther up the river, left them with some friends, and hurried back to Manchester, across the river from Richmond. He had been on horseback for thirty-six hours, and now his horse fell exhausted within sight of the besieged capital. Jefferson swung the saddle on his back and walked to a farmhouse, where he obtained a colt. When he got to Manchester he could see, from across the river, that the British had already taken Richmond.

As he watched, fire burst from the capital. Arnold and his men were burning public buildings and stores of food and tobacco. Then they left the way they came.

Two days after the invasion Jefferson "resumed his residence" in Richmond and proceeded to investigate the damage. The losses turned out to be not as severe as the blows to the Governor's reputation and to the State's prestige.

Only nine buildings were burned by Arnold's expedition, but there was enough smoke to blacken the reputation of the Governor.

4

The following months were the darkest that the American cause had yet experienced. The British had an iron grip on the seacoast and seemed to be slowly choking the breath of life out of the American defenders. When the British commander, Lord Cornwallis, entered Virginia in the spring of 1781, the State seemed lost. Cornwallis cut into Virginia like a knife into an apple. Despondency was universal. Even Jefferson, whose temper was usually serene, gave way to discouragement. He appealed to General Washington to save his native State.

For strategic reasons General Washington could not leave the North. Lord Cornwallis penetrated into Virginia as far west as the River Anna (Rivanna), about fifty miles from Jefferson's home.

Jefferson and the legislature fled to Charlottesville. Cornwallis conceived the clever idea of capturing Governor and legislature. He detached one of his officers, the "hunting leopard" Colonel Tarleton, and a troop of cavalry with instructions to dash swiftly to Charlottesville to capture Virginia's legislators and then to near-by Monticello to seize the Governor.

Tarleton and his troops got to the tiny town of Louisa,[2] within about forty-five miles of Charlottesville, before a single American realized what was afoot. Fortunately, there was one such American, Captain John Jouett. Stopping at the Cuckoo Tavern in Louisa to spend the night, he looked out of the window and saw the white-coated troopers galloping westward. Between Louisa and the Blue Ridge Mountains there was only one town of any importance—Charlottesville. It took no gift of divination on the part of Captain Jouett to guess whither the British were heading. The Captain quickly swung on his horse and galloped toward Monticello to warn the Governor. His Prince Charley was considered the "best and fleetest horse in

[2] In 1950 the population of Louisa was 344.

seven counties." Jouett, wearing a bright red coat and a plumed hat, was racing Tarleton over mountain paths known only to a few native Virginians. At four-thirty in the morning, after having ridden five and one-half hours over wild mountain paths, Jouett reached Monticello.

Awakened by the clattering of hoofs, Jefferson came out on the east portico to see what was doing. The scarlet-coated officer, his plume askew, rode up to the steps, dismounted, and delivered the news to His Excellency. Jefferson invited Jouett into the house, treated him to a glass of his best Madeira, and sent him down the road to Charlottesville to wake up the legislators who were sleeping at the Swan Tavern. The Governor woke his family and guests, among whom were the Speakers of the two houses and several members of the legislature. The gentlemen breakfasted leisurely and departed for Charlottesville, where they called a quorum and adjourned to Staunton, some thirty-five miles further west. Jefferson sent his wife, who was ill, and his children in a carriage down the mountain and remained behind, arranging his papers and putting things in order. His favorite horse, saddled and newly shod, was waiting for him at a designated spot on the road.

A few miles from Charlottesville, Colonel Tarleton detached a small troop under Captain McLeod to ride up the hill to Monticello, seize Jefferson, and hold the place as a lookout point. Monticello commanded a view of about a dozen counties. While Jefferson was packing his papers and the servants were storing valuables in the cellar, a man rode up with the news that the British were coming up the mountain. The Governor hurried to the spot where his horse was waiting. Before mounting, Jefferson looked at Charlottesville through a telescope. The town seemed quiet, and the Governor, who disliked unnecessary haste, concluded that the report of British occupation was exaggerated. He walked back to the house, but on the way he decided to take another look, and saw that the streets of Charlottesville were overrun with dragoons. Jefferson retraced his steps and got on the horse.

Five minutes later McLeod's troopers surrounded Monticello. They took over the estate like harmless guests. Tarleton had given McLeod "strict orders . . . to suffer nothing to be injured." They remained in Monticello for eighteen hours and then they left after having, in the words of Jefferson, "preserved everything with sacred care." They behaved with similar circumspection in Charlottesville, where Colonel Tarleton succeeded in capturing seven members of the legislature. For the rest, Jefferson tells, Tarleton "did little injury to the inhabitants."

Weary from their flight and full of anxiety for the future, the members of the legislature looked for a scapegoat and found one. Who was to blame for their plight? The Governor. Who was responsible for the defenselessness of the State? The Chief Magistrate. What the State needed in the crisis, cried a large number of the legislators, was a dictator, not a democrat.

They argued that events showed that a democratic government was no good in wartime—hence by implication no good at any time. They insisted that the constitution be suspended and one man (preferably Patrick Henry or some general) be given absolute powers. The very suggestion was outrageous to Jefferson. If self-government was worthless in a crisis, then it had no·worth at any time. For the test of an institution is its workability under the greatest point of tension. The "Dictator party" was determined to smash the State government, to prove that it did not work. Then a dictator would step in and "save" the State.

Jefferson's friends and followers united for a decisive struggle on the floor of the House. The vote for a dictator was taken in secret, and was barely defeated. "A few votes only" decided the issue in favor of democracy.

The "Dictator party" aimed a new dagger at the Governor. On June 12, 1781, just as Jefferson's term was coming to a close, a young member of the legislature named George Nicholas made his debut in the House of Delegates by asking that Governor Jefferson's conduct be officially investigated. Jefferson's friends were in no position to protest, since it would have exposed them to the charge of being afraid to face the truth. The legislature voted unanimously "That at the next session of the Assembly an inquiry be made into the conduct of the Executive of this State for the last twelve months."

Although there was nothing else the legislature could do, as Jefferson realized, it was nevertheless an unprecedented insult. He had entered office under popular approval and now, two years later, he was leaving under a cloud. Sick at heart, Jefferson retired to his home and asked George Nicholas, who was his neighbor and later his devoted friend, for a list of particular charges that would be made against him in the autumn, so that he could defend himself. Nicholas complied and Jefferson answered every point meticulously. The charges dealt mainly with Arnold's and Cornwallis's invasions of Virginia and Jefferson's behavior in those crises.

When autumn came, Jefferson's neighbors in Albemarle County unanimously elected him to the legislature in order that he be given a decent chance to defend his official character. He vowed to resign and leave politics forever as soon as he had vindicated himself.

Upon his arrival in Richmond, Jefferson found, to his surprise, that the legislature was not merely friendly but apologetic. As a mark of genuine esteem, and perhaps of a bad conscience, the House of Delegates honored him by naming him to important committees and by selecting him member of the Congress in Philadelphia, a position which Jefferson turned down. In the meantime, a committee of five was going through Nicholas's charges and Jefferson's replies.

In the middle of December the committee completed its report. Jefferson rose and said quietly that he was ready to answer all charges. He read the same replies that he had made to George Nicholas. No one on the floor either asked any questions or raised any objections. Then Colonel John Banister, chairman of the committee of five, brought his report to the House. Its findings were clear and sharp: "no information being offered on the subject matter of the said inquiry, except that some rumors prevailed," the committee concluded that "said rumors were groundless." Immediately after, the House of Burgesses unanimously adopted a resolution of thanks to the former Governor for his upright conduct and thus vindicated him:

> Resolved, That the sincere thanks of the General Assembly be given to our former Governor, Thomas Jefferson, Esq. for his impartial, upright, and attentive administration of the powers of the Executive, whilst in office . . . the Assembly wish therefore, in the strongest manner, to declare the high opinion which they entertain of Mr. Jefferson's ability, rectitude, and integrity as chief magistrate of this Commonwealth, and mean, by thus publicly avowing their opinion, to obviate all future and remove all former unmerited censure.

In the legislature and all over the State Jefferson's friends and followers celebrated his vindication. His Albemarle constituents and neighbors received him jubilantly upon his return home. A thick-skinned politician would have taken the affair as merely a passing, albeit a somewhat unpleasant, incident which turned out right. A scheming politician would have made capital out of his thorough vindication by the legislature. But not Jefferson. "I find," he once told Francis Hopkinson, "the pain of a little censure, even when it is unfounded, is more acute

an the pleasure of much praise." He could not forget that he
ad stood *accused* before his peers—he, the most well-mean-
ig and most honest of men. Never again, he told his friends
vith an undercurrent of bitterness, would he return to public
fe. That was the low-watermark period in Jefferson's life,
hen his philosophy deserted him.

He sulked for more than a year. His friends, even so de-
oted a one as James Madison, became annoyed. Such a petty
:action, though understandable under the circumstances, was
ot worthy of a man of Jefferson's caliber.

Another one of Jefferson's disciples, the twenty-three-year-
ld James Monroe, informed the former Governor that public
pinion was condemning him for his selfish behavior in with-
rawing from public life. In a long reply Jefferson admitted
.at, after all his years of sacrifice in the public service, the
:gislature's investigation of his conduct had given him an aw-
il shock. Only death could heal the wound that was inflicted
pon his spirit:

> I might have comforted myself under the disapprobation of
> the well-meaning but uninformed people yet that of their repre-
> sentatives was a shock on which I had not calculated. . . . I had
> been suspected . . . in the eyes of the world, without the least
> hint . . . being made public which might restrain them from
> supposing that I stood arraigned for treason of the heart and
> not merely weakness of the mind; and I felt that these injuries
> . . . had inflicted a wound on my spirit which will only be
> cured by the all-healing grave.

CHAPTER SEVEN

PHILOSOPHER

(1781-1783)

JEFFERSON was certain, at the age of thirty-eight, that never again would public life ensnare him. He had no need, he felt, for politics as a creative expression.

His country, he was sure, no longer had need of his services, particularly so since the military situation had changed in favor of the American cause. For almost simultaneously with Jefferson's retirement from the governorship, in the summer of 1781, the French fleet arrived and began to break the British stranglehold on America. In September, 1781, the French Admiral de Grasse battered the British fleet in the Chesapeake. Six weeks later came the electrifying news of Lord Cornwallis' surrender with his entire army to General Washington at Yorktown. British power was broken and American independence virtually assured.

Jefferson felt that he could now devote himself to the kind of life he craved, the life of a cultivated grand seigneur who was at the same time a scientist and a large-scale farmer who was also a philosopher.

His home, Monticello, a half-domed, Italian-styled structure perched in proud isolation amid shrubs and flowers on the crest of the hill, had windows facing every point of the compass. The windows in the house were open to every breeze that blew from the misty pastel-blue of the Blue Ridge and the darkling green of the surrounding hills. The house was not simply light and airy, but as spacious as ingenuity could make it and as comfortable as imagination could conceive it. "Mr. Jefferson," a French aristocratic visitor remarked, "is the first American who has consulted the fine arts to know how he should shelter himself from the weather." This visitor, the Marquis de Chastellux, spent four delightful days in Monticello in the spring of 1782. The observant Frenchman was impressed by the genius and charm of his American host:

> Let me describe you a man, not yet forty, tall, and with mild and pleasing countenance, but whose mind and understanding are ample substitutes for every exterior grace. An American who without ever having quitted his own country, is at once

56

musician, skilled in drawing, a geometrician, an astronomer, a natural philosopher, legislator, and statesman. . . . A mild and amiable wife, charming children, of whose education he himself takes charge. . . .

I found his first appearance serious, nay even cold; but before I had been two hours with him we were as intimate as if we had passed our whole lives together; walking, books, but above all, a conversation always varied and interesting.

At about the same time another Frenchman, the Marquis de Barbé-Marbois, secretary of the French Legation in Philadelphia, asked Jefferson to supply him with some data on the State of Virginia. The French Government was anxious to know something concrete about its American ally, and the Legation in Philadelphia was making inquiries in the various States. The result as to Virginia was an early American masterpiece.

Gathering and compiling information about his native State was a task entirely to Jefferson's taste. His notebooks were filled with observations on natural phenomena, and his mind was stocked with a vast store of scientific information. All he needed to do was to marshal his stuff on paper. But he did more: he presented his data not as dry facts, but as muscle reinforcing a point of view. He worked over and polished his *Notes on Virginia* for months. The "notes" were really sculptured essays on a variety of subjects, ranging from paleontology to history, from zoology to theology, from anthropology to economics, from geography to botany. He consulted no reference book but his own eyes and his memory.

The *Notes on Virginia* remained in manuscript for about two years, until Jefferson got to Paris. Then he had two hundred copies struck off at a cost of 1,254 francs. Copies were distributed among a circle of carefully chosen friends, with the request that they be kept absolutely confidential.

2

The retired philosopher at Monticello was not destined to enjoy his retirement. His fragile and beautiful wife Martha had given birth to five children in ten years. Three of those children died. In May, 1782, at the age of thirty-three and a half, the delicate and ailing Martha gave birth to a sixth child.[1] This last childbirth was too much for Mrs. Jefferson. She was the great love of his life, and he dared not think of what existence would be without her. For four months he never left her bedside, nursing her with desperate tenderness.

Edward Bacon, the manager of the Jefferson plantation, is

[1] This child, a girl, died two years later.

authority for the statement that the dying Martha exacted a promise from her husband not to give their children a stepmother: "Mr. Jefferson promised her solemnly that he would never be married again." In view of their passionate and unclouded love, the story is credible.

One noonday in September, Jefferson's "state of dreadful suspense," as he described it, came to an end. He had watched the last spark of his wife's life flickering out, and he was dazed into insensibility. His sister Mrs. Carr led him out of the room. Moments later Martha expired. Jefferson had seen her die for four months, but he was unprepared for the shock. He fell in a frighteningly long faint. For three weeks he kept to his room, a silent being, tortured with sorrow. Night and day he walked incessantly up and down his room, alone with his wild thoughts, as if he had lost his reason. When he went out at last, it was to mount his horse and ride into the mountains, aimlessly rambling along unfrequented paths, a solitary man weeping for his beloved. Occasionally his ten-year-old daughter accompanied him and was a silent witness "to many a violent burst of grief." For six months he was alone with his sorrow, never communicating with, never writing to, anyone.

Gradually the flames of grief died down, and Jefferson began to take himself in hand. A father of three orphaned girls, he could not go on torturing himself to madness. Martha, the eldest child, was ten, Mary four, Lucy an infant; they all needed care. Jefferson took his children to Ampthill, residence of Archibald Cary, and had them inoculated for smallpox. He was the children's "chief nurse."

Jefferson remained at Ampthill, not knowing what to do with himself. Martha's death had shattered his plans for retirement. Monticello was too intimately associated with ten years of "unchequered happiness," as he said, for him to be able to live there now alone. A decision as to his future was finally made by his friends, who had never given up the hope of enticing him back into politics, where they felt he naturally belonged.

In Philadelphia the Congress was then making arrangements for peace with England. This gave Jefferson's friends an idea. Someone in the Congress, possibly James Madison, suggested that Jefferson be appointed Minister Plenipotentiary to negotiate the peace. The proposal was unanimously approved. News of the appointment reached Jefferson in November and, to the delight of his friends, he did not turn it down.

Jefferson tore himself away from his two youngest children, whom he left with their aunt Mrs. Francis Eppes, and took the

ird girl, Martha, with him to Philadelphia. There he left her
a a private school. He was to sail for Europe from Baltimore
n the French frigate *Romulus*, but bad luck was with him.
he *Romulus* was blocked in the ice, and sailing was delayed
definitely. The old year went and the new year came, and
ill the ship was ice-blocked.

At the end of January, 1783, word came to Philadelphia that
ae *Romulus* might break from its icy grip and set sail from
altimore. Jefferson and his secretary, Major Franks, hurried
outh to catch the boat. It was a terrible journey of five days.
erry service across the various arms of the Chesapeake was
retched. The two travelers waited in miserable inns, cold
nd unhappy, for the chance to cross icy waters.

But the *Romulus* did not sail. Its captain, the Chevalier de
illebrun, was informed that a small British fleet of seven ships
totaling 268 guns) was lurking at the capes of the Chesapeake
• intercept the French ship with the American envoy. Jeffer-
on, with dry modesty, considered this "a most amazing force
or such an object." Jefferson could neither return to Philadel-
hia in comfort nor resign his position in honor. Like the
igate *Romulus*, the Plenipotentiary was himself caught in a
m—a Minister who could not go to his post, a father who
ould not rejoin his family.

While Jefferson was fretting, news came from Europe that
provisional treaty of peace had been agreed upon. Jefferson
turned to Philadelphia. By the middle of March, news of the
eace treaty was confirmed and Jefferson asked the Congress
 release him. It finally resolved to inform "the Hon. Thomas
efferson . . . that Congress consider the object of his appoint-
ent so far advanced as to render it unnecessary for him to
ursue his voyage."

For three and a half months of trouble and vexation, Jeffer-
on was given polite thanks. The Congress thanked him for his
readiness . . . in undertaking a service." He returned to
Monticello somber and uncommunicative. This was Jefferson's
ortieth birthday. For the first time in his life he was aimless.

Gradually he began to return to his normal occupations. As
oon as it was known that Jefferson was available again, the
gislature of Virginia chose him as delegate to the Congress,
• take his seat in November.

The Congress was sitting in Annapolis, and there Jefferson
ined it in the middle of December. He worked quietly, with
oncentrated energy, sitting on every important committee,
rawing up reports, and soothing exasperated tempers. His
astery of the assuaging word and the flattering phrase was
emarkable; his conciliatory temper was pervasive. In no time,

the quiet delegate from Monticello was regarded as the mo
influential member of the Congress.

In the six months that he was in the Congress he heade
most of the important committees and drafted no less tha
thirty-one essential state papers. Some of these papers hav
become foundation stones of the American republic. Amor
these reports was Jefferson's classic paper proposing the doll
unit and the present coinage of the United States.

CHAPTER EIGHT

AMBASSADOR

(1784-1787)

IN MAY, 1784, Congress once more appointed Jefferson to a foreign post. He was made Minister Plenipotentiary, with instructions to collaborate with John Adams and Benjamin Franklin in negotiating treaties of commerce with European nations.

Jefferson went to Philadelphia to fetch his daughter, Martha, and then set out with her for the North in quest of a passage to Europe. They spent eighteen leisurely June days covering the distance from New York to Boston.

They sailed on July 5 on the ship *Ceres*. The crossing was short and pleasant, taking only nineteen days from Boston to Cowes. Jefferson's young daughter described the trip in a letter to friends in Philadelphia: "We had a lovely passage in a beautiful new ship, that had made but one passage before. There were only six passengers, all of whom Papa knew, and a fine sunshine all the way, with a sea which was as calm as a river."

2

Paris has fascinated Americans since Americans began to cross the Atlantic. Jefferson was no exception. He had never seen a city larger than Philadelphia, with its population of about 25,000, and now he found himself in the biggest metropolis in Christendom. The impact of Paris upon the sensitive planter from Virginia was stunning.

The French capital had everything to offer to a man of Jefferson's tastes and habits, although he never learned to like either congested streets or the proximity of teeming proletarians. Paris, with its beautiful, shifting pastel clouds, with its boulevards and bridges and parks and palaces and river quays, was an artist's dream and a gentleman's paradise. The city had a population of about 600,000, some getting fat on capon, and others, many others, living miserably and half-starving. About one-fifth of the population was unemployed, their sullen and hungry faces seen everywhere along the thirteen hundred streets of the city. But over and above the restive masses of

the poor, who were soon to blow up the whole mess, there wa
a stratum of super-refinement, of exquisite living, of preciou
manners. Men of culture and of taste met frequently and talke
lofty ideas and read serious books; worldly men and wome
met, gossiped, flirted, and seduced. It was an exciting and stin
ulating world into which Jefferson entered.

His first step in Paris was to call upon Benjamin Frankli
who lived at Passy. His second was to take an apartment. H
found a place on the cul-de-sac Têtebout (now rue Taitbout
near the present Boulevard Haussmann. Later he moved to
house at the corner of the Grande Route des Champs Elysé
and the rue Neuve de Berry, where he remained for the re
of his stay in Paris.

Jefferson placed Martha in an aristocratic convent, the Al
baye Royale de Panthémont, "the best and most genteel scho
in Paris." The school was recommended to Jefferson by
"lady friend" of Lafayette's.

The young French hero of the American Revolution was on
of Jefferson's most loyal supporters. It was Lafayette who gav
his American friend the golden key to French society. Anyon
recommended and received by the Marquis de Lafayette, wh
was himself connected with the highest French families, wa
sure to find an opening almost everywhere in Paris. Throug
Lafayette, Jefferson met an ever-increasing number of uppe
class Frenchmen and Frenchwomen. Jefferson's home on th
Grande Route des Champs Elysées became a center of sophis
ticated men and women. He dined out regularly, and was
visitor to the better salons.

Though Jefferson enjoyed life in Paris socially, he suffere
climatically. Jefferson's tough, lanky constitution was no proo
against Parisian rains. Though his health had been well-nig
perfect in the high clear climate of his native Virginia, it gav
way before the humidity of Paris. The first winter he spen
largely indoors, in great discomfort.

He recovered in the spring, and began his routine of risin
early and riding or walking a few miles daily. By the time hi
forty-second birthday came around he was able to walk seve
or eight miles every day. On one of these walks he stumbled
fell, and broke his right wrist. It was set badly, and never quit
recovered its suppleness or strength. Jefferson learned to writ
very well with his left hand. Years later, when he was an ol
man, he fell again and broke his left wrist. Thenceforth writin
was to be an ordeal for him.

Mornings he would read, study, and write. By one o'clock h
was ready for his hike. Later in the afternoon he would g

browsing through the streets, shops, and stalls. Those were happy, adventurous hours.

There was progress and invention everywhere. Jefferson, like the equally inventive Dr. Franklin, even looked forward to the time when men would fly in machines, like birds. But above all, it was books that fascinated the Virginian. He roamed through the bookstores, browsed through the shops, touched rare and strange books with the suppressed thrill of the reverent bibliophile.

3

Jefferson's official duties were not heavy, though they were sometimes irksome. At first he was only a Minister Plenipotentiary, whose object was to arrange treaties of commerce. The actual envoy was Benjamin Franklin, a man whose popularity was as great as his wit was renowned. In the spring of 1785, however, Franklin retired and was succeeded by Jefferson. It was then that Jefferson made the bon mot that convinced Frenchmen that he was worthy of occupying the place which Dr. Franklin had so long graced. When France's Foreign Minister, the Count de Vergennes, said to the Virginian, "It is you who replace Monsieur Franklin?" Jefferson replied, "No one can replace him, sir: I am only his successor."

4

France taught Jefferson the horrors of bad government and the miseries of inequality. What he saw in Europe confirmed his conviction, so fully justified by history, that the future belonged to America. In a letter to Monroe he burst out:

> I sincerely wish you may find it convenient to come here. The pleasure of the trip will be less than you expect but the utility greater. It will make you adore your own country, its soil, its climate, its equality, liberty, laws, people & manners. My God! how little do my country men know what precious blessings they are in possession of, and which no other people on earth enjoy. I confess I had no idea of it myself. While we shall see multiplied instances of Europeans going to live in America, I will venture to say no man now living will ever see an instance of an American removing to settle in Europe & continuing there.

On his long daily hikes through the country he would stop and talk to peasants and laborers, and he heard tales of woe that wrung his heart with pity. One day he took a walk to Fontainebleau, and on the way met a workingwoman who talked freely about her wretched existence. That conversation gave him a shocking insight into the dark, smoldering depths

of prerevolutionary France. In a letter to the Reverend Jame
Madison he relates:

> This . . . led me into a train of reflections on that unequa
> division of property which occasions the numberless instance
> of wretchedness which I had observed in this country & . .
> all over Europe. The property of this country is absolutely con
> centrated in a very few hands. . . . These employ the flowe
> of the country as servants (some . . . having as many as 20
> domestics). . . . the most numerous of all classes, that is, th
> poor . . . cannot find work. I asked myself what could be th
> reason that so many should be permitted to beg who are willin
> to work, in a country where there is a very considerable propor
> tion of uncultivated lands . . . ? I am conscious that an equa
> division of property is impracticable. But the consequences o
> this enormous inequality producing so much misery to the bul
> of mankind, legislators cannot invent too many devices fo
> subdividing property. . . . The earth is given as a commo
> stock for man to labour & live on. . . . But it is not too soon t
> provide by every possible means that as few as possible shall b
> without a little portion of land. The small land holders are th
> most precious part of the state.

France the famous, the beautiful, the core of Europea
civilization, did not impress the "savage of the mountains o
America," as Jefferson described himself ironically. He mad
comparisons between Europe and America, usually to the dis
advantage of Europe. If he had been asked to state his objec
tions to Europe in one brief sentence, he probably would hav
replied: Misery at the bottom and mischief at the top. "Eu
rope," he concluded bluntly, "was hell."

He rejected the whole social and political system on whic
European society was based. The caste-ridden and poverty
stricken world, even though it received him with cordiality an
deference, was not for him, and still less for his countrymen o
the other side of the Atlantic! One year after his arrival i
France, in a letter to his Italian friend Bellini he summarize
his impressions:

> I find the general fate of humanity here most deplorable. Th
> truth of Voltaire's observation, offers itself perpetually, tha
> every man here must be either the hammer or the anvil.

Was there nothing good in Europe! Yes, there was. Jeffer
son wryly admitted that France's strawberries, cherries, plums
gooseberries, and pears were better than those in America. Th
grapes were likewise superior. So were the manners of French
men, their arts, and their architecture. Jefferson envied French
men their temperance, recalling the heavy drinking among th

entry of his own country. He also envied Europe its arts,
specially music, for which he always craved.

He hoped that no American would ever come to Europe to
ve or to study. "An American, coming to Europe for educa-
on, loses in his knowledge, in his morals, in his health, in his
abits, and in his happiness."

5

In March, 1786, Jefferson had occasion to confirm his im-
ressions of European civilization by a visit to England. John
dams had invited him to join him in London to help in the
egotiation of a treaty with the visiting Minister from Tripoli.
He stayed in England for seven weeks, by turns skeptical
nd appreciative. Together with Minister Adams, he was duly
resented at the court of George the Third. It was not a happy
xperience. His Majesty had an understandable prejudice
gainst "rebels," and he also may have read the Declaration of
ndependence, in which he was mercilessly castigated as a
rant. When the two Americans were introduced to him, His
Majesty promptly turned his back upon them—the insult being
ntended for Jefferson more than for Adams. The author of
ne Declaration of Independence took the cutting hint that he
as not welcome in Britain. "It was impossible," he tells with
touch of bitterness, "for anything to be more ungracious,
an their [the King's and Queen's] notice of Mr. Adams &
yself. I saw at once that the ulcerations in the narrow mind
f that mulish being left nothing to be expected on the subject
f my attendance."

Some of the English Ministers took their cue from the mon-
rch and were likewise rude to Jefferson. Deciding that it was a
aste of time to court politicians, he devoted himself to visit-
ng places in and near London. Except for gardens and ma-
hines, the land of his ancestors did not greatly impress him.

6

Some time after Jefferson returned from England, he fell
n love. The affair was brief and apparently not successful.
Maria Cecilia Cosway was a miniature-painter. Her husband,
Richard Cosway, was likewise a miniature-painter. They were
n English couple who had lived on the Continent for some
me, and Jefferson probably met Mrs. Cosway in one of the
aris salons.

Not very much is known of the Jefferson-Cosway relation-
hip, nor even that anything serious took place between them.
ut whatever happened, there is reason to believe that Jeffer-
on was smitten hard. He had repressed his emotions since his

wife's death, and now Mrs. Cosway caused a brief and, f
him, somewhat violent flare-up. When Mrs. Cosway left Pari
Jefferson was overcome with emotion, and he poured himse
out in a long, prolix, Wertherian, unsubtle epistle. As a lo
letter, it may perhaps not rank with those of Abélard ar
Héloïse, but as a psychological document it is invaluable. Th
letter to Mrs. Cosway reveals the conflict between the man
sentiment and the man of intellect. In the case of Jefferso.
sentiment was rarely a victor.

My Dear Madam,—Having performed the last sad office
handing you into your carriage . . . and seen the wheels g
actually into motion, I turned on my heel & walked, more de;
than alive, to the opposite door. . . . I was carried hom
Seated by my fireside, solitary & sad, the following dialog
took place between my Head & my Heart:

Head. Well, friend, you seem to be in a pretty trim.

Heart. I am indeed the most wretched of all earthly being
Overwhelmed with grief, every fibre of my frame distend
beyond its natural powers to bear, I would willingly meet wha
ever catastrophe should leave me no more to feel or to fear.

Head. These are the eternal consequences of your warm
and precipitation. . . .

Heart. Oh, my friend! this is no moment to upbraid n
foibles. I am rent into fragments by the force of my grief!

The letter continued in this vein. In one passage Jeffersc
confessed, "my mind broods . . . constantly over your depa
ture," but he never came out flatly and said that he loved he

Mrs. Cosway who, one suspects, had encouraged the flirt
tion in Paris, for some reason did not continue it. Her rep
to Jefferson's eighteen-page outpouring consisted of four line
Your four lines, he wrote her in effect, show that you at lea
still think of me—"little indeed, but better a little than none
Even that little soon ceased.

7

In the third year of Jefferson's residence in Paris, he decid
to see something of the other parts of France and Europe. H
object was to learn what Europe had to offer in the way of ar
crafts, and agriculture, and then to give America the cream
his observations.

Jefferson left Paris in March, 1787, and for three mont
he toured southern France and northern Italy. It was an e
perience as memorable as it was valuable, particularly since I
traveled with notebook in hand, looking for plants, forge
bridges, machines, gardens, chimneys, sidewalks, pumps, ar
everything that was ingenious or practical. Much of what t

saw and put down on paper was to bear practical fruit in America. His *Memoranda* of the tour cover fifty-four printed pages, or approximately twenty-one thousand words. "I have not visited all the manufactures at this place," he wrote from Lyon to his secretary William Short, "because the knowledge of them would be useless, and would extrude from the memory other things more worth retaining. Architecture, painting, sculpture, agriculture, the condition of the laboring poor fill all my moments."

At Nîmes Jefferson was powerfully impressed by the remains of Roman grandeur. No student of history and architecture could remain indifferent to the majestic ruins of the ancient Romans. And Jefferson, like the historian Edward Gibbon a few years earlier, succumbed to the moldering beauty of the ruins. He wrote from Nîmes to his Parisian friend Madame de Tessé:

> Here I am, Madam, gazing whole hours at the Maison quarrée,[1] like a lover at his mistress.

The south of France in late March was like Southern California in the spring, fresh with new life under a dazzling blue sky. Jefferson was enchanted. His notes and letters sang with joy. "I am now in the land of corn, vine, oil, and sunshine," he wrote to William Short. "What more can man ask of Heaven? If I should happen to die at Paris I would beg of you to send me here and have me exposed to the sun, I am sure it would bring me to life again."

Jefferson was an indefatigable questioner. "In the course of my journey," he tells, "[I] have sought their [informed persons'] acquaintance with as much industry as I have avoided that of others who would have made me waste my time." When he reached Marseille he was asking everybody about rice, a superior variety of which he was hoping to plant in America. He got no satisfactory answer, so he decided to find out in northern Italy.

Jefferson spent his forty-fourth birthday on muleback, crossing the Maritime Alps into Italy.

In Turin Jefferson tasted a new wine, the "red wine of Nebiule," which he found "as sweet as the silky Madeira, as stringent on the palate as Bordeaux, and as brisk as Champagne." He was still pursuing rice in Piedmont, but did not find it until he reached Vercelli two days later. "From Vercelli to Novara the fields are all in rice, and now mostly under water." Here he made the discovery he was looking for, that the supe-

---

[1] He made sketches of this building which he later used as a model in his design of the State Capitol in Richmond, Virginia.

riority of European rice to American (Carolinian) was inhe‐
ent in the species, and not, as he thought, due to a bett‐
cleaning machine used in Italy.

Jefferson decided to take with him some of the Piedmonte
rice and grow it in America. But to his surprise he was to
that he could take rice out of the country only at the risk of h
life. There was a death penalty attached to the exportation
rice from Piedmont. Jefferson considered that sort of regul‐
tion so arbitrary that he had no scruples about breaking tl
law. He filled his coat pockets full of rice and then, to mal
doubly sure that he would get his precious species out
Piedmont, he hired a muleteer to smuggle two sacks of ri
across the Apennines to Genoa.

From Genoa Jefferson sailed back to Marseille; for two mi
erable days on sea he was "mortally sick." Afterward he too
it easy. He rented a barge on the tree-lined canal of Langu
doc, dismounted his glass-doored carriage from its wheels, ar
had himself towed up toward Toulouse.

8

The following year Jefferson took another trip, this time
the Low Countries and western Germany. On March 3, 178
he left Paris by carriage and four days later arrived at Tl
Hague, where he saw John Adams, who was now America
Minister there, and talked over some diplomatic business.

From The Hague he went to Amsterdam, then to Utrecl
and Nimwegen and points east. Like Peter the Great a centu
earlier, Jefferson was impressed by the mechanical arts of tl
ingenious Dutch, and he spent considerable time makir
sketches.

What he did not sketch he described in detail. He saw an
described a machine for drawing empty boats over a dam
Amsterdam. He admired a bridge across a canal "formed b
two scows, which open each to the opposite shore and l
boats pass." Another bridge he liked was one set on a swive
which turned so as to permit boats to pass. A hexagonal lanter
over a street door also struck him as a fine idea.

He crossed the Rhine from prosperous Holland into Ge
many. Jefferson was surprised by the poverty of the German
The reason was obvious. "The soil and climate are the same,
he noted; "the governments alone differ." The Dutch had
comparatively free and comparatively responsible governmen
The Germans did not. "With the poverty, the fear also of slave
is visible in the faces of the Prussian subjects." The countr
was poorly cultivated. "Universal and equal poverty over
spreads the whole." German farmhouses, Jefferson observe

were made of "mud, the better sort of brick," covered with thatch.

In Westphalia Jefferson looked over the famous hogs—"tall, gaunt, and with heavy lop ears"—from which fine pork and ham were made. Cologne impressed him as a city with plenty of commerce and plenty of poverty. Trade was in the hands of a handful of Protestants, who were being discriminated against by the Government, "which is Catholic, and excessively intolerant." In the region of Coblentz Jefferson studied the wines, specially Moselle. In Coblentz itself, in the Elector's palace, Jefferson first saw an invention which was to become a household institution in later America—central heating.

Between Frankfort-on-the-Main and Hanau in Hesse-Cassel Jefferson again observed the devastating effects of a tyrannical government. Frankfort, an independent and self-governing free city, was rich and active; Hanau was a ghost town. "In Frankfort all is life, bustle, and motion; in Hanau the silence and quiet of the mansions of the dead. Nobody is seen moving in the streets; every door is shut; no sound of the saw, the hammer, or other utensil of industry. The drum and fife is all that is heard." Such was one of the "effects of tyranny."

From Frankfort Jefferson went to Mainz, then to Mannheim and Heidelberg, where he admired the wines and the aviaries. The return journey led through Carlsruhe, Strassburg, Nancy, and Château Thierry.

In the latter part of April, after a journey of about seven weeks, he was back at his post in Paris.

CHAPTER NINE

SPECTATOR

(1787-1789)

JEFFERSON's return from his southern tour in 1787 coincided with two events of world importance. At Versailles, the Assembly of Notables, invited by the bewildered and bedeviled Louis XVI to advise him on the sorry state of the nation, was squabbling furiously but at the same time was preparing French public opinion for a new world. At Philadelphia at about the same time, fifty-five Americans, many of them personally known to Jefferson, gathered to shape a Constitution for the thirteen American States.

Jefferson was vitally interested in both the American convention and the French assembly, but distance prevented him from personal participation in the one, and diplomatic rules kept him from direct intervention in the other. There was nothing, however, to keep him from giving advice.

Among the Notables at Versailles was Jefferson's friend, the enthusiastic Lafayette. Like General Washington, Jefferson was fond of the young Marquis, though he by no means overlooked his shortcomings. Lafayette's greatest weakness, Jefferson observed, was "a canine appetite for popularity and fame."

Jefferson's insight into political drifts is well illustrated by his advice to Lafayette against imitating the United States. Every society must follow its own patterns, based upon its background and culture, and Jefferson was convinced that it would be a tragedy for France—a monarchy for over a thousand years—to plunge precipitously into an antiroyalist revolution. France was not ready for such a sharp cleavage with her past. Jefferson urged upon Lafayette the need for gradual reforms, the slow and systematic seizure of position after position, rather than impetuous revolution. He told Lafayette, who was a leading figure in the nascent French revolution, to keep "the good model of your neighboring country before your eyes" and then to "get on, step by step, towards a good constitution."

This advice came from a man who hated monarchs. The author of the Declaration of Independence, who had lashed George III as a sanguinary despot, advised the French that there was nothing to be gained from overthrowing the absolutist Louis XVI by force. It was cheaper to buy off the French King, for whom Jefferson had no exaggerated admiration, than to fight him. "If every advance is to be purchased by filling the royal coffers with gold, it will be gold well employed." But there was not much chance that even excellent advice could halt the march of the revolution.

2

While across the Atlantic at Philadelphia a group of men were hammering out a new Constitution for the young American republic, Jefferson, though physically absent, was not silent. He corresponded with such luminaries of the Constitutional Convention as George Wythe and James Madison, as well as with other influential Americans.

In his correspondence Jefferson argued in favor of republican institutions, clarified democratic ideas, refuted the assumptions of aristocrats and monarchists. He set himself up, as Voltaire had done on another occasion half a century earlier, as a one-man agency of enlightenment and democratic opinion. Lacking a press of his own and not being in a position to make speeches for his cause, Jefferson wrote letters. Of democratic government in America, he wrote to David Hartley:

> I have no fear, but that the result of our experiment will be, that men may be trusted to govern themselves without a master. Could the contrary of this be proved, I should conclude, either that there is no God, or that he is a malevolent being.

On the subject of rumors that some individuals in America were advocating a monarchy, Jefferson wrote to Benjamin Hawkins:

> . . . No race of kings has ever presented above one man of common sense in twenty generations. The best they can do is to leave things to their ministers. . . . If the king ever meddles it is to do harm.

To Governor Edward Rutledge of South Carolina he wrote in the same bitter-contemptuous tone of European despotisms:

> The European, are governments of kites over pigeons. The best schools for republicanism are London, Versailles, Madrid, Vienna, Berlin, &tc.

The cruel misgovernment of the European absolutisms, as well as the revolutionary fever that obtained in Paris, drove the ordinarily cautious Jefferson to a defense of the principle of rebellion. The blood of patriots and tyrants, he said, must re-

fresh the tree of liberty, regardless of whether it is planted i
Europe or America. His letter to Colonel William S. Smith
John Adams's son-in-law, is probably the most extreme state
ment on the subject of revolution ever penned by a responsible
American:

> God forbid we should ever be 20 years without such
> rebellion. . . . What country can preserve its liberties if it
> rulers are not warned from time to time that this people pre
> serve the spirit of resistance? Let them take arms. The remedy
> to set them right as to facts, pardon & pacify them. What signif
> a few lives lost in a century or two? The tree of liberty must b
> refreshed from time to time with the blood of patriots
> tyrants. It is its natural manure.

But the man whom Jefferson influenced most was Jame
Madison, one of Virginia's five remarkable delegates to th
Constitutional Convention at Philadelphia.[1] Jefferson's admira
tion for the always black-clad and dry-humored little Madison
was exceeded only by his affection for him. This confidence
was fully justified, particularly during the crucial struggle a
the Constitutional Convention when the insignificant-lookin
Madison emerged as one of the great political minds of hi
time.

After sixteen weeks of strenuous work and inevitable com
promise, the convention finished its work at Philadelphia. O
September 17, 1787, the draft was signed "By unanimous con
sent of the States present." It now faced the severe test o
public debate in the thirteen States.

Sometime in November Jefferson knew the provisions of th
Constitution, at least in outline. His first reaction was not favor
able, but he waited for more details before stating his objec
tions. In the latter part of December he apparently had a cop
of the Constitution before him. It was to Madison that h
wrote in incisive detail his criticism of the instrument.
should be stressed that the Constitution was without a Bill o
Rights. That is what shocked Jefferson.

In his letter to Madison, Jefferson explained that there wer
a number of things he liked about the Constitution. He ap
proved the division of the government into legislative, judi
ciary, and executive branches. He liked the provision that gav
the legislature the power to levy taxes, which preserved "invio
late the fundamental principle that the people are not to be
taxed but by representatives chosen immediately by them

[1] The quality of Virginia's delegates may be judged from the fact tha
they included, besides Madison, George Mason, Edmund Randolph
George Wythe, George Washington, Thomas Nelson, Richard Henry Lee
and Patrick Henry. Some of them, however, never accepted their positions

lves." He was "captivated by the compromise" that gave the
g States and the little States the same representation in the
enate. He liked the idea of the veto power for the President.
ll that was excellent, as far as it went. But it did not go far
nough to satisfy a man who believed that human liberties
ere at least as important as property rights. The original draft
f the Constitution did not emphasize human rights. To Jef-
erson a Constitution that did not specifically guarantee civil
berties was hardly worth the effort it took to engross it on
archment.

He then went on to elaborate the meaning and the signifi-
ance of a Bill of Rights that should be perpetually riveted to
ie Constitution, and not be dependent upon the shifting bias
f judges or the whims of public opinion. The people them-
lves had to be eternally protected against the Govern-
ient.

> Let me add that a bill of rights is what the people are entitled
> to against every government on earth, general or particular, &
> what no just government should refuse, or rest on inferences.[2]

Another thing about the Constitution that aroused Jeffer-
on's fears was that it put no time limit to office, particularly the
residential office. Experience, contemporary and historical,
howed that officeholders who were not limited in their tenure
nded to hang onto their positions by fair means or foul. Po-
tical power, Jefferson knew, offered irresistible temptations
o those who had once tasted it. A wise Constitution must put
limit to office in order to minimize temptation. Moreover,
efferson dreaded the possibility of the intervention of foreign
owers in American elections in order to achieve their own
nds. Such was the tragic example of contemporary Poland,
vhich, because she had an elective Chief Executive, was the
onstant prey of her powerful neighbors. To avoid these
angers, Jefferson favored—though he later modified his posi-
ion—a President elected for one term and ineligible forever
fter.

Another point that Jefferson raised as to the Constitution
vas the question of how much power the Government should
ave. Here he faced the seemingly insoluble dilemma of every
emocrat—that of liberty versus order. He knew that while
trong governments have always been the enemies of the peo-
le, weak governments have never been able to protect them.
owerful governments, moreover, by their very exercise of
ower have encouraged insurrections. The solution, Jefferson

[2] After long agitation the Bill of Rights (the first ten amendments to the
Constitution) was finally ratified by Congress on Dec. 15, 1791.

argued, lay in a balanced democracy where public opinic
should be free and enlightened and where the majority shou
prevail. And in no case should the Government be given tc
much power on any trumped-up excuse, such as the fear c
insurrections.

Jefferson's final reaction to the Constitution, especially afte
a Bill of Rights was attached to it, was enthusiastic. He r
garded it as "unquestionably the wisest ever yet presented t
men."

3

On July 14 a crowd of wrathful Parisians, having seize
arms, stormed the massive-stoned Bastille and killed its go
ernor. That night Louis XVI, at Versailles, was informed of th
turmoil in Paris. "It's a riot!" the King cried. "No, Sire," h
was told, "it's a revolution."

A curious incident occurred nearly a week after the fall c
the Bastille, showing the prevailing excitement as well as th
respect in which Jefferson was held. On July 20, 1789, Chan
pion de Cicé, Archbishop of Bordeaux, having been appointe
by the National Assembly chairman of its Constitutional Con
mittee, wrote a letter to the American Minister, who was co
sidered to be a specialist in such things, asking him to hel
in drafting a constitution for France.

Fearing that such an invitation would compromise his diplc
matic position, Jefferson quickly replied—in somewhat stilte
French—excusing himself on the ground that as a stranger h
could not participate, and giving the committee his "most si
cere and most ardent wishes" for perfect success.

The conflict over the constitution split the ranks of the A
sembly, and the abler members decided to talk over the situa
tion in a calm atmosphere. Lafayette knew where to go. H
wrote to Jefferson asking him for permission to bring ove
some members of the Assembly for dinner. Jefferson assure
him of their welcome. The next day they came, eight of th
leading men of the Assembly—Lafayette, Duport, Barnav
Alexander La Meth, Blacon, Mounier, Maubourg, and Dagou

After dinner the tablecloth was removed, wine was set o
the table, and Lafayette took the chair. From four o'clock i
the afternoon until ten at night the discussion went on, whil
Jefferson sat by, a sympathetic and silent listener. In his *Auto
biography* Jefferson pays tribute to the patriotism and elc
quence of his visitors, many of whom were destined to los
their heads under the knife of the guillotine.

That was Jefferson's last connection with the French Revc
lution.

For over a year Jefferson had been asking Congress for
ave, hoping to spend a few months in America and then re-
rn "to my prison." Now, after Washington's inauguration,
made an urgent plea to the Chief Executive for permission
visit America. President Washington promptly complied,
d at the end of August Jefferson received the good news. He
ft Paris in the latter part of September, believing that he
ould return to his post within a few months. A great num-
er of admiring and devoted friends gathered to bid the popu-
r Minister farewell. Most of them he was never to see again.
In his *Autobiography*, written thirty years later, Jefferson
id touching tribute to the country where he had spent five
ears rich in friendships and ripe with experience:

And here I cannot leave this great and good country without
expressing my sense of it's preeminence of character among the
nations of the earth. A more benevolent people, I have never
known, nor greater warmth & devotedness in their select friendships. Their kindness and accommodation to strangers is unparalleled, and the hospitality of Paris beyond anything I had
conceived to be practicable in a large city.[3] Their eminence too
in science, the communicative dispositions of their scientific
men, the politeness of the general manners, the ease and
vivacity of their conversation, give a charm to their society to
be found nowhere else. . . . So ask the travelled inhabitant of
any nation, In what country on earth would you rather live?—
Certainly in my own, where are all my friends, my relations,
and the earliest & sweetest affections and recollections of my
life. Which would be your second choice? France.

The Jeffersons, father and pretty daughters (little Polly had
oined him and Martha in Europe in July, 1787), sailed from
e Havre to Cowes on October 8. In England Jefferson's vo-
minous baggage, including plants and shepherd dogs, was ex-
mpted from customs examination by special order of Prime
inister Pitt. Contrary winds kept the Jeffersons from sailing
or two weeks, which time they spent sightseeing, especially on
e Isle of Wight. On October 22, 1789, the Jeffersons sailed
om Yarmouth, and after a smooth passage of one month they
t foot on American soil at Norfolk. Never again was Jefferson
leave his native country.

3 In this respect Paris certainly underwent a drastic change since Jeffer-
n lived there. Whatever virtues twentieth-century Parisians may have,
ospitality is decidedly not one of them.

CHAPTER TEN

SECRETARY OF STATE

(1790-1793)

W HEN Jefferson arrived at Norfolk on November 23, 1789
he opened a newspaper and, to his surprise, read that he ha
been nominated to the newly created post of Secretary o
State. He hoped that it was not true, for his plans were t
return to Paris for a few months and then to retire from po
tics for good—"to sink into the bosom of my family an
friends, and devote myself to studies more congenial to m
mind," he tells in his *Autobiography*.

Politics, however, kept on pursuing him. On their way t
Monticello the Jeffersons stopped off at Eppington, the res
dence of their relatives the Eppeses, and there an expres
courier brought Jefferson a letter from President Washingto
offering him the Secretaryship of State.

It was a flattering offer and Jefferson was not insensible t
it. That General Washington, for whom he had admiration,
not blind worship, should select him was a compliment whic
Jefferson appreciated. Still, accepting another responsible po
litical job meant more years of sacrifice, of mounting debt, o
separation from his family. Yet he could not categorically tur
down a man like George Washington. "It was impossible t
give a flat refusal to such a nomination," he told a friend.

On his way to Monticello Jefferson pondered the offer, an
after several days of soul-searching he informed the Preside
that he would accept the Secretaryship of State if he, Wash
ington, believed that it was best for the public welfare. "It i
not for an individual to choose his post," Jefferson told hin

Having thus left the decision in the hands of Presiden
Washington, Jefferson continued on his way to Monticello
Two days before Christmas they finally reached the outskir
of their estate. Jefferson had not been home for more than fiv
years.

Never before had there been such jubilation as now too
place when the master and his two attractive daughters arrive
home. The Negroes had learned of the approach of the Jeffe
sons when they reached Shadwell, four miles from Monticello

nd they streamed down the mountain in a frenzy of excitement. Nothing, not even the entreaties of the master, could top the slaves from unhitching the four horses and pushing nd dragging the heavy vehicle up the steep mountain to the ouse. And when Jefferson, himself deeply moved, stepped out f the carriage, his slaves fell upon him in an orgy of orship. "When the door of the carriage was opened," Martha elates, "they received him in their arms and bore him to the ouse, crowding around and kissing his hands and feet—some lubbering and crying—others laughing. It seemed impossible o satisfy their anxiety to touch and kiss the very earth which ore him."

2

Monticello had one important and welcome visitor after Christmas. It was James Madison, recently come from New York, where he was a member of Congress. Madison, it seems, ad promised President Washington that he would personally ind out how Jefferson felt about accepting the Secretaryship f State. Madison was also to use some gentle persuasion. The wo friends discussed the matter in detail, and Madison was ble to set Jefferson's mind at rest on a number of points. One f them concerned the duties of the office, involving both domestic and foreign affairs—it would not be as great a burden s Jefferson feared. After this conversation, Madison wrote to President Washington hinting that Jefferson was receptive: "All whom I have heard speak on the subject are remarkably olicitous for his acceptance, and I flatter myself that they will ot, in the final event, be disappointed."

That was a green light to the President. Once again Washington repeated his offer, this time stressing the importance of he position. The success of the Government depended upon ble men, and he, the President, could think of no one better tted to fill the post than Jefferson:

> I consider the office of secretary for the department of state very important on many accounts, and I know of no person, who in my judgment could better execute the duties of it than yourself. Its duties will probably be not quite so arduous and complicated in their execution as you may have been led at the first moment to imagine.

There was also pressure from other quarters. Madison wrote im from New York that "a universal anxiety is expressed for our acceptance." The "general good" required that the ablest 1an serve the young republic, and Jefferson was recognized by oth friend and foe as one of the commanding figures in merica. So great were the urgings for him to accept the

Cabinet post that he felt he could not refuse without "the da ger of giving disgust, and I value no office enough for that In the middle of February he finally informed the Preside that he would leave for New York as soon as possible to ta up his new duties.

There had been no false modesty about his hesitation to a cept a distinguished position under George Washington. T truth was that Jefferson could hardly afford to leave Monticel at this time. On and off, he had been away from his estate f about ten years, and in the absence of the master the lan had deteriorated. The estate comprised 10,000 acres and tw hundred slaves, but its productivity had gone down dange ously. His salary of $3,500 as Secretary of State ($500 mo than that of the other members of the Cabinet) would b just enough to support him personally. A few days before Je ferson left for New York, he made an appeal to priva bankers for a loan of $2,000. "I am only a farmer," he wrot "and have no resource but the productions of the farms." H offered his personal bond on his land for the loan, at 6 p cent interest.

A week before Jefferson left Monticello his daught Martha, a tall girl of seventeen, was married to her brillia second cousin, Thomas Mann Randolph of Tuckahoe. Th "high-toned" Randolph and the distinguished Martha, who John Randolph had once called "the noblest woman in Vi ginia," made a fine pair. Jefferson was delighted with his so in-law, whom he described as "a young gentleman of geniu science and honorable mind." [1]

3

Once again Jefferson went North, traveling by way of Ric mond, Alexandria, and Philadelphia. When he arrived Alexandria on March 10, the mayor and the citizens gave hi a public reception.

A heavy snowstorm slowed his progress to about two three miles a day, and it took him about a week to reac Philadelphia. Almost his first act was to visit the "venerabl and beloved" Franklin, who was sick in bed. Both friends we excited by the meeting. The eighty-four-year-old Franklin, wh had only one month to live, was eager to know what was goin on in France and how his friends were faring. Despite age an illness, he had been anxiously following the course of th revolution. "Ah," he had exclaimed upon hearing the news fro Paris and Versailles, "they served their apprenticeship America, and now they mean to set up for themselves."

[1] In Jefferson's absence, his son-in-law Randolph farmed the estate.

Jefferson was able to satisfy the old sage's curiosity about is French friends: "He went over all in succession, with a apidity and animation almost too much for his strength." 'hen he gave Jefferson a confidential paper to keep. Jefferson ater returned it inadvertently to Franklin's heir.

Jefferson arrived in New York on March 21. After being ordially received by the President, he rented a small house n Maiden Lane. Foreign and domestic problems were pressng for attention, and the new Secretary of State had little precedent to guide him and even less assistance to ease the burden of work. The Department of State consisted of three copying clerks at $500 a year and two at $800. There was no money for new appointments. In terms of sheer work it looked as if Jefferson would have to devote every ounce of strength and every minute of time to the job. But he felt that at least he could be useful, particularly as regards revolutionary France, around which a host of enemies was already crystalizing.

The New York atmosphere, both in the Government and n society, was so rabidly antidemocratic that Jefferson, recently arrived from a France that was in fever with democratic ideas, was scared for the future of the American republic. On many occasions when he dined out the Secretary of State found himself the only democrat among the guests.

> I cannot describe the wonder and mortification with which the table conversations filled me. Politics were the chief topic, and a preference of kingly, over republican, government, was evidently the favorite sentiment. An apostate I could not be; nor yet a hypocrite; and I found myself, for the most part, the only advocate on the republican side of the question.

Certain eminent and powerful men in the Government were hostile to democracy. Fisher Ames, a member of Congress from Massachusetts and a friend of Alexander Hamilton, considered democracy to be like death, a dismal passport to a more wretched hereafter. Common people, like slaves, should be ruled, he felt. Another enemy of democracy was Gouverneur Morris, who helped to frame the Constitution (without the Bill of Rights). He believed in a Senate appointed by the President for life from the ranks of the rich and the aristocratic. John Jay, the Chief Justice of the Supreme Court, was skeptical as to the people's ability to govern themselves. George Cabot, Senator from Massachusetts, said bluntly that "Democracy in its natural operation is the government of the worst." Jefferson, despite his unfailing courtesy, could not avoid

getting into arguments. Madison tells that at one dinner par
somebody argued against an elective executive and in favor
a hereditary ruler. Jefferson, recalling Louis XVI and Geor
III and a long line of similar incompetents, smiled, and mac
the devastating remark that he had heard of a "Universi
somewhere in which the Professorship of Mathematics w
hereditary." That killed that argument.

4

The man with whom the Secretary of State clashed almo
immediately upon entering his duties was his next in rank
the Cabinet, Secretary of the Treasury Alexander Hamilton.

Hamilton, absurdly young for his position, was not the kin
of man whom Jefferson could either like or understand. Fo
one thing, the Secretary of the Treasury was too brilliant an
too facile—the volatile type described by the Scotch-Irish
a "skite." For another, he was obviously a climber and ol
viously a careerist. Jefferson distrusted the volatility in Hami
ton and despised his careerism.

Hamilton's political principles underwent a change after h
successful career in the army and a fashionable marriag
He became steadily more conservative, and made himself th
cogent spokesman of the upper classes. So effective was I
that even Jefferson paid reluctant tribute to his enemy. H
once referred to Hamilton as a "colossus" and "an host withi
himself."

He carried his hostility for the common people too far. T
him the people were a "great beast." At the Federal Conve
tion he said: "Take mankind in general, they are vicious.
For the poor and the lowly he had contempt. Men, he w
convinced, were governed by crude self-interest or blind pa
sion. Most men, he was sure, were incapable of taking care
themselves.

Jefferson had a word for the bouncing young Hamilton.
was "monarchist." Hamilton, he said, was "not only a mo
archist, but for a monarchy bottomed on corruption." At th
time "monarchist" had the connotation and the force of th
word "Fascist" today. To Jefferson everything that was po
litically evil and morally objectionable was comprehended i
the label "monarchist."

While in the Cabinet, the two men did maintain social co
tact, but there was a deep current of antipathy between then
They did not spare each other's views or feelings. Jefferso
relates that he once invited Vice-President Adams and Secre
tary Hamilton to dinner. Over the mellow wine the men—
three of the four most important men in the country—fell in

political conversation. They argued the merits of the British constitution, and Adams was saying that if some of its abuses were corrected, it would be the "most perfect constitution of government ever devised by the wit of man." Hamilton disagreed. He insisted that even with the existing defects, the British was the "most perfect government which ever existed." To Jefferson such views were nonsense, and even dangerous nonsense. There was, he knew, precious little self-government or equality in Britain. England was an oligarchy, a country ruled by the rich and the well-born for the benefit of the rich and the well-born. Laborers were wretchedly exploited. Most of the good land was held in the hands of a few landlords. Parliament was corrupt, elected by notoriously crooked methods. Press and opinion were not free. Despite all that, the Vice-President of the United States and the Secretary of the Treasury both considered the British to be a nearly perfect government! What chance, Jefferson wondered uneasily, did the young American democracy have when such men were at the helm?

The Secretary of State and the Secretary of the Treasury were sometimes able to collaborate, especially when they met at dinner. One such occasion had far-reaching consequences. The young republic had not yet solved the problem of where to locate the capital. In days when men were more attached to their home State than to their country, and when transportation was slow and difficult, the location of the national capital was a matter of vital importance. When Jefferson arrived in New York to take up his duties, Congress was wrangling bitterly over the problem. Congressmen from the South moved for a reconsideration of the "Federal Town" bill, whereby the capital would be located on the "easterly bank of the Potomac." Congressmen from the North defeated the bill. In May, 1790, a compromise was reached whereby Philadelphia was made the temporary capital for a period of ten years. Feeling, particularly on the part of the Southerners, was intense. There were mutterings of secession.

At about the same time Hamilton had introduced his Assumption Bill, which provided that the Federal Government assume the war debts of the various States. The bill was necessary to save the credit of the Union, but the Southern members had defeated it. That in turn created angry sectional feeling in the North. Jefferson, although no financier and reluctant to agree with Hamilton, realized that the Assumption Bill was needed to "save us from the greatest of all calamities, the total extinction of our credit in Europe." Moreover, there was too much sectional prejudice in Congress. For the good of the republic it must be dissipated; otherwise Jefferson feared "a

dissolution of our union at this incipient stage." Why not ar
range a horse trade?

The Secretary of State invited Hamilton and two Virgini:
Congressmen, Lee[2] and White,[3] for dinner. At the meal :
bargain was struck. Hamilton promised that he would get th(
Northern members of Congress to vote for the bill establish
ing the national capital somewhere on the Potomac. The Vir
ginians gave their word to switch their votes on assumption
Both sides carried out their pledges. Hamilton got his bil
passed, and the South got the Federal capital on its border or
the Potomac, "not exceeding 10 miles square."

Thus the credit of the United States and the city of Wash
ington, D. C., were born at the same time.

5

After the Government had moved from New York to Phila
delphia, Jefferson rented a house and settled down to frugal
bachelor housekeeping. His finances were not in flourishing
condition, and he was compelled to watch his expenditure. Ir
the first quarter of 1791 his living expenses exceeded his salary
by more than $100 a month. On a salary of a little less thar
$300 a month, Jefferson spent around $38 for rent, about $32
on his stable, and approximately $44 on groceries and food
Service, including laundry, cost him approximately $29 an(
firewood about $24 a month. Coffee cost $3.20 a pound, anc
Jefferson, ever the precisionist, figured out that every time h(
served a cup of coffee with sugar the "dish is worth 2 cents.'
Tea was a little less expensive, only $2 a pound. Jeffersor
noted in his account book: "March 8 Tea out, the pound ha:
lasted exactly 7 weeks, used 6 times a week; this is 8/21 or .4
of an oz. a time for a single person." After this experimen'
Jefferson figured that a cup of tea cost only 1.6 cents, as compared to 2 cents for coffee. Henceforth he served only tea. H(
also served wine and French cooking. Some patriots resentec
such un-American goings-on in the house of the author of the
Declaration of Independence. Patrick Henry, Jefferson's ol(
crony and later political enemy, denounced him on the stump
as a recreant to roast beef, a man who had "abjured his native
victuals."

6

Matters were not shaping altogether to Jefferson's liking
Under Hamilton's aggressive leadership, financiers, speculator
—"stock-jobbers," as Jefferson called them—were getting :

---

[2] Richard Bland Lee (1761-1827).
[3] Alexander White (1738-1804).

grip upon the Federal Government. Hamilton's financial policies—his Excise Bill, his Bank Bill, his Assumption Bill—were taking effect. The country was beginning to enjoy what even Jefferson admitted was "unparalleled prosperity." Mills and factories were springing up, particularly in the North. Merchants were making money; financiers were flourishing. Nevertheless, Jefferson was uneasy.

He was uneasy as he watched the republic, which he had envisioned as a commonwealth inhabited by men who tilled the fields, become "corrupt" and gradually fall into the hands of merchants and speculators. The incipient American capitalism, particularly of the Massachusetts and New York variety, filled Jefferson with dismay. The men of business were not interested in liberty or equality. What they wanted was the help of the Government in making money. Although the country was still overwhelmingly rural, the business interests, led by Hamilton, were getting what they wanted.

Secretary of the Treasury Hamilton was idolized by what a later generation called the "special interests." His work in the fields of finance and economics brought him into close contact not merely with businessmen but also with influential members of Congress. Inevitably he became the head of a powerful group, although it was not a "party" in the modern sense. These men, sharing common aims, furthered each other's interests: ... "all the business is done in dark cabals," complained Senator Maclay, a Republican who was not in sympathy with the Hamiltonians. "Mr. Hamilton is all-powerful, and fails in nothing he attempts."

Success increased Hamilton's power and power swelled his sumptuousness. More and more the Secretary of the Treasury took on the airs of a Prime Minister, not hesitating to tell others, over whom he had no jurisdiction, what to do. He intervened in other departments. As his contempt for democracy grew, so did his disregard for the Secretary of State. At Cabinet meetings the aggressive Secretary of the Treasury spoke his mind with vehemence and stated his opinions with dogmatism, while the Secretary of State, always soft-spoken, confined himself to quiet, unaggressive arguments.

In the field of finance Jefferson was no match for Hamilton. The Secretary of State, with his lack of sympathy for business and the business point of view, naturally developed no skills in that field. And it was precisely in matters financial and fiscal that Hamilton was a specialist. It is not surprising, therefore, that President Washington, whose viewpoint was neither strictly agrarian nor entirely commercial and who strove to steer a middle course between the two, accepted the financial ideas of his gifted Secretary of the Treasury. Jefferson could offer no acceptable alternative. And Jefferson was not happy as he viewed the shape of things present and to come.

7

The dissensions behind the impressive façade of the Washington Administration were bound to reach the ears of the public. Both sides, the Southern-agrarian group led by Jefferson and the Northern-commercial interests headed by Hamilton, were playing for the highest stake in civilized society—political power. Victory would go to the side that had, not the heaviest artillery, but the most public support.

Newspapers were employed to trumpet the views of their backers and to castigate those of their opponents. The press was partisan in its politics, unrestrained in its utterances, abusive in its tone, and altogether venal. Hamilton's mouthpiece was the *Gazette of the United States*, a sheet 17 by 2 inches, with a circulation not exceeding 1,400. This was not, to be sure, an impressive number, but the readers of the *Gazette* were influential and its views were those of the Government.

The editor of this Philadelphia newspaper was John Fenno, son of a Boston leather-dresser. Fenno was often in trouble. He was saved from bankruptcy by Alexander Hamilton, the Secretary of the Treasury, and he was caned by Benjamin Franklin Bache, the editor of the Philadelphia *General Advertiser* (later the *Aurora*). There is a connection between these two seemingly discrepant events. For Fenno hated republicanism and democracy, and the Philadelphia *Aurora* supported both. Editor Fenno wanted to see the United States Government transformed into a monarchy, and he hoped that his newspaper would become the gazette of the royal court. His sheet, in fact, gave itself the airs of a royal gazette. In his pretentious manner he imitated the pomposity of the royal court of Great Britain: "We are informed that the President, His Excellency, the Vice-President, His Excellency, the Governor of this State, and many other personages will be present—"

The voice of Fenno was the voice of Hamilton. Like the Secretary of the Treasury, the editor of the *Gazette of the United States* professed contempt for democracy. "Take away thrones and crowns from among men and there will soon be an end of all dominion and justice," wrote Fenno. He argued that in the past democracy had "immediately changed into anarchy." As for his patron Hamilton, the editor lauded him in the hushed terms of a courtier speaking of His Majesty. "He"—Fenno referred to the Secretary of the Treasury—"is the highest jewel in Columbia's crown."

The Secretary of State saw no reason why the enemies of

republicanism should have a monopoly of the printed word. Early in 1791, on the advice of James Madison and Henry Lee, Jefferson offered a job as translating clerk in the Department of State to one Philip Morin Freneau, poet, journalist, and ardent democrat. Freneau was an old college mate of Madison's. "The salary indeed,". the Secretary of State wrote him, "is very low, being but two' hundred and fifty dollars a year; but also, it gives so little to do, as not to interfere with any other calling the person may choose."

There was no secret as to what the "other calling" referred to. What Jefferson was offering Freneau was a sinecure in order to enable him to publish a newspaper in which the democratic ideal, of both the American and the French varieties, would be championed. Freneau at first refused the offer, but Jefferson and Madison persisted. In a letter to Madison, the Secretary of State frankly explained what he was expecting of and how he could help the poet-journalist:

> Though the printing business be sufficiently full here, yet I think he would have set out on such advantageous ground as to have been sure of success. . . . I should have given him the perusal of all my letters of foreign intelligence and all foreign newspapers; the publication of all proclamations and other public notices within my department and the printing of the laws, which, added to his salary, would have been a considerable aid.

It took nearly half a year of persuasion before Freneau agreed to take the job and do battle with Fenno. In the summer of 1791 he came to Philadelphia and in October began to publish the *National Gazette*, one of the earliest organs of American democracy. Freneau issued his newspaper every Monday and Thursday. In it the "Poet of the Revolution" took up the cudgels in defense of American republicanism and the French Revolution.

In the summer of 1791, after having made arrangements to put Freneau behind the journalistic battery that was aimed at Hamilton, Jefferson discovered that there were some interesting botanical specimens up the Hudson Valley in New York. He and Madison took a leisurely trip to New York State. But they did not go to pick flowers. They went to light fires. The fires were intended to burn some of Hamilton's political friends in New York State at the next presidential election, which was only a little more than a year off.

New York State was split between two factions, one led by Alexander Hamilton and the other by George Clinton. Hamilton, through his marriage, had the backing of the aristocratic

families in New York State; Clinton, through Aaron Burr, ha
the support of the Sons of St. Tammany society in New Yor
City. The Hamiltonians enjoyed Federal patronage; the Clir
tonians hoped to.

Jefferson and Madison came to an understanding with Clir
ton and Burr. The result of this agreement was that in th
presidential election of 1792, Virginia and North Carolin
threw their support to George Clinton, as against John Adam
for Vice-President.[4] It was an auspicious beginning, for
laid the foundations of a new political party. Since 1792, th
South and Tammany Hall, regardless of differences and despit
occasional separations, have been the two mainstays of th
Democratic party.

Satisfied with having quietly laid foundation stones for h
alliance with New York, Jefferson extended his botanical ex
cursions farther north. Up in the region of Lake George h
admired the sugar maple, the silver fir, the white pine, th
decumbent juniper, the wild honeysuckle, the velvet aspen, th
downy shrub-willow, and the abundance of wild berries.

8

The little fires that Jefferson lighted in New York were t
break into flame within a few years, but the big newspape
cannon which he planted in Philadelphia hurled its shells im
mediately. Jefferson and his Republican friends, considerin
Hamilton an enemy of the republic, set out to eliminate hir
from power and to destroy his prestige. Jefferson did not mak
the mistake of underestimating his opponent. Possibly he over
estimated him.

Editor Freneau used exactly the right technique in his wa
on Hamilton. Instead of arguing with the Secretary of th
Treasury, or trying to refute his ideas, Freneau ridiculed hir
Instead of attacking him as a worthy opponent, the poet-edito
made Hamilton appear odious. Freneau was a master of mock
ery. His barbs soon got into the skin of the Secretary of th
Treasury. Freneau's *National Gazette* sneered at Hamilton an
his friends as flunkeys of monarchy.

Freneau's editorial attacks were no laughing matter t
Hamilton. His ideas, as well as his person, were being rid
culed, and he could not afford to ignore the challenge. He wa
he said, "unequivocally convinced" that Jefferson was behin
Freneau. The Secretary of State and his lieutenant Madiso
the leader of the Virginians in Congress, were "hostile to m
and my administration," Hamilton wrote angrily. And since
anger is a wretched counselor, the high-tempered Secretary c

---

[4] Adams was elected with 77 electoral votes, as against 50 for Clinto

he Treasury committed a serious mistake. Stung by the *Nation-al Gazette,* he published an anonymous attack on Freneau.

Hamilton's article, printed under the anonymous signature "An American," caused a furore. It accused Freneau of being he tool of Jefferson, of being paid from government funds, and even of an ignorance of the French language, which he was upposed to translate. Then the article turned its attention to Jefferson and raked him for all his political sins—of omission as well as commission. It accused the Secretary of State of being an enemy of the Government, of advocating "national disunion, national insignificance, public disorder, and discredit."

Jefferson, true to his method, did not answer. Freneau did. He went before the mayor of Philadelphia and swore truthfully that Jefferson had never hired him to edit a newspaper, had never paid him to do so, had never written a line for it. His own conduct, Freneau said, was "free, unfettered and uninfluenced." That was true, if for no other reason than that Freneau, sharing the political views of Jefferson, did not have o be told what to print.

Hamilton, still writing as "An American," refused to accept Freneau's oath, saying in effect that the "pensioned tool" was as much a liar as his boss Jefferson. Ultimately Hamilton, unable to find proof that Jefferson had really established Freneau's newspaper, had to retract his charges. That did his prestige no good.

A few weeks after his first assault, Hamilton renewed the battle with a series of six articles signed "Catullus." [5] He repeated his former charges and added new accusations. "Catullus" flayed the Secretary of State as an enemy of the Constitution, a treacherous business adviser, and a hypocrite.

That "Catullus" was Hamilton soon became an open secret and a public sensation. Violent attacks by a member of the Cabinet upon a colleague were not usual events that could be disregarded. The person who was most mortified by these printed recriminations was the two antagonists' chief, President Washington. A man of moderation and prudence, the President could not understand such passionate outbursts as were printed in the warring gazettes. He was fed up with politics anyhow, and now his two lieutenants were at daggers' points. The President was afraid that such a feud might tear the republic to pieces.

Washington, a man of sixty and with failing health, wanted o retire. Only a few weeks before the journalistic war started,

[5] They were all published in Fenno's *Gazette of the United States.* The first ticle appeared on Sept. 15, 1791, the second on Sept. 19, the third on Sept. ?, the fourth on Oct. 17, the fifth on Nov. 24, and the sixth on Dec. 26.

the President had called in wise little James Madison an
talked to him about a successor. Washington wanted to kno
whether the Secretary of State would consider the Presidency
Madison, knowing his friend's mind, said that he doubted i
". . . . with respect to Mr. Jefferson," Madison told the Pres
dent, "his extreme repugnance to public life, & anxiety to ex
change it for his farm & his philosophy made it doubtful . .
whether it would be possible to obtain his own consent; and
obtained, whether local prejudices in the Northern States . .
would not be a bar to his appointment."

The President had not been in "any wise satisfied" wit
Madison's opinion. He did not want to run again in 1792, an
hoped to find a successor who had a chance of being electe
and who could be trusted to carry on. But there was no or
in America of sufficient political stature to replace Washingto
at a time when the country was threatened with disunity. Bo
Jefferson and Hamilton realized this and pleaded with Wash
ington to be a candidate for a second term. The precarious unit
of the republic hung upon the thread of the life of one man

An inflexible sense of duty had made Washington agree t
sacrifice his deepest inclinations and run for a second tim
But now the two ablest members of his Cabinet were at ope
war and threatened the republic with that very disunity whic
they had pleaded with him to avert by becoming a candidate
The President's patience was not inexhaustible, and in "
plague o' both your houses" state of mind, he made a shar
appeal to both men for moderation.

Jefferson was in Virginia when the letter reached him. H
knew the cautious President well enough to realize that th
"advice" was a rebuke. Stung by the implied criticism, Jeffe
son in a letter of nearly three thousand words made a vigorou
defense of his position. He criticized Hamilton sharply for hi
policies, accused him of corrupting Congress, and positivel
denied having instigated or influenced Freneau in his attack
on the Secretary of the Treasury. Selections from Jefferson
long letter follow.

He defended himself against Hamilton's charge that he ha
been hostile to the Constitution:

> The . . . charge is most false. No man in the U. S. I suppos
> approved of every tit[t]le in the constitution: no one, I believ
> approved of more of it than I did: and more of it was certain
> disproved by my accuser than by me, and of it's parts mo
> vitally republican. Of this the few letters I wrote on the subje
> (not half a dozen, I believe) will be a proof; & for my ow
> satisfaction & justification, I must tax you with the reading
> them when I return to where they are. You will there see th
> my objection to the constitution was that it wanted a bill

rights securing freedom of religion, freedom of the press, freedom from standing armies, trial by jury, & a constant Habeas corpus act. Colo Hamilton's was that it wanted a king and house of lords. The sense of America has approved my objection & added the bill of rights, not the king and lords.

He made a vigorous defense of the freedom of the press, both Freneau's and Fenno's:

As to the merits or demerits of his [Freneau's] paper, they certainly concern me not. He & Fenno are rivals for the public favor. The one courts them by flattery, the other by censure, & I believe it will be admitted that the one has been as servile, as the other severe. But it is not the dignity, & even decency of government committed, when one of it's principal ministers enlists himself as an anonymous writer or paragraphist for either the one or the other of them?—No government ought to be without censors: & where the press is free, no one ever will. If virtuous, it need not fear the fair operation of attack & defence. Nature has given to man no other means of sifting out the truth either in religion, law, or politics. I think it is honourable to the government neither to know, nor notice, it's sycophants or censors, as it would be undignified & criminal to pamper the former & prosecute the latter.

He concluded by announcing his desire to retire from office at the end of this Administration, and he warned the President that as a private citizen he would consider himself free to make a public defense of his character against the slanders of Hamilton. He had too high a regard for his reputation among the American people to permit it to be smeared by a man like the Secretary of the Treasury:

I will not suffer my retirement to be clouded by the slanders of a man whose history, from the moment at which history can stoop to notice him, is a tissue of machinations against the liberty of the country which has not only received and given him bread, but heaped its honors on his head.—Still however I repeat the hope that it will not be necessary to make such an appeal. Though little known to the people of America, I believe, that as far as I am known, it is not as an enemy to the republic, nor an intriguer against it, nor a waster of its revenue, nor prostitutor of it to the purposes of corruption.

9

Three weeks after the letter was dispatched, on September 30, Jefferson followed it with a visit to Mount Vernon. He spent the night at the President's cool house on the Potomac. In the morning before breakfast, the two Virginians had a long, frank talk. Jefferson recorded the conversation in his *Anas*, his confidential and somewhat indiscreet political diary.

The President expressed his wish that the Secretary of State would reconsider his decision to retire. He flattered his guest with the statement that he "could not see where he should find another character" to take Jefferson's place. Of course he sympathized with the Secretary of State's desire to leave his post since he too found the burdens of office onerous. "Nobody disliked more the ceremonies of his office, and he had not the least taste or gratification in the execution of it's functions."

But the call of duty, Washington told his guest, was stronger than personal desires. Therefore, he could not avoid making the "sacrifice of a longer continuance." Would not the Secretary of State do the same?

This brought the conversation around to the subject that was uppermost in the President's mind, his deep concern over the conflict between Jefferson and Hamilton. Washington said that he was pained that the political difference between the two men had gone so far as to become a "personal difference" and he wished that he could be "the mediator." Without defending or criticizing either of the two men, the President said that both of them were needed in the Cabinet, to balance each other—"he thought it important to preserve the check of my opinions in the administration in order to keep things in their proper channel & prevent them from going too far."

It was a shrewd appeal, but Jefferson said that he was disturbed by Hamilton's monarchistic machinations. The President denied that there was any monarchist movement in the country; and even if there were, it did not amount to much— "he did not believe there were ten men in the U.S. whose opinions were worth attention who entertained such a thought."

Jefferson countered that "there were many more than he imagined." He argued that "tho' the people were sound, there were a numerous sect who had monarchy in contempl[atio]n. That the Secy of the Treasury was one of these." He quoted Hamilton as having said that "this Constitution was a shilly shally thing of mere milk & water, which could not last, & was only good as a step to something better." There was, Jefferson said, a powerful group in Congress that had benefited from Hamilton's financial policies and was, therefore, "ready to do what he should direct."

The President frankly admitted that such a group did exist in the legislature, but he doubted whether it could be "avoided in any government." Jefferson refused to accept this point of view. "I told him there was great difference between the little accidental schemes of self interest which would take place in every body of men & influence their votes, and a regular system for forming a corps of interested persons who should be steadily at the orders of the Treasury."

The President admitted that Hamilton's financial system had any critics, but he was willing to leave it to the test of time. So far, Washington said, Hamilton's policies had been successful—"he had seen our affairs desperate & our credit lost, and that this was in a sudden & extraordinary degree raised to the highest pitch." Jefferson did not argue the subject, and the President reverted to "another exhortation to me not to decide so positively on retirement."

That same day Jefferson left Mount Vernon for Philadelphia. As soon as he arrived in the capital, he carried out his promise to Washington and forwarded to him copies of his letters on the subject of the Constitution, written during the struggle for its adoption. The letters disproved Hamilton's charge that Jefferson had been hostile to the Constitution. But that only made it worse, since it proved Hamilton's accusation false and thereby further widened the breach between the two men. The President made another effort to bring them together. He wrote to Jefferson a letter of warm esteem and made a touching plea for conciliation with Hamilton.

Much as Jefferson admired the President's character and appreciated his confidence, he saw no possibility of compromise between himself and the Secretary of the Treasury. Hamilton kept on saying that "there was no stability, no security in any kind of government but a monarchy," and he was deliberately creating a privileged class of financiers and rentiers. Members of Congress and of the Administration, encouraged by Hamilton, were being tempted to make money in stocks and speculation. That put an end to their independence. Such behavior on the part of representatives of the people shocked Jefferson. When he was approached with a proposition to make money in a financial enterprise, he replied:

> When I first entered on the stage of public life (now twenty-four years ago), I came to a resolution never to engage while in public office in any kind of enterprise for the improvement of my fortune, nor to wear any other character than of a farmer. I have never departed from it in a single instance; and I have in multiplied instances found myself happy in being able to decide and to act as a public servant, clear of all interest, in the multiform questions that have arisen, wherein I have seen others embarrassed and biased by having got themselves into a more interested situation. Thus I have thought myself richer in contentment than I should have been with any increase of fortune.

The Secretary of State was determined to leave his post so that he could be free to oppose Hamilton's policies. But for the time being the appeals of the President that he remain in office prevailed. James Madison likewise urged him to stay on

for a while longer. The shrewd Congressman from Virgin
had long argued with Jefferson about the danger of retirin
under fire. He reasoned with his friend that his "exit from pu
lic life" must not be made until he could do so with "just
fying circumstances which all good citizens will respect, & t
which your friends can appeal." Madison was to all intents an
purposes Jefferson's public relations counsel, and he was thin
ing of the future.

10

In the autumn of 1792, in an atmosphere of political bitte
ness so intense that old friends crossed the street in order
avoid speaking to each other, George Washington reluctantl
stood for re-election. He received the unanimous vote of th
Electoral College. The election was significant for a number
reasons, not the least of them being the emergence of Jeffe
son's own party, the Republican, as a political power of na
tional importance.

In a sense, the campaign of 1792 was a projection of th
Jefferson-Hamilton conflict onto the national arena. Ever
where the Republicans put up a stiff fight against Hamilton
Federalist party. Both sides agreed upon Washington fo
President, but there was a severe struggle for the Vice-Pres
dency. In the end John Adams, the Federalist candidate, d
feated George Clinton, Jefferson's choice, with 77 elector
votes against 50. The defeat of the Jeffersonians was not
serious as this would indicate, for they won a majority in Co
gress and were able to elect as Speaker of the House a ma
who was sympathetic to their views.[6] What was equally si
nificant, as foreshadowing things to come, was that most
the South had voted for Jefferson's Northern candidate fo
Vice-President.[7]

For the successful candidate there was no joy in the electio
Washington's second Administration started in an atmosphe
black with dissensions and rent by hatreds. Fires of animosit
the hatred of section against section and class against clas
burned throughout the Union.

The touchstone was the French Revolution. As the revol
tion in France spiraled (up or down, depending upon one
point of view) from protest to revolt and from revolt to ma
sacre, Americans, shaken or thrilled by the events, passionate

[6] The urbane Frederick Augustus Conrad Muhlenberg of Pennsylvan
a former Federalist who finally lined up behind Jefferson.
[7] George Clinton got Virginia's 21 electoral votes, North Carolina's
and Georgia's 4. Only two Southern States voted for John Adams—Mar
land (6) and South Carolina (7). Kentucky, admitted to the Union th
very year, gave its 4 votes to Jefferson (who was not a candidate).

ok sides. Feelings mounted to fever heat, for in the days
hen there was no baseball or cinema, politics was about the
ly catharsis that most men had to relieve pent-up emotions.
The French Revolution divided the United States according
class lines. Folk in the upper income brackets, particularly
ose engaged in commerce or industry, were inclined to re-
rd the French revolutionists much in the same way that like-
inded people regarded Bolshevists in a later day. In fact, the
ord "Jacobin" (it was applied in profusion to Jefferson) was
ed with the same purpose and effect as "Red" in recent years.
en who were not well-born or well-to-do tended to welcome
e French Revolution as a force for the liberation of man-
nd from the yoke of tyranny and oppression.

This split in public opinion was mirrored in the Govern-
ent, especially since Jefferson was a stanch friend of France,
French culture as well as politics. Around Jefferson, then,
e hatreds swirled, for alone among the members of Wash-
gton's Cabinet he stood out in defense of the newly created
rench Republic. President Washington, while he tried to
aintain a temperate middle course in foreign policy, was
ienated by the lengths to which the French revolutionists
ere going.

In aristocratic Philadelphia the "Jacobin" Secretary of State
as cut dead socially. Only three families would receive him
their homes. Former friends and acquaintances crossed the
reet when they saw his tall figure approaching.

Personal slights were insignificant compared to the national
akes involved. For the United States, depending as it did
pon shipping for its exports and imports, faced a crucial test
foreign policy. The country had had a profitable commer-
al alliance with France since 1778; at the same time Britain,
hich controlled the seas, was unfriendly to America. Jeffer-
n's policy was to continue the alliance with France, regard-
ss of the upheavals in Paris. The influential Hamilton, how-
ver, had always been in favor of co-operation with England,
ven to the point of subservience; and now, when France was
the hands of the revolutionists, the Secretary of the Treas-
ry impressed upon President Washington the desirability of
pro-British policy. Hamilton said that he saw no "solid
round of difference" between the rulers of England and the
usinessmen of the United States.

Jefferson had no objections to doing business with England,
ut to him the problem had political, rather than economic,
nplications. To be sure, he disliked the British ruling class and
e knew that the latter had only contempt for America. But
e matter went deeper than mere antipathy. A pro-British
rientation on the part of the United States meant, in the first

place, deserting the struggling French Republic at a period
when it was surrounded by a hostile world. It meant, further
more, an alliance with Europe's most vigorously antidemocratic
ruling group, which, by controlling the seas and seaborne
commerce, was in a position to dictate, or at least influence
internal politics in America. That may have appealed
to Hamilton, who admired everything British, but the very pros
pect was a nightmare to Jefferson.

But deeper than Jefferson's dread of British influence was his
conviction that upon the success or failure of the French Re
public depended the continued existence of American democ
racy. For Jefferson took a world view of politics. Unlike many
of his parochial-minded contemporaries, he felt keenly that
he lived in a revolutionary age and that the civilized world
especially the one lying on the edges of the Atlantic Ocean
was a unity. Successful revolution in France would bring
about emulation everywhere. Failure of the revolution in
France would cause a revulsion against republicanism every
where, including the United States. Jefferson's espousal of re
publicanism and democracy at home drove him relentlessly
to the position of becoming a champion of republicanism and
democracy abroad, especially in France. From that stand he
could not, he dared not, recede.

His faith in the French Revolution was put to a shocking
test when the Jacobins seized power and began to butcher their
opponents. Much as the killings outraged him, he did not let
his repugnance to bloodshed blind him to the larger issue,
namely, the success of the revolution. When William Short
Jefferson's friend and protégé in Paris, wrote him bitter let
ters about the massacres in which he had lost dear friends, the
Secretary of State replied with a vehement defense of the revo
lution. He said, in effect, What are the lives of a few people
compared to the liberty of the world? In many ways it is per
haps the most remarkable letter Jefferson had ever penned:

> In the struggle which was necessary, many guilty persons fell
> without the forms of trial, and with them some innocent. These
> I deplore as much as any body, & shall deplore some of them
> to the day of my death. But I deplore them as I should have
> done had they fallen in battle. It was necessary to use the arm
> of the people, a machine not quite so blind as balls and bombs
> but blind to a certain degree. A few of their cordial friends met
> at their hands the fate of enemies. But time and truth will
> rescue & embalm their memories, while their posterity will be
> enjoying that very liberty for which they would never have
> hesitated to offer up their lives. The liberty of the whole earth
> was depending on the issue of the contest, and was ever such
> a prize won with so little innocent blood? My own affections
> have been deeply wounded by some of the martyrs to this cause

but rather than it should have failed I would have seen half the earth desolated. Were there but an Adam & an Eve left in every country, & left free, it would be better than as it now is.

11

A wild gale blew across the Atlantic in the winter of 1793 nd no ships sailed the ocean. For three months there was no ews from Europe. Then, in April, 1793, when Washington's cond Administration was only a month old, ships landed and rought news that set the country agog.

From travelers and old gazettes Americans learned that, in anuary last, the French had cut off the head of Louis XVI. mericans now learned for the first time that France, their lly for fifteen years, had declared war on Britain and Spain. hat brought the conflict to the very doors of the United States. inally there was the news that a French Minister Plenipotenary had landed in Charleston, South Carolina, and was coming to Philadelphia to replace the royalist envoy, De Ternant.

The new Minister of the French Republic was an excitable oung civet named Edmond Charles Genet. Certain historians ave long since pretended that Genet was a species of jackass nd clown. That he was not. A man of aristocratic birth and a cholar, "Citizen" Genet had broken with royalism and aristcracy, although one of his sisters was the memoir-writing 1adame de Campan, lady-in-waiting to Queen Marie Antoiette. He was a widely traveled intellectual, a man of scientific terests, a friend of thinkers like Condorcet, and above all, an nthusiastic republican. In June, 1792, he achieved the republican badge of honor by being expelled from the domain of erfdom by Catherine II of Russia. The fact that the Czarina id not approve of Genet's republicanism made him acceptable o democrats everywhere.

Citizen Genet was a man of faults. His chief defects were a ick of modesty and an absence of reserve. To him the French epublic was not simply a *patrie;* it was a cause. He was not erely a representative of his country; he was a missionary r an idea. And being a zealot, he had no discretion.

Americans helped to fan the flames of his enthusiasm. From harleston to Philadelphia, Genet traveled through the back ountry, where people showed their warm approval of the sister republic overseas. He was gaped at like a great personge and received like a hero. That did nothing to whittle down is vanity. "I live in the midst of continual parties," he wrote xcitedly. "Old Washington is jealous of my successes, and the nthusiasm with which the whole town flocks to my house."

To give Genet his due, he was not sent to carry out the

conventional diplomatic duties of an ambassador. His instructions were to use the United States as a center of operations
against Britain. He was ordered to fit out privateers to prey
upon British shipping, to recruit troops for the seizure of
Spanish-held Florida and Louisiana, and to obtain the active
participation of the United States in the war. His Government
had instructed him to influence American opinion secretly—
"to direct opinion by means of anonymous publications."

While Genet was coming to present his credentials to President Washington in Philadelphia, there was a clash of opinion
in the Administration on the subject of his reception. Hamilton, who loathed the French Revolution, particularly since the
execution of the King, argued against recognizing the regicide
republic and against receiving its Minister. The Secretary of
the Treasury advocated a break with France and a renuncia-
tion of the treaty of 1778, on the ground that since the monarch who had signed that treaty was dead, the alliance was no
longer binding.

Hamilton was now on ground that was thoroughly familiar
to the Secretary of State, and the latter had no difficulty in
polishing off his opponent. Jefferson demolished Hamilton's
position by stressing a few principles that were self-evident
among liberal thinkers. The monarch, Jefferson pointed out, is
not the state, but the agent of the state. Source of authority in
any country, the Secretary of State emphasized, is not the king,
who is transient, but the people, who are permanent. The monarch is merely the symbol of authority. "Consequently the
Treaties between the U. S. and France, were not treaties between the U. S. & Louis Capet,[8] but between the two nations
of America & France." So long as the two nations remain in
existence, regardless of the change in the form of their government, their treaties are binding.

Jefferson then raised questions that were lined with sarcasm.
The American republic, he said, had been eager to ally with
despotic France, but now that France was herself a republic
some American gentlemen did not like her. Would these gentlemen, Jefferson asked sarcastically, never have allied with
France if the latter had been a republic?

President Washington and Attorney-General Randolph
agreed with the Secretary of State that the treaty with France
was still valid, and it was decided to receive Genet. Hamilton
ostentatiously joined the former French Minister, De Ternant,

8 "Louis Capet" was the sobriquet which the French revolutionists con-
temptuously applied to Louis XVI. The latter resented it strongly (see
S. K. Padover's Life and Death of Louis XVI, Appleton-Century, 1939,
p. 293). Jefferson, ordinarily a scrupulous observer of conventions, probably used the nickname in order to annoy Hamilton.

putting on mourning for the guillotined Louis XVI. "A ·rfect Counter-revolutioner," was Jefferson's grim comment. Early in May there arrived in Philadelphia the French igate *L'Embuscade*, which had brought Genet to America. n the way from Charleston the frigate had captured a British ·ip and brought her as a prize to port. The republican tizenry of Philadelphia went mad with enthusiasm. *L'Embus- ·de* was received by a wildly cheering crowd. "Upon her com- g into sight," Jefferson wrote to Monroe, "thousands & thou- nds of the *yeomanry* of the city crowded and covered the harfs. Never before was such a crowd seen there, and when e British colours were seen *reversed*, & the French flying ·ove them they burst into peals of exultation."

At about the same time Genet in person arrived in Phila- ·lphia. He was received like a conquering hero. A "vast con- ·urse of people," in the words of Jefferson, received him at ·ray's Ferry and shouts of welcome thundered in the volatile ·renchman's ears. The rousing cheers went to his head and ·ayed there. His ardor was not quenched by President Wash- ·gton's correct but not ardent reception. The Minister went · the Secretary of State and presented his credentials with ·e words: "We see in you the only person on earth who can ·ve us sincerely & merit to be so loved." Jefferson was pleased. ·e felt that Genet would serve as a center around which pro- ·rench opinion would crystallize.

But Genet brought only embarrassment and trouble to the ·cretary of State. His presence and activities raised some ·essing problems. To what extent was the United States bound ·y treaty to aid her ally France against Britain? Was the ·nited States justified in permitting the fitting out of French ·rivateers? What would be England's reactions if the Wash- ·gton Administration permitted such privateering?

If Genet did not raise these questions, Hamilton emphati- ·lly did. During furious Cabinet squabbles, the Secretary of ·e Treasury warned the President against the dangers of ·ing involved in war with a mighty Naval Power such as ·ritain. He urged not merely neutrality in the Anglo-French ·ar, but an alliance with Britain, a country that the over- ·helming majority of Americans distrusted and feared.

Jefferson argued that the least the Administration could do ·as to remain an honest neutral in the war, helping neither ·untry. That was not fair to France, but it was safe for ·merica. "If we preserve even a sneaking neutrality," Jeffer- ·n confessed early in May, "we shall be indebted for it to the ·resident, & not to his counsellors." In the end an uneasy ·utrality was agreed upon, for the young republic, even if it wished to aid France, was in no position to expose itself t attacks by the powerful British fleet.

Genet, convinced that public opinion was behind him, wa not satisfied with passive neutrality. He felt that under th treaty of 1778 he had a right to demand positive assistanc such as the free use of American ports. Moreover, he aske for funds in the form of advance installments on the debt th United States owed to France.[9] In this the Secretary of th Treasury was thoroughly unco-operative. But the Secretary State, the friend of France, proved in the end to be no mor helpful.

"Sneaking neutrality" was not to Jefferson's taste or convi tions, but since the situation demanded it and the Preside favored it, the Secretary of State could only obey. When Gen came to him and demanded that the treaty of 1778 be strictl executed, the uneasy Secretary of State sought refuge in jurid cal subterfuge, a kind of chicanery that Jefferson despised others. "This Secretary of State," Genet reported to Pari "hunts excuses in the dusty tomes of Vattel and Grotius."

Citizen Genet impatiently refused to accept Jefferson's ju ridical subtleties. France was fighting for life and liberty, had the American colonies a decade back, and she needed ai The United States was the ally of France; the American Secr tary of State was the vaunted friend of France. Then why a these tortuous subterfuges when help was required?

Early in August, to the vast relief of the Secretary of Stat the Cabinet decided to request the French Government recall its Minister Plenipotentiary. "He will sink the republica interest if they do not abandon him," Jefferson told Madiso

But Genet, like the shrew in Shakespeare, had the last wor Before being replaced, he did exactly what Jefferson had bee trying to persuade him not to do—he published some of h correspondence with the Administration, thereby appealing t the people against the Government. He also attacked Pres dent Washington, for whom Americans, even those who di agreed with him, entertained universal admiration. Criticizin the President was a privilege reserved for Americans, n foreigners. The effect of this "intermeddling by a foreigner was, as Jefferson had foreseen, to alienate French sympathizer and to throw public opinion in the direction of the pro-Britis Federalists.

Even the cool and patient Washington was affected by th strain of events, especially by criticism of his foreign policy the Republican press.

9 Between 1775 and 1782 France had advanced 18,000,000 livres in ca to the American colonies to help fight Britain.

President Washington was particularly incensed by the attacks upon him that appeared in the *National Gazette*, for Freneau did not follow his patron Jefferson in either accepting or condoning a policy of neutrality toward France. In his championship of the French Republic, the poet-editor did not spare the President.

At a Cabinet meeting, the President again raised the question of Freneau. Washington, his nerves on edge, lost his temper and flew into one of his rare and terrifying rages. He "got," Jefferson records in his confidential diary, "into one of those passions when he cannot command himself . . . defied any man on earth to produce one single act of his . . . which had not been done on the purest motives . . . that *By god* he had rather be in his grave than in his present situation. He had rather be on his farm than to be made *emperor of the world*."

Like Washington, Jefferson reached the point where he also felt that he would rather be on his quiet farm than "emperor of the world." He had been in the public service for almost a quarter-century, during which time he had neglected his estate and his personal affairs. What did he get out of office but hatred, misrepresentation, and a host of enemies? At the age of fifty, he decided, he was too old to cope with the political world.

He handed in his resignation to the President. Again Washington urged him to stay, but this time even the personal appeals of the weary President could not alter his determination. He consented to remain in office only until the end of the year 1793.

Three days before Christmas, 1793, Washington made another personal appeal to his Secretary of State to remain in office. Jefferson's decision could not be shaken. "In this," he said, "I am now immovable by any considerations whatever."

On December 31, 1793, nearly four years after he had become Secretary of State, he sent in his resignation to the President: "I now take the liberty of resigning the office into your hands. . . . I carry into my retirement a lively sense of your goodness."

There was nothing for President Washington to do but to let his Secretary of State go. Reluctantly he accepted the resignation, and he sent Jefferson on his way with his blessings: "Let a conviction of my most earnest prayers for your happiness accompany you in your retirement."

CHAPTER ELEVEN

VICE-PRESIDENT

(1797-1801)

ON THE fifth day of the year 1794 Jefferson said farewell to Philadelphia—forever, he hoped. On the sixteenth of January he climbed the winding road to Monticello, the peaceful nest that would shelter him from further storms.

He had taken a rough beating at the hands of Hamilton in the last three years. Never again, he repeated, would he be enticed into the political arena, where jackals and wolves were in the habit of tearing at the vitals of a man's character and reputation. He felt himself old and ill. But he was neither old nor ill. At fifty he was as vigorous as ever, showing few signs of age except a graying around the temples. But he was weary and hurt. The cure for his soul-sickness was work in the open air.

Jefferson plunged into farming with a zeal he had never felt before. "I return to farming," he wrote to John Adams, "with an ardor which I scarcely knew in my youth. . . . Instead of writing 10. or 12. letters a day, which I have been in the habit of doing as a thing of course, I put off answering my letters now, farmer-like, till a rainy day."

Farming was his sole means of support. Financially, he was broke, "money-bound," as he called it when he asked a man to lend him $100. The plantation was run down, and it needed hard work and careful cultivation to make it productive again. Jefferson possessed 10,000 acres of land, but only 2,000 were in use. The rest was uncleared timber, or otherwise unproductive. Two thousand acres in use sounds like a lot of land, but in reality it was little. These acres had to support not only Jefferson's family, including many relatives, but also one hundred and fifty-four slaves and their progeny. For the plantation depended upon slave labor.

Jefferson hated and dreaded the whole institution of slavery. He felt that it degraded both the master and the man. One of the most eloquent condemnations of slavery ever written is to be found in his *Notes on Virginia:*

> The whole commerce between master and slave is a perpetual exercise of the most boisterous passions, the most unremitting

100

despotism on the one part, and degrading submissions on the other. Our children see this, and learn to imitate it; for man is an imitative animal. . . . The parent storms, the child looks on, catches the lineaments of wrath, puts on the same airs in the circle of smaller slaves, gives a loose to the worst of passions, and thus nursed, educated, and daily exercised in tyranny, cannot but be stamped by it with odious peculiarities. The man must be a prodigy who can retain his manners and morals undepraved by such circumstances.

But there was not much that an individual planter could do about it. In a slave economy the planter had little choice but to continue using slave labor or to bankrupt himself by liberating his Negroes. Freeing the slaves, however, was no solution either, for such freedmen, unable to find free work in a slave world, would be certain to be exposed to beggary or starvation. Moreover, the slaves were neither morally nor technically prepared to make an independent living in a competitive world.

On the Jefferson plantation there were also 249 head of cattle, 390 hogs, 5 mules, and 34 horses. Of the latter, 8 or 9 were devoted exclusively to riding. It took Jefferson several months after his return from Philadelphia before he was able to borrow $50 to buy two or three score of sheep.

During his absence, Jefferson discovered, his lands had been ravaged to a "degree of degradation far beyond what I had expected." It was necessary, therefore, to heal the wounds of the soil and give the land a breathing spell. To do that, Jefferson divided his lands under cultivation into four large farms. These farms were in turn subdivided into six fields of 40 acres each. This permitted a six-year period of rotation. For example, the first field would be planted to wheat, the second to corn, the third to rye or wheat, the fourth and fifth to clover, and the sixth to buckwheat. Rotation, together with contour plowing on hills to stop runoffs (Jefferson and Washington were among the American pioneers in this form of plowing), saved the land from exhaustion and wastage.

Jefferson brought system into management and invention into work. Each farm was an independent unit, directed by a steward and worked by four male slaves, four female slaves, four oxen, and four horses. But slaves and oxen were not the only ones cultivating the Jefferson lands. The master, with his lively sense of inventiveness, was one of the first Americans to use farming machinery. On the Jefferson plantation there was a threshing machine which was carried on a wagon, and weighed about a ton. It was capable of threshing as many as one hundred and fifty bushels a day. There was also a drilling machine, invented by one of Jefferson's neighbors.

Intelligent management and careful planning finally broug[h]
results. Within two years after his return from Philadelphi[a]
the agricultural yield of Jefferson's plantation compared wi[t]
the best in the State.

In his early fifties Jefferson was a lean, grizzled, quizzic[al]
farmer, as happy as a busy mortal and a loving parent can b[e]
No political ambition slumbered in his breast, he was co[n]
vinced. He shunned all "intermeddling with public affairs" an[d]
refused participation in political activities. "I have returned[,]
he told a French friend, "with infinite appetite, to the enjo[y]
ment of my farm, my family & my books, and had determine[d]
to meddle in nothing beyond their limits."

But Jefferson deceived himself. He made a mistake when h[e]
assumed that the outside world would leave him alone with h[is]
books and his family. He also fooled himself into believing th[at]
he was nothing more than a farmer in retirement. Jeffers[on]
found it hard to admit, even to himself, that he could not resi[st]
the call of a good cause or the temptation of acting in an aren[a]
larger than Monticello. For all his patience and philosophi[c]
poise, he could not shut his susceptible mind to the clam[or]
from the outside world. Up to the hill of Monticello the[re]
came a steady stream of letters, and many friends.

His friends, especially Madison, played delicately upon h[is]
emotions to bring him out from his retirement. Madison w[as]
always dropping skillfully baited hints to stir up Jefferso[n's]
dormant ambitions. Judiciously distributed rumors to the effe[ct]
that Jefferson was a candidate for the Presidency found the[ir]
way into the newspapers. Such gossip was in turn relayed t[o]
Jefferson in letters.

Jefferson protested that he did not seek the Presidency, b[ut]
his protests were couched in ambiguities. He insisted that h[e]
did not want the high office, but he never said emphatically th[at]
he would not take it. In a letter to Madison written in th[e]
spring of 1795 Jefferson disclaimed all political ambition[s]
"The little spice of ambition which I had in my younger da[ys]
has long since evaporated, and I set still less store by [a]
posthumous than present name." But at the same time he to[ld]
his friend that he was interested in seeing that his own part[y,]
the Republican, did not lose votes in the next election. He als[o]
confessed to another one of his correspondents that he was "[a]
warm zealot for the attainment & enjoyment by all mankind [of]
as much liberty, as each may exercise without injury to th[e]
equal liberty of his fellow citizens." It is hard to square a desi[re]
for retirement from politics with a wish to see one's part[y]
victorious and one's fellow men in possession of full libert[y]

Both aims had to be fought for, and no one knew that better than Jefferson.

His letters show the inner struggle that he must have gone through—a conflict between a happy but politically inactive retirement and a strong ambition to direct events. To dampen the flame of ambition, he even went so far as to refuse to read newspapers. "I read but little," he wrote to Mrs. Trist in the autumn of 1795, "take no [newspaper] that I may not have the tranquility of my mind disturbed by falsehoods & follies."

But try as he would, he could not drown out the political voices that reached all the way to Monticello.

2

When the election year 1796 came around it was generally known that President Washington would not be a candidate for a third term. He had accepted a second term with the utmost reluctance, and now he was weary, unwell, and utterly sick of politics.

It was certain that the Vice-President, John Adams, would be a candidate for the Presidency. He would have the support of the Federalists and the conservative interests in general. But who would be the candidate of the Republicans and radical-democratic elements? The answer was obvious to Jefferson's friends and followers. To the planters of the South, the farmers of the West, the mechanics of the North, there was only one man to lead the Republican forces, and that was Thomas Jefferson.

There were no formal nominating conventions in those days. Candidates were selected and programs adopted by a few leading figures in their political parties. Some such figures, like Aaron Burr of New York, were political bosses; others, like Alexander Hamilton, were leaders by dint of sheer intellectual weight.

As early as February, 1796, James Madison, who was to the Republican party what Hamilton was to the Federalist, urged Jefferson to come out and declare himself a candidate. Madison's appeal was based upon the ground of historical destiny. He was so eager to nail Jefferson's candidacy that he actually told him that it was his "historical task" to run for the Presidency: "I intreat you not to procrastinate, much less abandon, your historical task"—Madison underlined the word. "You owe it to yourself, to truth, to the world."

Madison's plan was to have the Republican leaders draft Jefferson, thereby facing him with a fait accompli. His only fear, as he confessed to his fellow lieutenant in the Republican party, James Monroe, was that their candidate might balk publicly and thereby ruin the party in the election.

Jefferson's political seclusion and his known disinclination be a candidate for the Presidency made his opponents war They suspected him of playing a crafty game. A Federal pamphleteer, William Loughton Smith, ridiculed Jefferson i pretending to retire. According to Smith, Jefferson's retireme was merely a trick in order to "mature his schemes of co cealed ambition, and at the appointed time, come forth t undisguised candidate for the highest honors." [1]

As the period of election was approaching, Jefferson co tinued to play the sphinx. He wrote no political letters to l friends and never a word to the press. "From a very ear period of my life," he confided to Monroe at this time, "I h laid it down as a rule of conduct, never to write a word for t public papers." He kept them guessing.

His ambiguous attitude was such that his enemies found easy to accuse him of hypocrisy, a charge that dogged him de ing his life and clung to his reputation thereafter. But there w no hypocrisy in his behavior. In his wish to have nothing to with public affairs he was sincere, but he was equally since in his desire to see his ideas triumph. He believed deeply th what he did was not only right, but in the best interest of t public. If, therefore, there was deception in his course, it w nothing more than self-deception.

Autumn came and Jefferson was still noncommittal. Silen being taken for consent, the Republicans nominated him f the Presidency. Aaron Burr of New York was selected as l running mate. The Federalists chose John Adams and Thom Pinckney. Jefferson accepted the nomination by the simp process of not protesting against it. To the world, and even his own family, he gave the impression of indifference.

A presidential election in those days was neither simple n direct. In each State the Electoral College voted for both c fices, without designating which of the candidates was to g first place (the Presidency) and which second (the Vic Presidency). The votes were then sent to the national capit to be counted. The candidate who had the highest number votes was declared President and the next highest, Vic President. If the two leading candidates had an equal numb of votes, the election was to be decided by the House of Repr sentatives, wherein each State cast one vote. Communicatic

[1] W. L. Smith, *The Pretensions of Thomas Jefferson to the Presidency Exa ined; and the Charges against John Adams Refuted,* Philadelphia, Octob 1796. A copy may be found in the Rare Book Room of the Library Congress.

eing slow and uncertain, it took several weeks for all the votes o come in from States so far apart as Georgia and Massahusetts.

In the middle of December Jefferson had a feeling that the lection would go against him. As a political strategist, he knew hat elections cannot be won without careful groundwork, and e had done practically nothing to organize the campaign. He nstructed Madison that in case of a tie the Republicans should ive their vote to Adams. "I pray you and authorize you fully, o solicit on my behalf that mr. Adams may be preferred."

By that time Madison, who was pulling political strings at 'hiladelphia, sensed that Adams would get the Presidency and efferson would have to content himself with second place. nowing Jefferson's sensitiveness, Madison was worried lest he vould refuse the Vice-Presidency. That would hurt his political eputation. Madison, who was looking to the future, wrote him rgently: "You are bound to abide by the event whatever it nay be. On the whole, it seems *essential* that you should not efuse the station which is likely to be your lot."

Jefferson, in the meantime, half hoped that he would be deeated. To a friend he confessed that if he lost: "I protest efore my god, that I shall, from the bottom of my heart, reoice." While the Presidency was tempting in one sense, it was rightening in another. He remembered the torments suffered y George Washington under attack. He knew that the presilential office was one in which the occupant was the whippingoy for every irresponsible critic and the target of every venal cribbler. Such a prospect was not encouraging to a man who iked to plant corn in peace and who had no lust for power.

As soon as Jefferson received Madison's letter about the Vice-Presidency, he hastened to assure him that he would not e hurt at getting second place. No question of pride was involved in being second to a man as esteemed as John Adams. As for the position itself, he had no strong feelings about it ither way.

The result of the election was as Jefferson had anticipated. Vhen the electoral votes were finally counted in February, 797, it was found that John Adams had 71 votes and Jefferson 8. That made Adams President and Jefferson Vice-President.

But the surprise of the election lay in the distribution of the otes. As Jefferson analyzed the ballot he realized that he had ome within a hairbreadth of being elected. A shift of two votes vould have given him the Presidency. For three votes of the arrow margin which elected Adams were actually cast in solid efferson States. Adams got a single vote in each of the States f Pennsylvania, Virginia, and North Carolina; all the rest of ie votes in those States went to Jefferson.

Jefferson realized that the election of 1796 contained the ke‖ of future success. If the South could be kept solid for th‖ Republicans—and there was no reason to assume that it woul‖ not be—then all that was needed to win in 1800, and subse‖ quently, was Pennsylvania. He had just carried thirteen out ‖ Pennsylvania's fourteen votes. Next time his party would mak‖ sure to win them all. "Let us," he wrote to Madison, "cultiva‖ Pennsylvania, & we need not fear the universe."

4

On February 20, 1797, Vice-President-elect Thomas Jeffe‖ son left Monticello for Philadelphia. He drove a phaeton ‖ Alexandria and then, after sending his servant Jupiter hom‖ with the horses, took a stagecoach to the capital. He arrived ‖ Philadelphia two days before the inauguration.

Having lost the Presidency by three votes, Jefferson viewe‖ the Vice-Presidency with a considerable degree of coolnes‖ The Vice-Presidency was a position of honor and of obscurit‖

The inauguration was not quite Jefferson's show, and so h‖ planned to slip into Philadelphia unobserved and without an‖ fuss. But his friends were on the lookout, and as soon as the‖ spotted him they fired artillery in his honor. A troop of militi‖ accompanied him to the city, carrying a banner: JEFFERSON THE FRIEND OF THE PEOPLE.

On the morning of Saturday, March 4, Jefferson entered th‖ Senate room to be sworn in as Vice-President, and President ‖ the Senate. The fifty-four-year-old Vice-President, dressed ‖ black, was an uncommon figure. Still as lean and bony as in h‖ youth, there were now streaks of gray in his reddish hai‖ Long-limbed, long-chinned, long-browed, speaking in a lo‖ voice and without any gestures, he gave the impression of ‖ strongly poised man who keeps his thoughts to himself. "H‖ spoke," a contemporary who listened to him relates, "like on‖ who considered himself entitled to deference."

A dramatic little incident occurred after President Adam‖ had delivered his inaugural address. As Adams left the ha‖ Vice-President Jefferson had started to follow when he notic‖ the tall figure of George Washington rising and making read‖ to leave. With quick courtesy the Vice-President fell bac‖ to let Washington pass. But the outgoing President was just ‖ courteous; he insisted that the new Vice-President precede hi‖ The embarrassed Jefferson did so, to the accompaniment ‖ hearty cheers.

No longer protesting that he was through with politics, Jef‖ ferson, with measured steps, went about his plans for the deme‖

ition of the Federalists and their ideology. Two methods were available. One was to tighten the Republican party into a powerful fighting instrument. The other was to pounce like a hawk upon every Federalist blunder and make the most of it.

Jefferson had a fresh, and essentially democratic, view of the function of political parties. Others, including Washington, looked upon political parties with distaste, considering them as breeding grounds of factionalism and cradles of strife. Jefferson, however, was one of the first great modern leaders to realize that political parties were essential to self-government. Opposition parties were necessary not only as vehicles for the expression of political aims and passions, but also as checks upon the party in power. Without political parties there could be no self-government:

> . . . in every free and deliberating society, there must, from the nature of man, be opposite parties, and violent dissensions and discords; and one of these, for the most part, must prevail over the other for a longer or a shorter time. Perhaps this party division is necessary to induce each to watch and to delate to the people the proceedings of the other.

Jefferson conceived a political party as a tough and yet flexible instrument. In itself a party was not sufficient to win power. It needed a cause. And the Federalists were not slow in supplying it. Led by Hamilton, the Federalists urged President Adams to declare war on France. The President refused to do so, his aim being to extort respect for the American flag rather than to shed American blood. But a considerable defense program was inaugurated. Men-of-war were built, armed merchant vessels were put to sea, the regular army was greatly increased, a marine corps was raised, $7,000,000 was borrowed, and the treaty with France was abrogated. Vice-President Jefferson signed a contract with Eli Whitney, the Yankee inventor, for 10,000 muskets. The country was in a state of undeclared war with France.

But the defense program was accompanied by a fever of belligerency, and that in turn gave rise to the well-known diseases of intolerance and political witch-hunting. Excuses for intolerance and persecution were not lacking. The country was in a state of unrest, and fear gripped the members of the ruling elements. They blamed Jefferson, the Jacobins, and, above all, the foreigners. The country harbored many refugees, exiles, and agitators born abroad. Most of them were good men and few among them, particularly the French and the Irish, were radicals. Among the more eminent foreign-born were Thomas Cooper, the English scientist; James Thomson Callender, the Scotch political writer, du Pont de Nemours, the French economist and founder of the present-day Du Pont dynasty; Joseph Priestley, the English chemist; Albert Gallatin, the Swiss economist and statesman. Upon the heads of many of these people there descended a torrent of Federalist calumny.

Stories were being circulated about Irishmen and Jacobins arming to invade and overthrow the United States. One Federalist Senator said that the Commonwealth of Pennsylvania was full of "United Irishmen, freemasons, and the most God provoking democrats this side of hell!" Professional patriots grew hysterical and club ladies (or their contemporary equivalents) were trembling with expectation. The upper classes, particularly in New England, "scared easy." Good ladies expected to be murdered in their beds, or meet a fate worse than death at the hands of the godless Frenchmen and wild Irishmen. And who was to blame? That man Jefferson!

5

In the summer of 1798, Congress, against the advice of the cooler heads in the Federalist party, passed the Alien and Sedition acts, designed to choke off agitation and to stifle criticism of the Adams Administration. The Alien Acts authorized the President to expel all those whom he should "judge dangerous to the peace and safety of the United States" or should have "reasonable grounds to suspect are concerned in any treasonable or secret machinations against the government."

The Sedition Act provided for a fine of no more than $2,000, and imprisonment of no more than two years, for the writing, printing, uttering, or publishing of "any false, scandalous and malicious writing or writings against the government of the United States . . . with intent to defame . . . or to bring them . . . into contempt or disrepute; or to excite against them . . . the hatred of the good people of the United States, or to stir up sedition within the United States, or to excite any unlawful combinations therein."

The Sedition Act was so broad and inclusive that it virtually abolished the Bill of Rights. The Federalists were out to destroy republicanism, Jeffersonianism, Jacobinism, and radicalism in one fell swoop. If in the process they also blasted away the democratic foundations of the republic, so much the better, they thought.

The acts were passed right under Jefferson's gavel, so to speak. As presiding officer of the Senate, however, he scrupulously refrained from interfering. He felt that the Federalists were doing their best to commit suicide, and he did not think it his bounden duty to stop them.

Not that he could have checked the outburst of reaction

ven if he had tried. To Jefferson's Republicans, the Alien and
edition acts were, naturally, poison. Some of the more re-
ponsible Federalists agreed. John Marshall, for example, con-
idered these acts useless and unwise. Alexander Hamilton,
espite his hatred for Jeffersonianism and democracy, likewise
eared the effects of the repressive legislation. "Let us not
stablish a tyranny," Hamilton urged. "Energy is a very differ-
nt thing from violence." But these men were powerless to
heck the hysteria.

While Hamilton feared the consequences of the acts, Jeffer-
on coolly waited for their effects. "For my own part," he said,
I consider those laws as merely an experiment on the Ameri-
an mind, to see how far it will bear an avowed violation of
he constitution." He was certain that they would boomerang.

With the passing of the Sedition Act a "Federalist reign of
error," to quote Jefferson's words, descended upon the land.
Vithin a few months after the act was passed, the Federalist
idges created a sufficient number of martyrs to the cause of
berty to do Jefferson a world of good.

The first man to be convicted under the act, in October,
798, was Matthew Lyon, a Jeffersonian Congressman from
Vermont. He had been born in Ireland and had a fine record
s a patriot and a soldier in Washington's army during the
Revolution. Lyon's conviction was typical and scandalous.
he indictment charged him with the intent "to stir up sedi-
on, and to bring the President and government . . . into
ontempt." Actually he had not stirred up sedition; he had
erely committed lèse majesté by criticizing President Adams.
Ie had printed a statement that he could not support Adams
vhen he saw "every consideration of the public welfare swal-
owed up in a continual grasp for power, in an unbounded
hirst for ridiculous pomp, foolish adulation and selfish ava-
ice," and "men of real merit daily turned out of office for
o other cause but independency of sentiment," and the
sacred name of religion employed as a state engine to make
nankind hate and persecute each other." This language may
ave been somewhat intemperate, but it was not treasonable
—at least not under the Bill of Rights.

But Justice William Paterson of the United States Supreme
Court and the jury thought otherwise. In his defense, Lyon
aid that the Sedition Act was unconstitutional, his publication
nnocent, and its contents true. Point-blank he asked the Judge
vhether he had not often dined with President Adams and
bserved "his ridiculous pomp and parade." The Judge de-
ied it, and instructed the jury to ignore the constitutional
alidity of the act (since juries could not pass upon that) and

to decide merely whether the defendant had published "sedi
tiously." The jury convicted Lyon and sentenced him to fou
months in prison and $1,000 fine. This conviction of a Revo
lutionary soldier, a patriot, and a member of Congress came
as a tremendous shock to the nation. It was to be the first na
in the Federalist coffin.

The second conviction also took place in Vermont and wa
directly connected with Matthew Lyon. Anthony Haswell, the
editor of the *Vermont Gazette*, printed an advertisement which
Lyon had inserted. It was for a lottery to raise money to pay
Lyon's fine. It stated that Lyon was "holden by the oppressive
hand of usurped power in a loathsome prison, deprived al
most of the right of reason, and suffering all the indignitie
which can be heaped upon him by a hard-hearted savage [the
U. S. Marshal] who has, to the disgrace of Federalism, beer
elevated to a station where he can satiate his barbarity on the
misery of his victims."

For this Haswell was indicted by the same judge and jur
who had convicted Lyon. Haswell offered evidence to prove tha
Lyon was being brutally treated by the Marshal. But the jury
had no admiration for republicans and no love for foreigners
The English-born Haswell, father of seventeen children, wa
sentenced to two months in jail and $200 fine.

Still another victim of the "Federalist reign of terror" wa
Thomas Cooper, the English-born educator and scientist. I
his capacity as an editor of a pro-Jeffersonian Pennsylvania
newspaper, Cooper had criticized President Adams, saying tha
he was "hardly in the infancy of political mistake" and othe
such generalities. For this act of lèse majesté Cooper was in
dicted.

A student of the law, Cooper spoke in his own defense. He
addressed the jury in dignified terms, pointing out that he had
published only the truth, that his criticism was legitimate, an
that he had expressed his opinions as a member of a lawfu
political party. It did him no good. In charging the jury, Jus
tice Samuel Chase of the United States Supreme Court wen
out of his way to praise the Sedition Act—which it was no
within his province or jurisdiction to do—and to attack the
falsity of Cooper's statements. The jury found Cooper guilty—
six months in prison and $400 fine.

Perhaps the most scandalous case under the Sedition Ac
took place in Jefferson's own Virginia. In Richmond, James
Thomson Callender, a Scottish-born political writer, was in
dicted for the grave crime of criticizing President Adams
What made the case sensational, however, was the behavior o
the judge. Three of the greatest lawyers in Virginia—William
Wirt, Thomas Nicholas, and George Hay—volunteered to

defend Callender. But Supreme Court Justice Chase, the same one who had convicted Cooper, was not impressed. In the court he did everything to show his contempt for the lawyers. He cut them short, cracked jokes, and made them shut up. When William Wirt started to tell the jury that the Sedition Act was unconstitutional, Justice Chase snapped, "Take your seat, sir." George Hay, the other lawyer, was so angered at the Justice's bullying tactics and insulting interruptions that he refused to go on with the case. Callender was convicted, sentenced to nine months in jail, and assessed a $200 fine. Virginia rocked with indignation, and Jefferson chalked off another mark against the Federal judiciary.

6

As Vice-President, Jefferson could not openly do very much about the persecutions under the Sedition Act, but as leader of his party he could not abstain from acting. Throughout the country men and women—all those who were not zealous Federalists—looked to Jefferson to raise his voice in protest and to supply the leadership against the raging reaction.

Jefferson acted in his own indirect way. Secretly, in collaboration with such friends and aides as George Nicholas and James Madison, he drew up a manifesto, the so-called Kentucky Resolution, which elaborated the theory of States' rights as a club with which to beat the Federalists. The theory was based upon three basic propositions—that the Federal Government was created by the individual States; that it was the agent of the States; and that its actions were subject to criticism, or even nullification, by the States. Underlying the long resolution there was a tone, faint but discernible, of rebellion, a threat of ultimate secession in the face of Federal tyranny— "these and successive acts of the same character, unless arrested at the threshold [will] necessarily drive these states into revolution and blood."

The Kentucky Resolution was adopted, with virtual unanimity, by the Kentucky legislature. In Virginia, a similar resolution, drawn up by James Madison, was also overwhelmingly carried in the legislature. These resolutions were the first heavy shots fired in the war on the Federalists. That Jefferson was the instigator and coauthor of the resolutions few people knew, but many suspected.

Jefferson continued to preside over the Senate with scrupulous impartiality and impressive serenity. Only his most intimate friends knew of his plans. To many lieutenants of his party throughout the country he wrote letters of advice and encouragement, urging them to keep calm and steady. That he was a candidate for the Presidency, the center and hope of resistance to the Federalists, was a wide-open secret. But his was a low-visibility strategy that disconcerted the opposition. He left no crack open into which they could shoot an arrow.

In the darkest days of Federalist reaction Jefferson's function was that of inspirer, stimulator, and clarifier. He wanted his friends and followers to understand the basic issues involved and to act upon them in the light of reason. His object was to educate the people, so that they could not fall victim to phony arguments and false appeals. For this purpose he wrote long letters which he knew would be read in circles, around stoves, in stores, in taverns, in shops.

CHAPTER TWELVE

CANDIDATE

(1800)

THE CAMPAIGN of 1800 was unlike anything ever known in America before. For sheer virulence and bitterness it has hardly been surpassed since. The gloves were off. On the Federalists' side it was a struggle to preserve power for the rich and the privileged. On the Jeffersonian side it was a battle to keep America a democracy, with liberty and opportunity for all the people.

There was a surprising political awareness on the part of simple artisans, farmers, workers, and little people in general. To them, as to millions of later Americans, America "was promises." Adams, Hamilton, and other conservatives despised the common people, and made no secret of their contempt. But Jefferson championed their cause and spoke in their name. He not only formulated their inarticulate hopes, but also believed in their intelligence, trusted their judgment, respected their character. Jefferson wanted every man to have a chance or life, liberty, and the pursuit of happiness.

The common people's trust in Jefferson is something to marvel at. Except for his immediate neighbors, he had literally no contact with the masses, and he sought none. The people who were behind him had never seen him. They had never heard him speak. They had never shaken his hand. And yet to hundreds of thousands of them Tom Jefferson was a symbol and a hope.

Here was a great paradox. The aristocrat of impeccable taste and of exquisite manners, the hypersensitive gentleman who was shy of meeting with the common people in the mass, was the man who had devoted his life to the popular cause. He was the strangest leader of democracy ever known.

He was also, in the strictest and non-invidious sense of the word, the master politician of the age. For sheer political adroitness Jefferson has probably never been excelled in America, except possibly by Abraham Lincoln, whose physical and mental resemblance to Jefferson, frequently overlooked, is startling. Like the far better known Lincoln, Jefferson had the knack of crystallizing popular ideas and aspirations in unfor-

gettable words. Again like Lincoln, Jefferson had the priceles
gift of knowing how to get along smoothly with those wh
were ambitious for power and prestige. And like Lincoln, Jef
ferson knew when and where to strike the telling blow.

The way Jefferson organized the campaign of 1800 was
masterpiece of political strategy. Every move was calculate
in advance, with an eye to the maximum political effectiveness
Each step was carefully weighed by Jefferson's chief aides
particularly Madison and Monroe. No possible advantage wa
overlooked; no flank left exposed. In every section of th
Union key figures were set in motion by the Vice-President
They kept in touch with Jefferson by correspondence, and oc
casionally through personal contact. Among these men wer
Albert Gallatin and Thomas McKean of Pennsylvania; Charle
Pinckney of South Carolina; John Taylor of North Carolina
Robert R. Livingston and George Clinton of New York. The
made up a sort of Jeffersonian general staff.

The actual work of winning over the voters and of keepin
them in line was entrusted to local agitators and politica
bosses. Jefferson carefully cultivated and inspired these men
writing them letters which contained judicious mixtures of ad
vice and encouragement. They were a tough lot, used to shout
ing their arguments in taverns and country stores. But the
were as American as homespun; stanch and aggressive indi
vidualists who despised the silk-breeched gentry. Jefferson wa
brought up among such men, and he had a deep-rooted appre
ciation of their worth. His father had been such a homespu
frontier type of American.

They were hard-bitten, hard-driving men, these Jeffersonia
leaders. In Georgia there was James Jackson, a man withou
birth or position. By sheer will and ability Jackson became
lieutenant-colonel in the Revolutionary War, Governor o
Georgia, and United States Senator. He had been born ir
England and was a stout democrat. Perhaps the toughest po
litical boss in the Jeffersonian party was Benjamin Austin o
Boston. Austin of Boston was a member of the Massachusett
Senate and a first-rate democratic speaker. A lean, lank, lan
tern-jawed figure, he was the terror of the blue-blooded Fed
eralists. He would flood town meetings with his followers, mer
"who looked as if they had been collected from all the Jails o
the continent," according to John Quincy Adams.

Jefferson also made systematic use of the press and th
printed word. As far back as 1799, one year before the cam
paign actually got under way, Jefferson wrote to Madison:

We are sensible that this summer is the season for systemati energies and sacrifices. The engine is the press. Every man must lay his purse and his pen under contribution. . . . Let me pray and beseech you to set apart a certain portion of every post-day to write what may be proper for the public.

Note the expression "what may be proper for the public." It is a good definition of propaganda, for which Jefferson had a twentieth-century appreciation.

Both the Republican and the Federalist newspapers were unrestrained and vindictive. Their contents, after being read by a few, spread by word of mouth, gathering poison from tongue to tongue.

To Jefferson the press, with all its shortcomings, was a weapon in the battle for democracy. He planned his campaign from behind the scenes, striking swift, invisible blows. When he suggested to one of his lieutenants that he distribute several dozen copies of a certain pamphlet in "every county comm[itt]ee in the state," he added a warning that his sponsorship of the pamphlet should be kept secret. "You will readily see what a handle would be made of my advocating their contents." Secrecy was his strategy and his predilection. In describing the political situation in North Carolina, he explained that Republican propaganda there should be carried out under cover. "The medicine for that State must be very mild & secretly administered. But nothing should be spared to give them true information."

He used pamphlets like ammunition. One of the Jefferson-inspired pamphlets was Thomas Paine's *Rights of Man*. Jefferson also dropped hints and suggestions into the ears of political organizers and editors. One of his ideas which speakers and writers were asked to take up and hammer at was government expenditure. Jefferson suggested to his followers that they keep on assailing the Adams Administration on the ground of costliness and extravagance. This, he said coolly, would "open the eyes of the nation." It did.

The Jefferson writers—Freneau, Duane, Callender, Cooper —and the Jefferson organizers played together like an orchestra under the master's baton. And when the campaign was over, the outmaneuvered and outgeneraled John Adams was to pay bitter tribute to the political skill of the Jeffersonians: "A group of foreign liars, encouraged by a few ambitious native gentlemen, have discomfited the education, the talents, the virtues, and the property of the country."

2

In the spring of 1800, after Congress adjourned, Jefferson and Burr were unanimously nominated by a congressional caucus. "The campaign," Jefferson wrote to John W. Eppes, "will be as hot as that of Europe, but happily we deal in ink only; they in blood."

In taverns and courthouses, at meetings and barbecues, men began to exchange arguments, handbills, and blows. But the central figure around whom all the heat was generated never made any public appearance. He made no speeches, shook no hands, but calmly continued with his routine. A young man named Thomas Lee Shippen visited Jefferson during the campaign and was struck by his charm and serenity. Jefferson invited Shippen to join him and Madison in a little outing. There was no campaign talk or worry. "I never knew men more agreeable than they were," Shippen tells. "We talked and dined and strooled [sic] and rowed ourselves in boats, and feasted on delicious crabs."

Jefferson needed all the philosophy and self-confidence he could muster to ride through the campaign storm. He was made the target of such abuse and defamation as was never before heaped upon any public figure in America. The Federalists portrayed him as a thief, a coward, a libertine, an infidel, and an atheist. The religious issue was dragged out, and stirred up flames of hatred and intolerance. Clergymen, mobilizing their heaviest artillery of thunder and brimstone, threatened Christians with all manner of dire consequences if they should vote for the "infidel" from Virginia. This was particularly true in New England, where the clergy stood like Gibraltar against Jefferson. In Virginia itself the clergy had no overpowering influence. In Jefferson's home State gentlemen were inclined to be agnostic, and ordinary folk were imbued neither with theological prescience nor with intolerance. There is the anecdote about the Reverend Mr. Garrettson, a Methodist clergyman, who while traveling through the Virginia backwoods met a man and asked him whether he was acquainted with Jesus Christ. "Sir," came the unexpected reply, "I know not where the gentleman lives."

The most violent attack on Jefferson's religion was made by William Linn in a pamphlet entitled *Serious Considerations on the Election of a President*. Linn, who was a Dutch Reformed minister in New York City, accused Jefferson of the heinous crimes of not believing in divine revelation and of a design to destroy religion and "introduce immorality." Linn set out to show that Jefferson was a "true infidel," quoting from Jefferson's writings, real and imaginary, to prove his case. He quoted Jefferson as saying that "It does me no injury for my neighbor to say there are twenty gods, or no god. It neither picks my pocket nor breaks my leg." [1] Linn wrote that Jefferson once pointed to a dilapidated church and remarked, *"It is good enough for him that was born in a manger."* Such a remark, the Reverend Mr. Linn concluded, could "issue from the lips of no other than a deadly foe to His name and His cause." "Does Jefferson ever go to church?" the Reverend asked. "How does he spend the Lord's day? Is he known to worship with any denomination of christians?" The answer was a resounding NO!

> Let the first magistrate to be a professed infidel, and infidels will surround him. Let him spend the sabbath in feasting, in visiting or receiving visits, in riding abroad, but never in going to church; and to frequent public worship will become unfashionable. Infidelity will become the prattle from the highest to the lowest condition in life, and universal desoluteness [sic] will follow.

An infidel like Jefferson could not, should not, be elected. The Reverend Mr. Linn concluded his pamphlet with a fiery appeal to Christians to defeat the "infidel" from Virginia:

> Will you then, my fellow-citizens, with all this evidence . . . vote for Mr. Jefferson? . . . As to myself, were Mr. Jefferson connected with me by the nearest ties of blood, and did I owe him a thousand obligations, I would not, and could not vote for him. No; sooner than stretch forth my hand to place him at the head of the nation "Let mine arms fall from my shoulder blade, and mine arm be broken from the bone." [2]

The Jeffersonian side did not make the mistake of underestimating the effectiveness of Linn's pamphlet. Cogently stated, it undoubtedly sounded convincing to thousands of sincere Christians. In an age when ministers were the most potent members of the community, an accusation of infidelity was dangerous. The pamphlet put Jefferson on the defensive and made it necessary for his followers to clear his religious character. A number of vigorous pamphlets were issued in reply to Linn's *Serious Considerations*. Perhaps the best of them was Tunis Wortman's *A Solemn Address to the Christians and Patriots upon the Approaching Election of a President of the United States*. Wortman started out by establishing the propositions that Jefferson was a fine republican citizen and a good Christian:

---

[1] Linn quoted correctly. The quotation is to be found in Jefferson's *Notes on Virginia*, Query XVII.

[2] Job XXXI, 22. Another pamphlet that repeated Linn's charges was John Mitchell Mason's *The Voice of Warning to Christians in the Ensuing Election*. It was a trumpet blow in Zion, asking for the defeat of the Virginia "infidel."

That the charge of deism . . . is false, scandalous and ma-
licious—That there is not a single passage in the Notes on
Virginia, or any of Mr. Jefferson's writings, repugnant to christianity; but on the contrary, in every respect, favourable to it

Wortman praised Jefferson, whom he described as the "sage
of Monticelli" [sic], as a great scholar, a great patriot, a
great scientist, and a great statesman. He pointed out that the
religious issue was nothing more than what a later generation
has called a "red herring," in order to confuse and mislead
the people. His conclusion was eloquent:

People of America, patriots and electors, be assured that it is
not religion, but the state which is in jeopardy—Jefferson, who
has been the object of so many unmanly but unavailing calumny, is one of the strongest bulwarks of its safety; remember
that at this moment, your liberty, your constitution, your families, your children, the fate of the empire, depend upon the
rectitude of your decision.

De Witt Clinton, Jefferson's New York ally, likewise came
to his defense in *A Vindication of Thomas Jefferson, against
the Charges Contained in a Pamphlet Entitled "Serious Considerations."* Clinton's aim was to make out the difficult case
that "we have the strongest reasons to believe that he is a *real
Christian.*" He argued that Jefferson was a highly moral man
of lofty character. "I feel persuaded that he is a believer." "I
feel happy to hail him a Christian." And he clinched his argument with

And let me add . . . that he has for a long time supported
out of his own private revenues, a worthy minister of the Christian church—an instance of liberality not to be met with in any
of his rancorous enemies, whose love of religion seems prin-
cipally to consist in their unremitted endeavors to degrade it
into a handmaid of faction.

Another defender of Jefferson's religious character was John
James Beckley, whose *Address to the People of the United
States* lauded Jefferson for having established the Statute of
Religious Freedom in Virginia:

Read, ye fanatics, bigots, and religious hypocrites, of whatsoever clime or country ye be—and you, base calumniators
whose efforts to traduce are the involuntary tribute of envy to
a character more pure and perfect than your own, read, learn
and practice the RELIGION OF JEFFERSON, as displayed in th
sublime truths and inspired language of HIS ever memorabl
"Act for establishing religious freedom."

In days when religion was firmly tied to morals, a man accused of irreligion was automatically branded a moral outcast

If you did not believe in God, so the clergy argued, you were ipso facto a thief and a seducer. If you did not attend church regularly, you naturally hated your mother and beat your wife.

They accused Jefferson of everything. If the sermons of the clergy were to be believed, there was no crime in the calendar of which Jefferson was not guilty and no unspeakable evil which he had not committed. One clergyman, the Reverend Cotton Mather Smith, accused Jefferson of having obtained his property by fraud and of having robbed widows and orphans. Others warned their congregations that their Bibles would be confiscated if the Republican ogre were elected. They compared him to Rehoboam, the evil son and successor of King Solomon, from whom the ten tribes revolted.

The clerical fulminations did not budge Jefferson from his determination to ignore them. He had too great a contempt for his detractors to dignify them with a reply. To Uriah McGregory of Connecticut he wrote:

> From the moment that a portion of my fellow citizens looked towards me with a view to one of their highest offices, the floodgates of calumny have been opened upon me. . . . I know that I might have filled the courts of the United States with actions for these slanders, and have ruined perhaps many persons who are not innocent. But this would be no equivalent to the loss of character. I leave them therefore, to the reproof of their own consciences.

But from friends he could not conceal his anger at the clerical character-assassins. At the height of the campaign of vilification, Jefferson gave voice to one of his angriest yet immortal statements. In a letter to Dr. Rush he wrote: "they [the clergy] believe that any portion of power confided to me, will be exerted in opposition to their schemes. And they believe rightly; for *I have sworn upon the altar of god, eternal hostility against every form of tyranny over the mind of man.*" [3]

The religious issue—freedom versus intolerance—undoubtedly had its educational effect upon many people. Whether it influenced any votes is another question, and one that it is not possible to answer either way. It is certain, however, that so much mud was hurled at Jefferson that some of it stuck. For generations many communities, particularly in the North, continued to regard Thomas Jefferson as Antichrist. As late as 1830 the Philadelphia Public Library refused to keep any works

[3] Italics mine. S.K.P. Incidentally, these words, suggested by former Secretary Ickes and this author, are engraved on the Jefferson monument in Washington, D. C.

dealing with the life or writings of Jefferson. In New England he was pursued by relentless clerical hatred. A Puritan clergyman during a baptism asked the father for the child's name. "Thomas Jefferson," the father replied. "No such unchristian name!" thundered the clergyman. "John Adams, I baptize thee."

The religious question that was raked up was only a side issue. The real struggle was over popular government. It was a battle for democracy.

The frankness with which the opposing sides faced the issue of democracy versus oligarchy is astonishing to modern ears that are accustomed to sounds which do not mean what they seem to mean. In 1800 the men who fought the war of democracy against privilege, and of privilege against democracy, minced no words; they said exactly what they thought. Both sides hated and feared each other too much to pretend to have any other feelings. In the Jeffersonian ranks there were men who did not conceal their conviction that the moneybags and the aristocrats were ripe for the ax. Among the Federalists there was a blunt contempt for and fierce hatred of the "rabble."

It took courage to be a democrat, a follower of Jefferson. A democrat had no caste and no character. He was not respectable, did not belong to the best clubs, wore no silk on Sunday. A democrat, a follower of Jefferson, was a common man, an ordinary American who worked with his hands and hoped for a better life. The Federalists regarded such men as the lowest dregs of humanity. Henry Adams, the great-grandson of John Adams, has given the following mental picture of Jeffersonian democrats as conceived by the Federalists:

> Every dissolute intriguer, loose-liver, forger, false-coiner, and prison-bird; every hare-brained, loud-talking demagogue; every speculator, scoffer and athetist,—was a follower of Jefferson and Jefferson was himself the incarnation of their theories.

The Federalists, terrified at the prospect of propertyless people winning the campaign, made the mistake of overlooking an elementary fact in arithmetic—a fact that Lincoln well knew when he said that God must love the common people because he made so many of them. The Federalist campaign was based upon an appeal to men of property and a contempt for men without much property. It happened that men without much property were in the majority.

The Federalists made another mistake: every time they at

tacked Jefferson as a leader of democracy, they identified him with democracy. And the common people were quick to draw the conclusion, if any were needed, that Jefferson must be their friend, since he too believed in self-government for ordinary folk.

The Federalists indulged in a spree of hatred for democracy that intoxicated them. They marshaled antidemocratic arguments that appealed to an upper-class minority which needed no convincing. They did not reach, or even try to reach, the common people. Dennie's *Portfolio* wrote:

> A democracy is scarcely tolerable at any period of national history. Its omens are always sinister. . . . It is on its trial here, and the issue will be civil war, desolation, and anarchy. No wise man but discerns its imperfections, no good man but shudders at its miseries, no honest man but proclaims its fraud, and no brave man but draws his sword against its force.

This was reprinted in all the Federalist newspapers.

At a dinner in New York City, Alexander Hamilton struck his hand on the table and shouted to a man who had expressed a democratic sentiment: "Your people, sir,—your people is a great *beast!*"

As the election of Jefferson seemed to be more and more of a certainty, the hysteria of the Federalist press redoubled in violence. The *Columbian Centinel* exclaimed that the election of Jefferson was "equivalent to a Revolution" and warned the country: "Citizens beware, you are on the margin of a precipice." An appeal was made to the citizens to "crush the monster" before it was too late.

"The Jeffersoniad," an anonymously written essay in thirteen installments, raked Jefferson's character with fanatical savagery. It smeared the Republican candidate as an anarchist and a coward, and even went so far as to start a hopeful rumor of his death.

3

During all this excitement, throughout the spring and the summer of 1800, Jefferson stayed home at Monticello and attended to his private affairs. He neither orated nor campaigned. The only evidences of his participation in the campaign were a gift of $50 to the political writer James T. Callender (victim of the Sedition Act) and a subscription to an extra newspaper or two. Otherwise he followed his routine with unshatterable serenity. He never doubted the outcome of the struggle.

In the latter part of November Jefferson left Monticello for Washington, which was the capital of the nation since June.

As Vice-President, he had to be in Washington for the opening of the Congress. In the swampy village on the Potomac Jefferson awaited the result of the election with cool confidence. In this he differed from the rest of the country, which was on tenterhooks. News of the election was trickling in slowly, in inconclusive fragments. Early in December Jefferson learned that he had carried Virginia by a smashing plurality. Out of 27,335 votes cast, he received 21,111. This was a great personal triumph, particularly since the Federalists had been using the potent name of George Washington (who had died in 1799) against Jefferson.

A few days later Jefferson learned that he had carried South Carolina. "I believe we may consider the election as now decided," he wrote. Soon it was known that the Republican party had swept the country and had won majorities in both houses of Congress. Du Pont de Nemours, Jefferson's French friend, was quick to congratulate him with a Gallic compliment (in French, as he always wrote Jefferson): "Behold you at the head of your wise nation. She has freely placed her greatest man in her greatest position."

The Jeffersonians began a round of celebrations with speeches, songs and toasts.

But the celebrations were premature. When the electoral vote was counted, it was found that though Adams was defeated, Jefferson was not elected. This paradoxical situation was the result of the confused electoral law, which did not stipulate that the electors should specify which of the candidates was to be President and which Vice-President. Each elector voted for two candidates, and the one with the highest number of votes was declared President. It was true that Adams and Pinckney were defeated—with 65 and 64 electoral votes respectively—but it was likewise true that Jefferson did not get a majority over his running mate, Aaron Burr. The Republican vote stood 73 electoral votes for Jefferson and 73 electoral votes for Burr.

The Jeffersonians thus had a majority of the total vote cast, but they had no President. The election now had to be thrown into the House of Representatives, which, under the Constitution, had the power to break the tie. This was a heaven-sent opportunity for the Federalists. They considered the election of Jefferson to be a national calamity and were determined to do everything to prevent it. Although it was universally known and assumed that Jefferson, and not Burr, was the presidential candidate, and although the people had voted for Jefferson, and not for Burr, for President, the embittered Federalists in Congress were resolved to throw their votes to Burr.

Not all the Federalists, however, were willing to be a party to this unscrupulous scheme. The two greatest, John Adams and Alexander Hamilton, would have nothing to do with the intrigue. In view of the hatred that both men bore Jefferson, their behavior in this instance was a tribute to their patriotism. Perhaps they did not object so much to the dishonesty of the plot to defeat Jefferson as to the character of Burr. For Aaron Burr was not famous for virtue or steadfastness of character, and the idea of such a man's occupying the presidential chair was disturbing to responsible men.

To Alexander Hamilton, Burr was "bankrupt beyond redemption." When that arch-Tory, Gouverneur Morris, told Hamilton that "Burr must be preferred to Jefferson" because the latter was "infected with all the cold-blooded vices," Hamilton gave a determined No. The career of the machine politician Burr, he replied, proved that he had "formed himself upon the model of Catiline, and that he is too cold-blooded and too determined a conspirator ever to change his plan."

Before the election was thrown into the House of Representatives, Hamilton announced that he would support Jefferson against Burr. He did that because he considered Jefferson to be the lesser of two great evils.

As for John Adams, in this crucial struggle he felt less strongly about Jefferson, whose principles he disliked, than he did about Burr, whom he feared and despised. Jefferson, despite his ardent democratic views which were anathema to Adams, was at least honest and a gentleman, Adams knew. But Burr, in Adams's eyes, was a "humiliation" to America.

Jefferson may have known of the underground intrigues that were designed to rob him of victory, but he went about his vice-presidential duties as if the election concerned two other fellows. Before the House of Representatives took up the balloting, Jefferson visited President Adams on official business. In the breast of Adams, the defeated candidate, there dwelt no love for Jefferson. But the President was a gentleman, and he spoke to his visitor words of magnanimity which he did not feel.

"Well," the President said to the Vice-President, "I understand that you are to beat me in this contest, and I will only say that I will be as faithful a subject as any you will have."

Jefferson did not think that this was the right interpretation of events. To him the election was not a matter of persons but of principles.

"Mr. Adams," he said, "this is no personal contest between you and me. Two systems of principles on the subject of government divide our fellow citizens into two parties. . . . Were we both to die to-day, to-morrow two other names would be in the place of ours." . . .

"I believe you are right," Adams admitted, "that we are but passive instruments, and should not suffer this matter to affect our personal dispositions."

But he did not really feel magnanimous. The defeated President was bitter and unforgiving.

4

On February 11 the House of Representatives in Washington began to ballot in order to break the Jefferson-Burr tie. Each of the sixteen States was allowed one vote. Nineteen times the ballot was taken on that day, and nineteen times the result was the same—eight States cast their votes for Jefferson, six for Burr, and two were divided. Neither candidate had a clear majority. On February 12 the ballot was taken nine times, and the result was the same. On February 13, 14, and 16, the House of Representatives voted six times. And the results were identical. The Federalists were determined to subvert the will of the people and to defeat Jefferson at all costs.

At the height of the bitter deadlock President Adams said to Jefferson with an undertone of anger: "Sir, the event of the election is within your own power. You have only to say you will do justice to the public creditors, maintain the navy, and not disturb those holding office, and the government will instantly be put into your hands."

Jefferson replied quietly: "I will not come into the government by capitulation."

"Then," Adams said, "things must take their course.'

Jefferson knew himself to be the lawful choice of the majority of the people, and he would not under any circumstances be a party to any kind of compromise. "Many attempts," he informed Monroe, "have been made to obtain terms & promises from me. I have declared to them unequivocally, that I would not receive the government on capitulation, that I would not go into it with my hands tied."

The Federalists' intrigues to deprive him of the Presidency were so blatant that there was fear of secession in case the House of Representatives voted for Burr. As a matter of fact, the Jeffersonians, whose leader in Congress was the intelligent Albert Gallatin, declared openly and firmly that if the House did so, there would be an armed uprising in the Middle States.

Animosity on one side was matched by loyalty on the other. Joseph H. Nicholson, a Congressman from Maryland, is a case in point. While the House was voting, Nicholson was gravely ill. But, nursed by his wife, he had himself daily carried in a litter to the Capitol and scribbled *Jefferson* on every ballot. Other Republican Congressmen were equally stanch. That winter Jefferson lived with thirty Republican members of Congress

t Canaird's boardinghouse, in an atmosphere of comradeship
nd democratic simplicity. When someone suggested that
ne Congressmen give their fellow boarder Jefferson, who after
ll was Vice-President of the United States and the leader of
neir party, a seat of honor at the long table, they replied with
ffectionate laughter that "he must not be allowed to forget
nat he is one of the people and that all were equal." Jefferson
as proud of his pupils in democracy.

President Adams did everything to embarrass Jefferson. A
ew days before the final vote in the House, Adams appointed
ohn Marshall, who hated Jefferson, to the Supreme Court.
he President also put a number of other tories, Federalists
ll, into lesser judicial posts. These appointments were a con-
mptuous challenge flung into the face of Jefferson, for the
ew judges disliked both his person and his ideas. Adams's ac-
on could undoubtedly be defended on legal grounds, but to
addle a new President with hostile judges, appointed for life,
as not altogether cricket. Jefferson did not consider it
air.

By this time there was a secessionist air in Washington, and
nany people, especially the more responsible Federalists, began
o fear that the anti-Jeffersonian intrigue might lead possibly
o a dissolution of the Union and certainly to widespread un-
est. Under pressure of opinion and upon the urgent advice of
Iamilton, some Congressmen shifted their votes, and broke
ne week-long deadlock. On the thirty-sixth ballot ten States
nally cast their votes for Jefferson and four for Burr. Two
oted blank.

This took place on February 17, 1801. On that day, after
nirty-one hours of balloting, Jefferson was elected third Presi-
ent of the United States.

CHAPTER THIRTEEN

PRESIDENT

(1801-1809)

THE INAUGURATION took place in a bleak and deserted city
John Adams, frustrated and embittered, left Washington th
night of March 3. The defeated old President would not do hi
hated successor the honor of being present at his installation
and Adams's example was followed by other high officials and
gentlemen. The gentry ostentatiously turned its collective back
on the victorious apostle of democracy.

Washington, the capital since the preceding summer, was a
swampy village that accentuated the bleakness of the occasion
The settlement was without any proper streets or urban facili
ties. It possessed a few wretched houses, "most of them small
miserable huts," according to Oliver Wolcott, Adams's Secre
tary of the Treasury. Gouverneur Morris described it ironicall
as "the best city in the world for a *future* residence. We wan
nothing here but houses, cellars, kitchens, well informed men
amiable women, and other trifles of this kind, to make our cit
perfect."

The inauguration was as extraordinary as the capital itself
On the morning of March 4 the sun was shining over the mu
of the capital. Jefferson rose and donned green breeches, gray
woolen stockings, and a gray waistcoat. The tall, bony Presi
dent-elect left the boardinghouse and walked the two blocks t
the unfinished Capitol as if he were performing an ordinary
errand. He was accompanied by a number of friends and col
leagues, also on foot. This was in striking contrast to John
Adams, who in 1797 had ridden ceremoniously to the inaugu
ration in a coach and six.

Jefferson entered the Senate Chamber as unostentatiously a
he came. The Republican members of Congress rose and
greeted him warmly. There were few visitors present. He
walked up to the table, shook hands with Vice-President Burr
A Bible lay on the table. Near by stood a tall, thin, black
haired man. He was a Virginian named John Marshall, Chie
Justice of the Supreme Court. Marshall and Jefferson, althoug
distant kinsmen, felt a deep aversion for each other. But th
august occasion left no room for the play of antipathy. Th
Chief Justice delivered the oath of office to his enemy, and hi

emy repeated the sacred oath to uphold and defend the Constitution of the United States.

After a brief pause, Jefferson—President Jefferson—began
read his inaugural address in a clear, well-modulated voice.
was a beautiful speech, an eloquent appeal for national unity
d conciliation. He stretched out a friendly hand to all his
pponents and all those who hated him. "We are all repub-
cans; we are all federalists," he exclaimed. He reminded the
untry that the rights of the minority were as sacred as those
the majority. He reassured the people that there would be
injustice and no persecution, and he appealed to the whole
untry to unite with "one heart and one mind."

2

The President's immediate problem was what to do with the
ederalist officeholders. His own party insisted that John Ad-
ns's appointees be dismissed. Jefferson knew that many, pos-
bly most, Federalist appointees, particularly those holding ju-
icial posts, were his personal enemies and, in general, no
iends of democracy. Yet he felt ashamed to have to throw men
ut of their jobs simply because he disagreed with their ideas.

James Monroe, writing from Richmond, warned the Presi-
ent to proceed cautiously in the matter of removals. "The
rinciple," Monroe advised, "is sound that no man ought to
e turned out for mere difference of political sentiment. . . .
y retaining them in office you will give a proof of tolerance,
oderation & forbearance, which must command the respect
f the benevolent."

The theory was excellent, but it clashed with the needs of
e occasion, as well as with the larger aims. Jefferson felt that
e welfare of the republic required that its avowed enemies
e ferreted out of office. The country, he said, was in the "ene-
ies' hands."

About the Federalist judges who were appointed for life,
e President could do nothing; but he could sweep out Ad-
ns's district attorneys and marshals. Removing people from
fice was an ordeal. "In this horrid drudgery," Jefferson once
onfessed to William Short, "I always felt myself as a public
xecutioner."

One of Jefferson's earliest acts was to nullify the appoint-
ents made by Adams in December, 1800, when the President
iew already that he had been defeated at the polls. Among
ose "midnight appointments," as Jefferson dubbed them con-
mptuously, were forty-two justices of the peace. Jefferson
isted seventeen of them. At that time there were 316 Federal
fices at the disposal of the President. When Jefferson took

over power, all of these officials were Federalists. Within two
years he removed 105 of them—collectors of customs, marshals,
district attorneys, and consuls. But of the 105, only 9, according to Jefferson, were dismissed for purely "political principle."

In their place Jefferson appointed men who were friendly to
his ideals and on whose loyalty he could rely.

3

On one point the President was adamant. He absolutely refused to appoint kinsmen. Nepotism was a hateful idea. It was
also bad politics. No one, Jefferson said, would believe that
a relative was given a job because he happened to have merit.
"I . . . laid it down as a law of conduct for myself, never to give
an appointment to a relation."

Jefferson disliked the task of making appointments to office.
He found it disagreeable to have to disappoint people, and yet
there were not enough jobs to go around. The worst of it was
that every position that he filled caused enmity on the part of
those who did not get the job.

The Cabinet, when it was finally constituted, reflected Jefferson's dual aim: to achieve national unity and to surround himself with men of ability. As a gesture of friendship and appease-
ment, he chose half of his Cabinet from New England. And to
avoid the kind of conflict that disrupted Washington's Cabinet, Jefferson chose men whose ideas did not clash with his.

For Secretary of State, he appointed James Madison. For
Secretary of the Treasury, he chose Albert Gallatin. The Secretaryship of War went to Henry Dearborn. The position of Attorney-General was given to Levi Lincoln. The Postmaster
Generalship was obtained by Gideon Granger. The recently
created Secretaryship of the Navy was filled by Robert Smith.
Secretaries Dearborn, Lincoln, and Granger were New Englanders. Smith was from Maryland. Gallatin was a Swiss, via
Pennsylvania. The only Southerner in the Cabinet was Madison. In so choosing his Cabinet, Jefferson wanted to show the
country that his was not a factional or sectional Administration, but a truly national one.

Secretary of War Dearborn was born in New Hampshire,
where he had once practiced medicine, but was a resident of
Maine, which State he had represented in Congress. He had had
a fine war record, and had achieved the rank of colonel. A
big and imposing man, he was cool-tempered and able. Levi
Lincoln, the Attorney-General, was in his early fifties, Massa-
chusetts-born and Harvard-bred. By profession he was a lawyer
and by conviction an ardent Jeffersonian Republican. Like Dearborn, he also had been a member of Congress. Gideon

Granger, the Postmaster-General, being only thirty-four, was the youngest member of the Cabinet. He was born in Connecticut and was a Yale graduate. By profession a lawyer and by inclination a politician, he was a member of the State legislature, where, despite his youth, he had achieved distinction for his energy and efficiency. Robert Smith, the Secretary of the Navy, succeeded his brother Samuel after the latter had served a few months under Jefferson in the same post. The forty-four-year-old Smith was a lawyer from Maryland, and his family, particularly his brother Samuel, was intimate with Jefferson. The Smiths came from an eminent family of Baltimore and they knew something about shipping and finance. Robert Smith, being a man of elegant manners and distinguished appearance, was popular with the navy people.

But the ablest and most interesting members of the Cabinet were not the men from New England or from Maryland, but a Virginian and a Swiss. In ability, as well as rank, Secretary of State James Madison excelled all others except the President. Madison combined a massive intellect with a jolly disposition. The homely little Secretary of State was both a fine scholar and an amusing storyteller. Sir Augustus Foster, the British Minister, said of Madison that he was better informed even than Jefferson himself—a superb compliment, even if not altogether true—and, moreover, "a social, jovial and good-humored companion, full of anecdotes, sometimes rather of a loose description, but often of a political and historical interest." Unlike the President, Madison was also a cogent speaker. He had a fine legal brain. Only his appearance was against him. Washington Irving's description of him is famous: "But as to Jemmy Madison—ah, poor Jemmy—he is but a withered little Apple-john."

If "Jemmy" Madison was physically unimposing, his wife, Dolly, made up for it in sparkle and looks. Washington Irving said of her admiringly: "Mrs. Madison is a fine, portly, buxom dame who has a smile and a pleasant word for everybody." Jefferson being a widower, the "buxom dame" was his official hostess. The famous Dolly was perhaps the liveliest lady in Washington.

In Secretary of the Treasury Albert Gallatin, Jefferson had a real jewel. Neither Jefferson nor his party, made up as it was of agrarians and mechanics, was famous for knowledge of finance or intimacy with commerce. But when it came to figures and finance, Gallatin was a wizard. In the realm of money he was as smart as a Yankee trader and as tough as Alexander Hamilton.

Like Hamilton, Gallatin was foreign-born. It is a peculiar coincidence that the two ablest financiers of their day should have been born abroad; both of them left a deep imprint upon their adopted country, particularly in the realm of financial administration. Gallatin was born in Geneva, Switzerland, of an aristocratic family, and came to America in his teens. Unlike Hamilton, the noble-born Gallatin was an ardent democrat. He was also a first-rate administrator. In appearance he was tall, long-nosed, long-faced, blue-eyed, and bald-headed. There was great power and drive in that long figure. His eyes were those of a man who knew the value of money.

For his chief, President Jefferson, Gallatin had an admiration that amounted to reverence. He always kept a portrait of Jefferson on his desk. The latter, in turn, held Gallatin in warm esteem and was deeply grateful for his efficient handling of the national finances. Gallatin, Jefferson said, was a man "of a pure integrity, and as zealously devoted to the liberties and interest of our country as its most affectionate native citizen." Jefferson's admiration and affection for the Secretary of the Treasury lasted a lifetime. As late as 1823 Jefferson, a very old man, wrote to Gallatin that a visit from him to Monticello would be a "day of jubilance" and added: "I shall love you forever, and rejoice when you rejoice, and sympathize in your evils."

It was, on the whole, a remarkable Cabinet, and it functioned in exceptional harmony. Largely this was due to Jefferson's tact and his graciousness; he knew how to handle difficult individuals with silk gloves. The President's cheerful disposition, his genuine affection for those who worked with him, and his willingness to discuss ideas on their merit, kept the Cabinet clicking like a well-oiled machine. Every member, moreover, recognized and bowed to the President's intellectual superiority.

Jefferson held a loose rein over the Cabinet. "I have no pleasure in the exercise of power," he told one of his political lieutenants. He never interfered or dictated except in cases of exceptional gravity. At Cabinet meetings, even when matters of unusual importance were discussed, the President acted only as primus inter pares. In true democratic fashion, he retained for himself an equal vote with the others, and decisions were made on the basis of majority opinion. "So that," Jefferson explained to one of his intimates, "in all important cases the Executive is in fact a directory, which certainly the President might control; but of this there was never an example."

The members of the Cabinet were encouraged to ring the doorbell of the Executive Mansion any time something important came up. There was no need, he told them, to wait for ceremony, appointments, or protocol. They were told to "call on me at any moment of the day which suits their separate convenience." His Cabinet, Jefferson later said,

> presented an example of harmony in a cabinet of six persons, to which perhaps history has furnished no parallel. There never arose, during the whole time, an instance of an unpleasant thought or word between the members. We sometimes met under differences of opinion, but scarcely ever failed, by conversing and reasoning, so to modify each others' ideas, as to produce a unanimous result.

4

Jefferson's first Administration began under a lucky star. For the first time in years, no vital problems plagued the country. Business was good, the people were comparatively well off, and there was no threat of war. The French Revolution had run its violent course inside France. Its frustrated hopes and distorted idealism were seized upon by a swarthy little Italian adventurer who dreamt a typical "Fascist" dream of a new order in the world. The new order was to be shaped by the ambitious Corsican, who had a genius for political brigandage, for the exclusive benefit of himself, his family, and his professional condottieri. Napoleon's lust for domination was to plunge the world into fourteen years of violence and bloodshed. Its reverberations were to be felt in the United States and to affect President Jefferson as deeply as the French Revolution had shaken President Washington. But now, during Jefferson's first years in office, Bonaparte had signed a truce with the British and was not yet at war with the world.

Broadly speaking, Jefferson pursued two general lines of policy: economy at home, peace abroad. Although he was personally in debt, the notion of a public debt was repugnant to him. Not being an economist, he viewed economic problems from a political angle. He considered it an axiom that "Debt & revolution are inseparable as cause and effect." A rising national debt was like a flood. If permitted to go on unchecked, it would destroy the whole fabric of society—"if the public debt should once more be swelled to a formidable size," he once wrote to Gallatin, ". . . we shall be committed to the English career of debt, corruption and rottenness, closing with revolution."

Jefferson was convinced that a government that owed a lot of money to private individuals was no longer free but a pawn of its creditors. Under no circumstances must the United States Government borrow so much money as to become obligated to the bankers and thereby lose its freedom. Economy, he said, meant liberty; borrowing spelled servitude.

There was another reason why Jefferson, the agrarian democrat, abhorred the idea of a big national debt. It was clear that debt meant interest, interest called for higher taxes, and higher taxes involved a reduction in the standard of living of the common people. Coddling the bankers and robbing the toilers was not Jefferson's idea of the good society. He once explained in a letter to Samuel Kercheval:

> If we run into such debts, as that we must be taxed in our meat and in our drink, in our necessaries and our comforts, in our labors and our amusements, for our callings and our creeds, as the people of England are, our people, like them, must come to labor sixteen hours in the twenty-four, give the earnings of fifteen of these to the government for their debts and daily expenses; and the sixteenth being insufficient to afford us bread, we must live, as they now do, on oatmeal and potatoes; have no time to think, no means of calling the mismanagers to account; but be glad to obtain subsistence by hiring ourselves to rivet their chains on the necks of our fellow-sufferers.

The President and his Secretary of the Treasury attacked the problem of economy along three lines. There was to be no more borrowing. The national debt was to be extinguished by systematic payments of principal and interest. Expenditures were to be drastically reduced. Wherever possible, Jefferson tried to shift the burden of taxation from the poor to the rich. A large portion of the Government's income came from imposts on imported goods and shipping. This, in Jefferson's eyes, was as it should be, since he believed that it affected mainly those who could best afford to pay. "I wish," he told Gallatin in 1802, "it were possible to increase the impost on any articles affecting the rich chiefly, to the amount of the sugar tax, so that we might relinquish that at the next session."

One of the direct taxes that Jefferson abolished was the excise on distilled liquors. This did not make him unpopular with the whisky-drinkers. Wine-imbibers, who belonged to the upper crust, continued to pay a tax and to curse the President.

Jefferson inherited a national debt of over $80,000,000. The President and Gallatin elaborated a system whereby $7,500,-000 were set aside annually for the payment of principal and interest. This worked so well that by the end of Jefferson's Administration—despite the purchase of Louisiana and losses due to the Embargo—the national debt was decreased by $27,-500,000. This economizing was achieved, to some extent, at the expense of the army and the navy. The army was reduced from 4,000 to 2,500 men.

In the realm of finance, the Jefferson Administration insti-

uted two major reforms. Under Hamilton and his successors,
government finances had been handled in the English way—an
account was given to the legislature after the money had been
spent. In Jefferson's eyes, such a system was both undemocratic
and potentially corrupt. He believed that Congress should
know beforehand what the Government intended to spend in
the coming year. The representatives of the people should have
the power to approve or disapprove of each detailed item. This,
in Jefferson's opinion, was the only way the people could control the Government and check upon its actions. He therefore
proposed to Gallatin that he institute a system of strict account-
ing and submit to Congress detailed appropriations bills.

5

In foreign affairs Jefferson's course was as simple as his economics. To him the United States was a great island of freedom
in the midst of a world of tyranny. He blessed the Almighty
Being for the fact that America was "separated by a wide
ocean from the nations of Europe," and he hoped to keep it
that way.

If Jefferson had been able, he would have put up a Chinese
wall around America, not as a bulwark against invaders, but as
a means of keeping out the Old World's patterns of hate and
injustice. This was not chauvinism or narrow patriotism. Jefferson's love of country was, indeed, tinged with the universal.
He loved America as a wise father proud of his offspring, not
as an anxious lover jealous of his mistress. He was so proud of
America that he wanted his land to be a beacon of freedom to
mankind. Always he was conscious of world opinion. He knew
that if the democratic experiment succeeded in America it
would be followed elsewhere.

Jefferson also wanted America to be a haven for the world's
oppressed. In his first Annual Message to Congress, he made
an eloquent appeal for an open door for refugees:

> And shall we refuse the unhappy fugitives from distress that
> hospitality which the savages of the wilderness extended to our
> fathers arriving in this land? Shall oppressed humanity find no
> asylum on this globe?

But he did not desire any large-scale immigration to America, fearing that men brought up in the school of despotism
would not make ideal citizens of a free republic. "In proportion
to their numbers," he had written in 1792, "they will share with
us the legislation. They will infuse into it their spirit, warp and
bias its directions, and render it a heterogeneous, incoherent,

distracted mass." Jefferson preferred small groups of immigrants, particularly skilled artisans and craftsmen.

Of all emigrating peoples, Jefferson preferred Italians. They were among the world's finest artisans and artists, as well as energetic farmers and viticulturists. He felt that skilled and hard-working Italians could transform many areas of America from a wilderness into a garden. In connection with another emigrating people, the Germans, Jefferson played with the idea of carrying on an experiment to compare German labor with Negro labor. He wanted to import "as many Germans as I have grown slaves" and to settle them "and my slaves, on farms of 50 acres each, intermingled." He was sure that, given a chance the German immigrants, particularly their children, would become "good citizens."

It was the European aggressors and oppressors that Jefferson wanted to keep out of America. One way of doing it was to cut contact with the outside world down to an irreducible minimum. Such an aim sounds quixotic in the radio- and airplane encircled world of the 1950's, but it was not altogether visionary in the sailing-vessel days of the early 1800's. Jefferson wanted no truck with Europe, except a minimum of necessary trade. He meant to let all the existing treaties die and to make no new ones; and if an emergency should arise, he would send a representative abroad to settle it, and then have him return home. There would be no permanent American diplomatic agents abroad.

In this instance policy coincided with a certain bias. Knowing many diplomats, Jefferson distrusted them as deeply as he disliked bankers. He regarded diplomats with suspicion as the spoilers of peace and their craft as the smithy of war. To his friend William Short, who was in the diplomatic service, the President wrote: "I have ever considered diplomacy as the pest of the peace of the world, as the workshop in which nearly all the wars of Europe are manufactured."

Gradually the President liquidated America's diplomatic missions in Europe. He called in the diplomats, not like a mother hen anxious for her chicks, but like a cautious businessman closing his foreign branches because they did not pay . . . "as we wish not to mix in the politics of Europe," the President stated, "but in her commerce only, Consuls would do all the business we ought to have there." He withdrew William Smith from Portugal, William Murray from Holland John Quincy Adams from Prussia. He intended to withdraw the rest—Rufus King was in London and Robert R. Livingston in Paris—but Napoleon's international adventures threw a wrench into Jefferson's plans.

Events beyond the control of Presidents or philosophers nullified Jefferson's dream of political isolation from the rest of the world. But the destruction of the President's isolationist fences brought to America a gift of priceless value and incomparable importance. In the spring of 1803 the paths of two great ambitions met for a brief moment, and a bargain was struck. Napoleon, ambitious to build a personal dynasty, sold territory that was of no use to his family. Jefferson, ambitious to secure a free republic for posterity, bought the territory that was of use to his people.

The background of the story, involving the greatest real-estate deal in history, was essentially geographic and commercial. West of the Mississippi, and extending a thousand miles to the Rocky Mountains, lay a vast no man's land of forests and rivers and prairies and bison. It was a wilderness paradise, full of scenic wonders and overflowing with natural resources; and except for several thousand Indians and a few hardy whites, there was no one to admire the one or to exploit the other. Over this tremendous area, since 1763, had flown the flag of decaying and decrepit Spain.

Louisiana was the name of the whole region. Out of it were subsequently to be carved the States of Arkansas, Colorado, the Dakotas, Iowa, Kansas, Louisiana, Minnesota, Missouri, Montana, Nebraska, Oklahoma, and Wyoming. The Louisiana Territory comprised an area of almost a million square miles—about the size of the Argentine. The region was so big that all of Western Europe, including Scandinavia, could be tucked away in it.

The gate to the territory was New Orleans at the mouth of the Mississippi River. The latter, in turn, was the life line of the commerce of the American West. He who controlled New Orleans was in a position to affect the destinies of the American people who did not live on the Atlantic seaboard. So long as a feeble Spain held the key to New Orleans, the American West could grow and trade without fear of effective interference. But should New Orleans fall into the hands of a powerful and ambitious state, then the United States would face the choice of either submitting to dictation and a permanent status of inferiority, or fighting for the control of the Mississippi and the West. As Jefferson said categorically, any foreign Power that controlled New Orleans was the "natural and habitual enemy" of the United States. This was elementary politics, dictated by the stubborn facts of geography.

Napoleon, bent on building an empire in the Old World as well as in the New, pounced upon the Louisiana Territory at

his first opportunity. In October, 1800, by the secret treaty of
San Ildefonso, he obtained Louisiana and the adjoining Floridas from Spain. Since he did not take immediate possession,
the treaty was kept secret for about a year. But late in 1801 the
news leaked out. It came as a cruel shock to Jefferson. In one
blow it knocked out all his hopes for isolation from European
affairs.

With painful clarity the President saw that the French occupation of New Orleans meant inevitable war with Napoleon.
But the United States had neither enough troops nor sufficient
warships, and so Jefferson faced the bleak prospect of having to
ally with England, the nation he most distrusted, against
France, the nation he most liked. It was a bitter choice. The
day, Jefferson said grimly, that Napoleon's troops set foot on
the soil of New Orleans, that day "we must marry ourselves to
the British fleet and nation."

Public opinion was not prepared for the bad news about the
transfer of Louisiana to France, and when it came, there was
great agitation throughout the land. In the autumn of 1802
the country heard that the Spanish authorities in New Orleans
had withdrawn the "right of deposit" from American merchants. This meant more than the mere loss of $1,000,000
worth of produce annually; it meant stunting the growth of
the West by choking its outlet. Throughout the country there
was an outburst of indignation, particularly among Jefferson's
own stanch supporters, the men of the West.

Jefferson, having foreseen the emergency, gave the country
an impressive example of calm and imperturbability. He knew
he was taking steps to carry into effect his determination either
to buy New Orleans or to fight for it.

Quietly he had Congress pass a secret appropriation of
$2,000,000 to be used in the "intercourse between the United
States and foreign nations." Then, in March, 1803, he sent
James Monroe as envoy extraordinary to France to help Livingston make a deal with Bonaparte. Monroe was instructed to
offer Napoleon as much as 50,000,000 francs for New Orleans
and the Floridas, or two-thirds of that sum for the island of
New Orleans alone. The least the American negotiators were to
insist upon was a permanent guarantee of the rights of navi-
gation on the Mississippi. If the French refused, Jefferson instructed his envoys to play for time and get secretly in touch
with the British. The instruction that was sent to Monroe and
Livingston read:

  . . . as soon as they find that no arrangement can be made
with France, to use all possible procrastination with them, and

in the mean time enter into conference with the British government, through their ambassador at Paris, to fix principles of alliance, and leave us in peace till Congress meets; and prevent war till next spring.

As it turned out, this was not necessary, for Napoleon moved quicker than Jefferson could have hoped. While Monroe was sailing for France, Livingston had begun to negotiate with Napoleon and his Foreign Minister, the venal Talleyrand. The American Minister, who spoke French poorly and was hard of hearing to boot, got nowhere at first. Neither the imperious First Consul nor his corrupt Foreign Minister paid much attention to the patrician Livingston with his upright manners. The sincere republican from America was probably unaware that Talleyrand was making a fortune out of his office. Three months after he entered the Ministry of Foreign Affairs, Talleyrand had piled up a nest egg of 12,000,000 francs which he received in the form of "gifts" from foreign Powers that were currying favor with Napoleon.

The first thing that the cynical Talleyrand said to the gentlemanly Livingston was, "Have you any money?"

"I do not understand," stammered Jefferson's shocked plenipotentiary.

"In this country," Talleyrand said blandly, "matters are difficult to manage without it. With the aid of an abundance of money all difficulties are surmounted. Reflect well on this." [1]

In the meantime the uneasy Franco-British truce was rapidly deteriorating and a renewal of war between Napoleon and Great Britain was imminent. Since in case of war the British fleet could easily capture New Orleans, Napoleon thought it a clever idea to sell the territory to the United States and get money for something that would be a dead loss anyhow. The First Consul acted quickly. On April 11, 1803, he deliberately insulted Lord Whitworth, the British Ambassador in Paris, and raised his hand as if to strike him. Whitworth gripped his sword. Later in the day Talleyrand called in Livingston and asked him whether the United States wanted to have the "whole of Louisiana."

"No," the surprised Livingston replied, "our wishes extend only to New Orleans and the Floridas."

Without New Orleans, Talleyrand explained, the rest of the territory was of little value. He wanted to know what America would be willing to pay for the whole. Livingston was completely unprepared to make an offer, since Monroe had not yet arrived with instructions from Jefferson. But he tentatively offered Talleyrand 20,000,000 francs. "Too low," said the For-

J. W. Thompson and S. K. Padover, *Secret Diplomacy*, London, 1937, p. 207.

eign Minister, and asked Livingston to think it over and s
him tomorrow. The following day brought Monroe to Par
and Livingston went to see Talleyrand with a new offer, b
the Foreign Minister was evasive, perhaps because there w
nothing in it for him. On April 13, which was Jefferson's birt
day, Livingston had an interview with Marbois, the Minister
Finance, into whose hands Napoleon had put the negotiatio
Marbois told Livingston that Napoleon had said to him: .
"let them [the Americans] give you one hundred millions
francs, and pay their own claims and take the whole country

Livingston would not commit himself without Monroe. C
the following day the two Americans went to see Marbois a
made an offer of 50,000,000 francs. Marbois thought it was n
enough, but Livingston and Monroe, knowing that France w
on the verge of war and in need of the sinews of war, decid
to bide their time before giving away any more money th
they had to. On the last day of April the two American repr
sentatives and the French Ministers came to terms. Two da
later, on May 2, the historic treaty was signed. For the pri
of 60,000,000 francs—about $15,000,000—Napoleon cede
the whole Louisiana Territory to the United States.[2]

It was a phenomenal bargain. After Livingston had signe
his name to the treaty he exclaimed prophetically: "From th
day the United States take their place among the powers of t
first rank."

Livingston urged Jefferson that the treaty be immediate
ratified, lest Napoleon change his mind. Though questions
constitutionality were raised, Jefferson's party was stron
enough in the Senate to overcome opposition. On October 1
1803, the Senate ratified the treaty by a vote of 24 to 7.

Before the year was out, the country was given a memorab
Christmas present. On December 20, the French authoriti
handed over the Louisiana Territory to the United States, an
Jefferson's "island of freedom" thereby became an empire
liberty, stretching from the Atlantic to the Rockies. It was Pre
ident Jefferson's crowning glory.

In one stroke, and with superlative luck, he had doubled tl
territory of his country, not by war but through purchase—a
achievement rarely, if ever, excelled in recorded history. Tl
Louisiana Territory, Jefferson was convinced, would be opene
to immigration, and the new settlers would bring prosperity
the United States and happiness to themselves.

In the third year of his Administration, Jefferson came

---

[2] Fifteen million dollars was of course a lot of money in those day
Since wages in a city like New York amounted to about $10 a month, or
may roughly estimate the value of the dollar then to be about twen
times what it is today.

grips with the Federal judiciary. It was the first conflict of its kind in the United States; the last, so far, took place in 1937. The struggle is not yet over, for neither Thomas Jefferson in 1803-04 nor Franklin D. Roosevelt in 1937-38 can be said to have achieved brilliant success in his conflict with the judiciary.

Jefferson was driven to the conflict by the dynamics of his ideas, as well as by the logic of his position. The Federalists, especially John Adams, had packed the judicial posts with their own appointees. These judges liked neither Jefferson nor his type of democracy. The antipathy, needless to say, was reciprocal.

How Jefferson felt about the judiciary can be gathered from an anecdote. A few years after he retired from the Presidency, Jefferson entertained at dinner a number of guests, including his enemy, Chief Justice John Marshall. The conversation turned to the training of lawyers. Jefferson criticized the narrow, legalistic education of lawyers and said that they should have "More general science, and more common sense." Then he told of an experiment that he had made when he was President.

To fill the Supreme Court of the Michigan territory, Jefferson had chosen three utterly different men from different parts of the country. Only one of them was a lawyer—"a dry technical lawyer," Jefferson remarked smiling, "and would not believe two and two made four, unless you could prove it by an adjudged case." The second, Woodward of Virginia, was a philosopher and a scientist, a "visionary." The third was a "large strong-handed and strong-minded Vermont farmer" who never saw a textbook and despised legal learning.

Chief Justice Marshall asked ironically: "And how did your plan operate, Mr. President; did your machine go well?"

"Upon my word," Jefferson replied candidly, "it would not go at all."

From the beginning of his Administration Jefferson had intended to put a bridle on the Federal judiciary. The draft of his first message to Congress, in December, 1801, carried a concealed bomb that was designed to blow up the powers and pretensions of the judges. In that original draft the President declared the Sedition Act of the Adams Administration unconstitutional and denied the Supreme Court the exclusive right to construe the Constitution.

But the bomb was not placed. At the last moment the President changed his mind. The nation, he knew, had not yet recovered from the election; bitterness still lingered in many parts of the country. The time was not ripe to start a judicial war. Hence Jefferson struck out the passage in the speech that might give offense to the moderates among the Federalists.

His speech to the Congress was conciliatory and soft-spoke. It was, to borrow a phrase used by the *Republican Advocate* "like the oil of the good Samaritan to the wounded stranger gratefully healing to the public mind." The "oil" worke. When the next congressional election came around, Jefferson party carried the country overwhelmingly.

While Jefferson was biding his time, his judicial opponent jumped the gun. This came about in an incident which did no lack drama. The story, fateful in its influence on American history, is famed as the case of *Marbury* v. *Madison*.

William Marbury was a petty Federalist politician. In th last hours of his Administration, President Adams had ap pointed him justice of the peace for the District of Columbia The Senate ratified the appointment. The Secretary of Stat (who was John Marshall) signed and sealed the commissio. Everything went according to schedule, but there was one slip up. The outgoing Administration was so busy making arrang ments to move out that it failed to deliver the commission t Marbury.

When the new Administration came in, Marbury asked fo his commission, which was still lying on the Secretary of State desk. Jefferson, who resented Adams's "midnight appoint ments," ordered Madison, his Secretary of State, not to delive it. Marbury applied to the Supreme Court for a writ of man damus, under Section 13 of the Judiciary Act of 1789, to orde Secretary Madison to give him his commission. In February 1803, Chief Justice Marshall delivered his decision in the cas of *Marbury* v. *Madison*. It turned out to be epoch-making.

First of all, Marshall pointed out, Marbury's commission wa valid, regardless of whether it was delivered or not. Madi son acted illegally in withholding the commission. Therefor Marbury had the right to seek a remedy—the writ of man damus. Round one for Marbury.

The real problem, the Chief Justice argued, was whether th Supreme Court was competent to grant Marbury the mandamu he was seeking under Section 13 of the Judiciary Act o 1789. Here came the crux of Marshall's decision. The subtl Chief Justice pointed out that under the Constitution the Su preme Court had no power to issue writs against executive of ficers. Should, therefore, the court follow Section 13 of the Ac of 1789, or should it follow the Constitution? Marshall's an swer was obvious. "It is a proposition too plain to be contested, he wrote, "that the Constitution controls any legislative ac repugnant to it." In other words, the Constitution was superio to Section 13. In other words, Section 13 was unconstitutiona

In other words, the Supreme Court decides what legislative act is unconstitutional. Round two was thus against Marbury (who was only a pawn, anyhow) but for the Supreme Court.

Thus Marshall asserted the supremacy of the Supreme Court and at the same time rebuked Jefferson. The "crafty chief judge," as Jefferson called him, had delivered a hard blow. Incidentally, Justice Marshall passed judgment upon a case in which he had been previously involved, since he himself had signed Marbury's commission. Not everybody considered this ethical.

The dangerous implications of the Marshall decisions were not lost on Jefferson, who was convinced that this was a potential threat to free government in the future. A court that usurped the power—never granted by the Constitution—to pass upon legislative acts endangered the whole structure of democracy and challenged, in effect, the right of the people to legislate unhindered for themselves.

Jefferson's theory was—and James Madison, the "Father of the Constitution," agreed with him—that the framers of the Constitution had intended the three branches of the Government to check, not to dominate, each other. Any presumption of power on the part of one against the other, he considered as despotism.

Jefferson's greatest attempt to break the usurped power of the judiciary was the impeachment of Justice Samuel Chase of the U. S. Supreme Court. This was the same highhanded Chase who had presided at the trial of Thomas Cooper and James Thomson Callender. It was the same judge who had told some of Virginia's most eminent attorneys in court to shut up. It was the same Justice who once ordered the Federal Marshal to strike off the panel "any of those creatures or persons called democrats." It was the same Chase who, in addressing a grand jury in Baltimore, went out of his way to attack the new Maryland constitution because it provided for manhood suffrage, which, he said, would "certainly and rapidly destroy all protection to property and all security to personal liberty, and our republican Constitution will sink into a mobocracy."

Chase was, in short, an intemperate individual of exceptional virulence. As far back as 1778 he had been, in the words of Alexander Hamilton, "universally despised" (because he had tried to corner the market on flour). Now Jefferson decided that the time had come when the judge should meet his proper deserts at the hands of the representatives of the people whom he reviled.

The President, in a letter to Congressman Nicholson, urged

that the House impeach Chase, and early in 1804 a committee
was appointed to "enquire into the judicial conduct of Samuel
Chase." A year later the House, by a vote of 73 to 32, voted to
impeach the Justice on eight counts of misfeasance and mal-
feasance. The brilliant John Randolph of Roanoke acted as
prosecutor for Congress. Five of the greatest lawyers of the day
appeared on behalf of Chase.

The trial took place in the Senate, which was set up like the
English House of Lords. A majority of two-thirds was necessary for conviction on any one of the eight counts. Of the
thirty-four Senators who acted as the court in the impeachment, twenty-five belonged to Jefferson's party, and nine were
Federalists. Only twenty-three votes were necessary for conviction. But the President was either unable or unwilling to
crack the whip. Six of the Republican Senators refused to follow the majority of their party.

The trial, which lasted for nearly a month, was the most sensational of its day. The drama was heightened by the fact that
the man who presided at the trial was the Vice-President of the
United States, Aaron Burr. He had just slain Alexander Hamilton in a scandalous duel and was an object of public indignation.

On a number of counts a majority of the Senate found Chase
guilty—but no two-thirds majority could be found. Article 4,
for example, charging that Chase's conduct in the Callender
case was marked by "manifest injustice, partiality and intem-
perance," got 18 Senators for conviction, and 16 against. On
Article 8, accusing Chase of delivering "an intemperate and
inflammatory political harangue" before the grand jury at
Baltimore, the vote was 19 guilty, 15 not guilty. The upshot
was that the impeachment fell through. It is possible that what
saved Justice Chase was a "trade-union" feeling on the part of
the lawyers in the Senate. They did not like to set a dangerous
precedent against one of their kind, and in not finding Chase
guilty they also nullified the value of impeachment as a check
on officeholding lawyers. After the Chase case Jefferson said
that impeachment was a "farce."

The failure of the Senate to impeach Chase was a defeat for
Jefferson. If the Justice had been convicted, the President
would probably have followed it with an impeachment of the
whole Supreme Court. But as it was, he saw no reason for re-
peating the "farce." What was left of Federalist power now
sought entrenched shelter behind the battlements of the Supreme Court, where the judiciary bided its time to tear Jeffersonian idealism to rags and tatters.

If Jefferson failed in his attempt to put a permanent curb on the judiciary, he succeeded in scaring it. For the time being, the Federal judges were on the run. Chase himself delivered but one opinion afterward. Richard Peters, a District of Columbia judge who had sat with Chase in the trial of Callender, was so frightened by the threat of impeachment that for five years he refused to sign an order to carry out a decision that he himself had made in the District Court.

But while the judiciary was momentarily silenced, the Federalist press was not. Their numbers dwindling and their influence waning, the Federalists fought a bitter last-ditch press campaign against "that man" who had driven them from power. Die-hard Federalists carried on a guerrilla war against the President, sniping at his Administration and besmirching his character. One of their toasts was "Damnation to Jefferson forever!"

Jefferson's patience was severely tried and his democratic philosophy was put to a hard test. The temptation to strike back, to punish the libelers and to silence the calumniators, was exceedingly strong. But Jefferson, conscious of his mission and convinced that the eyes of the world were upon his democratic "experiment," resisted the temptation to curb the offenders. The test of freedom of speech, he well knew, was in its practice, not in its theory. No matter how greatly the newspapers abused their freedom, Jefferson felt, it was vital for democracy that that freedom be not checked.

The President suffered deeply from the poisoned barbs of the printers. Nevertheless, he was determined that nothing should block the "experiment" in freedom. He wrote to John Tyler:

No experiment can be more interesting than that we are now trying, which we trust will end in establishing the fact that man may be governed by reason & truth. Our first object should therefore be to leave open to him all the avenues to truth. The most effectual hitherto found is the freedom of the press. It is therefore the first shut up by those who fear the investigation of their actions. The firmness with which the people have withstood the late abuses of the press, the discernment they have manifested between truth & falsehood shew that they may safely be trusted to hear everything true and false & to form a correct judgment between them.

Madison was right when he told Lafayette, after Jefferson's death, that "no man more than Mr. Jefferson, regarded the freedom of the press as an essential safeguard to free Govt."

Jefferson also taught the country democratic manners. After all the talk about a monarchy under Washington and about pomp under Adams, Jefferson decided to set the country a deliberate example of republican simplicity. One of his earliest acts as occupant of the President's House was to abolish the weekly levee, a pretentious institution borrowed from monarchy. As practiced under Washington and Adams, the levee meant that once a week starch-bosomed ladies would appear before the President to do homage to the throne. Here was the incubation of snobbery, and Jefferson considered it unseemly in a democracy.

The President did away with the levee in a manner worthy of a play by Molière. When the word spread that Jefferson would not longer hold any levees, the ladies of Washington put on their best dresses and "mustered in force" at the President's House. But they found no President. He was out riding. Grimly they waited; they would have their levee whether the President liked it or not.

He came from his ride booted, spurred, dusty, hat in hand. Seeing the ladies, he beamed at them with all the suavity of a courtier and the graciousness of a Virginia gentleman. What a splendid surprise! What a delightful visit! He was overjoyed to see them! And would they not stay a bit longer? Speechless and bewildered, the ladies left in a hurry. Some had the humor to laugh at their discomfiture. The country laughed too. And the levee was buried forever after.

Jefferson also put the rules of precedence and etiquette, which had been rigidly observed under Washington and Adams, under the ax. He abolished formal state dinners and entertained only privately. At the table, which was round so that no one should claim precedence over the other, everyone was seated alike. The idea was, Jefferson said, that "nobody shall be above you, nor you above anybody."

Not without malice, the President instituted what he called the rule of "pêle mêle" which meant that no individual, regardless of his rank or importance, was to have precedence in going from one room to another. Women in the mass simply preceded men in the mass, on the principle that "When brought together in society, all are perfectly equal." This principle knocked the bottom from under the social climbers and caused at least one minor international incident.

The droll affair involved Anthony Merry, the British Minister in Washington, who did not understand how a diplomat could function without precedence and without gold lace. It was not dignified. It was not cricket. And it just was not done. But the dreadful thing did happen to Mr. Merry. When he arrived in Washington, Secretary of State Madison took him to see the President. Merry, resplendent in full regalia, gold lace, dress sword, and all, expected a formal state reception. Instead, he found the audience hall empty. This was his first surprise. But the real shock came when Madison led him through a narrow passageway, to the President's study and introduced him. Jefferson was cordial, but his appearance—! The amazed Merry, clinging to his dress sword, saw before him a man, he tells indignantly, "not merely in an undress, but actually standing in slippers down at the heels, and both pantaloons, coat and underclothes indicative of an indifference to appearance." The British Minister considered Jefferson's appearance a studied insult to His Majesty. Perhaps it was. When Jefferson was introduced at the court in London in 1786, George III had been deliberately rude.

This did not end the Merry affair. Jefferson invited Merry and his wife—a shrew and a snob, whom the President privately called a "virago"—to dinner. Among the other guests were the Spanish Minister, the Marquis de Yrujo, and his snooty wife (née Sally McKean of Philadelphia); the French Minister, Louis Pichon, and his wife; and James Madison and his wife, Dolly. Minister Merry had not been warned about "pêle mêle" and he, the diplomat representing the ranking Power, expected to be given precedence and be seated ahead of the other guests. Instead, Jefferson calmly offered his arm to Dolly Madison and seated her on his right; the others were left to follow and seat themselves "pêle mêle."

This was too much for the infuriated Merrys. They considered themselves outraged, demeaned, affronted, humiliated, and never so insulted in their lives. Merry protested the "incivility" to his Government in London and asked for further instructions. Jefferson, who was quietly amused at all this ado, tried to soothe the British Minister. He told him that this was a democracy and that everybody was equal. No insult was intended.

But it was no use; the Merrys would not be appeased. Never again did they appear socially at the President's House. Mrs. Merry wept outraged tears when uncouth American democrats visited her house and sometimes stepped on her gown. They also commented occasionally on her diamonds. The city of Washington under President Jefferson was, indeed, hard on the Merrys, the Yrujos, and the Sally McKeans.

The Merrys were not the only visitors to be offended by Jefferson. There was also Tom Moore, the Irish poet. When Merry introduced Moore to the President, the latter, from his towering height, looked down upon the perfumed little dandy (he had never heard of him before), courteously acknowledged the introduction, and passed on to other matters. Moore, hypersensitive as very short men are apt to be, was cruelly stung. Later he traduced the President and castigated America in savage verse.[3]

Moore's description of the President was, nevertheless, fair and graphic:

> He is a large man; in fact, I never met a man of loftier stature. He has a noble face, with a Scotch-Irish cast of feature, and with curly hair of a reddish tint, although greatly mixed with gray. His mouth is large and firm set, while his nose is of the true Scottish type and unusually wide at the nostrils. As to his eyes, I would say that they are of a grayish and light blue tint mixed, and steely in expression. His brow is broad and white and very free from wrinkles. His whole appearance denotes a man of vigorous actions, and did I not know that he was President of the United States, I would judge him to be a gentleman of landed property, with all the inclinations of a fox-hunting squire.

One of the presidential guests in 1802 was Thomas Paine, the freethinker who shocked the pious, the radical who scandalized the tories. Jefferson welcomed him warmly and appeared with him on the street arm in arm. The stuffed shirts in and around Washington were outraged. One citizen suggested that the President and his "blasphemous crony" should be hanged on the same gallows.

8

The President's house was fitted out in the utmost comfort, designed for living and not for show. Every room reflected Jefferson's tastes, habits, and interests. In the study the walls were lined with books, maps, and charts. In the window recesses were plants and flowers. Among the geraniums and the roses hung a cage containing a mockingbird, which Jefferson loved for its melodious voice and its devotion to him. The bird was his faithful companion during work. When there were no callers, the President let the bird fly freely about the room. Frequently it would perch on his shoulder while he was working and sing in his ear. It ate from his lips. And when Jefferson went to his room for a rest the affectionate bird would hop after him and chirp.

[3] In his *Epistles* (2d ed., 1806) Moore thus slandered Jefferson:

> "The weary statesman for repose hath fled
> From halls of council to his Negro's shed,
> Where blest he woos some black Aspasia's grace,
> And dreams of freedom in his slave's embrace!"

To make sure that he would not be misunderstood, the poet explained in a footnote that this allusion was to the President of the United States.

The Presidency, although not yet as burdensome as it was to become a century later, nevertheless absorbed virtually all of Jefferson's time. He complained to his friends that he did not have a free moment. The job compelled him to give up his favorite studies and books, as well as to interrupt his correspondence on scientific and speculative subjects. "It is rare I can indulge myself in the luxury of philosophy," he confessed to du Pont de Nemours in 1802. As for mechanics and mathematics, two of his favorite subjects, he told Thomas Paine: "I am obliged to abandon them entirely."

The President found little time to read, and when he did read, it was poetry. He read and reread Homer and Tasso, Shakespeare and Milton, Dryden and Pope; also the British ballads, particularly Ossian, the favorite of his youth. Occasionally he would clip verses from newspapers and, with his usual methodicalness, paste them in a scrapbook. In Jefferson's scrapbook there is a stanza from Thomas Sackville's *Mirror for Magistrates*, a poem first published nearly two centuries before the President was born:

> What doth avail to have a princely place,
> A name of honour, and a high degree;
> To come by kindred of a noble race,
> Except we princely, worthy, noble be!
> The fruit declares the goodness of the tree.
> Do brag no more of birth, or lineage then;
> For virtue, grace and manners make the man.

Characteristically, Jefferson thought this a great poem.

Under Jefferson the President's House became renowned for its hospitality and its manner of living. Often there were as many as twelve guests at the table. The guests were selected for their suitability, not for their rank or position. Warmed by the drinks and encouraged by the ever cheerful host, everybody had a great time at the presidential dinners.

At the table Jefferson was dressed in snowy linen and in black garments whose severe simplicity only underlined their expensive quality.[4] His genuine liking for people was reflected in his face, which, according to a contemporary, "beamed with benevolence and intelligence." It was a face marked with generosity and humankindness. In personal matters he could not say No; "it is so much pleasanter to *give* than to *refuse*," he used to say, smiling.

---

[4] The old clothes and heelless slippers which so struck Merry and other visitors were worn by the President on democratic principle. Actually Jefferson possessed and wore fine and expensive clothes. He spent a considerable amount of money on his wardrobe. His accounts show that he paid as much as £13 sterling for a suit and 50s. for a hat. A pair of lace ruffles, bought in France, cost him 120 francs.

The dinners were not exclusively for pleasure. They were also one of Jefferson's methods of governing the country. Washington was a "little village in the midst of the woods," as Senator Plumer, remarked. There were no amusements, and the members of Congress were bored. In the midst of the social desolation, the President's House was one of the places where Congressmen and Senators could go for relaxation, good wine, and genial talk. Jefferson took advantage of this situation.

Congressmen and Senators, in effect, had little choice but to visit the President's House, and Jefferson, with his exquisite tact and insinuating manners, rarely failed to put over his point of view. The dinners, delightful as they were in themselves, thus also served as political instruments.

The President was fond of using the person-to-person method in overcoming opposition. He would invite an opponent or a potential opponent for a confidential chat, and the two would iron out their difficulties in the mellow atmosphere of the President's study.

When the President wanted to discuss something confidential, he would have only a few members of Congress at the table, and no listening waiters or prying servants. Near each guest was placed a dumb-waiter which contained the whole dinner, from soup to wine, and each guest served himself, the while talking freely and uninterruptedly.

Usually there would be about ten legislators at the table, Federalists one time and Republicans another. Jefferson rarely mixed them, for he disliked discord and had a prejudice against argumentative talk. He would state his opinions in a quiet, persuasive fashion, without undue emphasis; and he would listen patiently and sympathetically to opposing ideas. He refused to argue a point if anyone differed with him; discussion, he said, did not change opinions but riveted them. Moreover, he was tolerant of every point of view. He once told his grandson:

> When I hear another express an opinion which is not mine, I say to myself, he has a right to his opinion, as I to mine; why should I question it? His error does me no injury, and shall I become Don Quixote, to bring all men by force of argument to one opinion? . . . If he wants information, he will ask it, & then I will give it in measured terms; but if he still believes his own story, & shows a desire to dispute the fact with me, I hear him & say nothing.

From a financial point of view Jefferson could hardly afford the Presidency. His manner of living went beyond his income. In the first year in office he spent $32,634, while his salary was only $25,000. In that year he derived around $3,000 from the sale of tobacco, so that he had to borrow more than $4,000 to make up the deficit. It might be argued that he could have economized on Madeira and Champagne, but then he also spent a considerable sum on charity—nearly $1,000 in 1801 and $1,585 in 1802.

9

The election year 1804 found Jefferson at the top of his political career. He was riding the wave of immense popularity. The people were prosperous. The country was at peace. "Never," said John Randolph in after years, "was there an administration more brilliant than that of Mr. Jefferson up to this period. We were indeed in the 'full tide of successful experiment!' Taxes repealed; the public debt amply provided for, both principal and interest; sinecures abolished; Louisiana acquired; public confidence unbounded."

Public confidence in Jefferson, despite the screechings of Federalist newspapers, was indeed "unbounded." On February 25, 1804, a congressional caucus in Washington unanimously nominated the President for re-election. Vice-President Burr was ignored. In his stead, the Republicans selected George Clinton, also of New York. The Jeffersonians had not forgotten that in the bitter election of 1800 Burr had permitted himself to be used by the Federalists in their attempted knifing of Jefferson, and now they would have nothing to do with him. And since Vice-President Burr had slain Alexander Hamilton, and was under indictment for murder both in New York and in New Jersey, the opposition party would not touch him either.

There was a pathetic scene in the President's House. Burr had decided to return to New York politics, but he knew that he could get nowhere without the approbation of the powerful President. He went to see Jefferson and pleaded with him for a token of public approval. If only the President would say a good word for him, he, Burr, could recoup his fortunes in New York. Jefferson was not encouraging. He had a feeling that he was dealing with a dangerous and desperate man. He had never quite trusted him, anyhow. "His conduct"—the President was speaking of early days—"very soon inspired me with distrust. I habitually cautioned Mr. Madison against trusting him too much."

Jefferson's enjoyment of the triumph of his unanimous renomination was dampened by a personal tragedy. His beautiful young daughter Maria, a brilliant and gifted girl whose aim in life had been to be worthy of her father, fell gravely ill. In the spring the anxious father hurried to Monticello to be at her bedside. He came just in time. Maria's death at twenty-six was a merciless blow to her father. Jefferson, now sixty-one and with only one surviving child, was shaken as he had not been since his wife's death. For hours after the young woman died, the stricken President stayed in his room with a Bible in his hand. Once again he was alone with his soul in the presence of death.

To his boyhood friend John Page, now Governor of Virginia, Jefferson poured out his overburdened heart. The letter to Page is a mixture of grief and philosophic reflections, with undertones of bitterness:

> Others may lose of their abundance, but I, of my want, have lost even the half of all I had. My evening prospects now hang on the slender thread of a single life.

There was not much campaigning that summer. The fury of the anti-Jeffersonian press, so fierce in 1800, had subsided to a low growl in 1804. The leadership of the Federalists was demoralized and their ranks were depleted by desertions to the Jeffersonian cause. Everywhere the Republicans were on the march. Their leader, who had successfully planned the defeat of the Federalists, was the most commanding figure in America. Nobody in the land had even a fighting chance of beating Jefferson. He was loved by common men as few leaders had been loved before. And the Federalist candidates who opposed him, General Charles Cotesworth Pinckney of South Carolina and former Senator Rufus King of New York, were cultured and able gentlemen, but not national figures.

The election turned into a rout of the Federalists. Of the seventeen States that voted (including Ohio, recently admitted to the Union), Jefferson got fifteen. In most States there was not even a contest; they simply went to Jefferson. The President even carried Massachusetts, where John Adams, who was one of the electors, voted for Jefferson, perhaps because he got tired of playing King Canute to the democratic tide. Except for Connecticut and Delaware, Jefferson got nearly all the electoral votes that were cast—162 out of 176.

It was an overwhelming triumph for Jefferson and a vindication of his democratic ideas. His popularity was so phenomenal that some observers, such as John Adams, thought that the President would be elected again in 1808. But Jefferson had no such intentions. He was convinced that there was a danger to democracy in more than two terms. Before the votes were counted he told a friend that he would not run for a third term.

Accompanied by enthusiastic citizens and militia, Jefferson went down muddy Pennsylvania Avenue, which he had planted with poplars, to Capitol Hill to deliver his second inaugural address. It was a simply written speech delivered in so low a voice that only a few people in the crowded auditorium were able to hear it. The sixty-two-year-old President gave an account of his national stewardship, and his barely audible words reflected a sense of quiet pride.

He told how he had cultivated friendship with all nations. He explained how the abolition of unnecessary offices had enabled the Government to eliminate internal taxes—"what farmer, what mechanic, what laborer, ever sees a tax-gatherer of the United States?" the President asked. The acquisition of Louisiana, Jefferson continued, enlarged the area of republicanism and secured the opposite bank of the Mississippi through the future settlement of "our own brethren and children." Freedom of the press, despite its abuse of the President, had been upheld, in order to prove to the world that self-government could function without suppression. That policy had been vindicated by the electorate.

Jefferson dwelt at some length on his successful policy of conciliating the Federalists. The election showed what great unity now prevailed throughout the country, and the President hoped that the rest of the Federalists would lose the "veil" from their eyes. He ended with an appeal for even greater national unity and for the aid of "that Being in whose hands we are."

> . . . let us cherish them [the Federalists] with patient affection; let us do them justice, and more than justice . . . and we need not doubt that truth, reason, and their own interests, will at length prevail, will gather them into the fold of their country, and will complete their entire union of opinion, which gives to a nation the blessing of harmony, and the benefit of all its strength.

10

Jefferson's second Administration, which began in an aura of goodwill and peace, was pock-marked with trouble and ended in adversity.

One of the troubles that caused greater annoyance than harm was the Aaron Burr conspiracy against the unity and welfare of the United States. The Burr plot is still cloaked in considerable mystery; its details are blurred and its motivations are vague. It seems that after Burr left the Vice-Presidency, discredited as a man, ruined as a politician, he approached Jefferson's enemies with offers to do harm to the President and the country. One of those approached was Merry, the British Minister, who still smarted from having been kicked in his dignity by Jefferson's slippers. Merry actually advised his Government in London to give Burr $500,000 for a promise to detach the Western States from the Union. Burr also got in touch with the Spanish Minister Yrujo, as well as a number of high United States Army officers, among them General William Eaton (who gave away the scheme to Congress), General James Wilkinson, and General Andrew Jackson. The former Vice-President was also active among certain people in the West, on the Ohio, on the Mississippi, and in New Orleans. The schemes that were hatched and the promises that were made sound more like a Grade B Hollywood thriller than veracious history.

Wind of the intrigues and machinations reached Jefferson sometime in 1806. Among those who warned the President of Burr's devious doings was the same General Wilkinson who had originally lent an ear to the conspiracy. In the autumn of 1806, after the incredulous President was convinced that the Burr intrigue was not altogether a comic-opera affair, he issued an order for the arrest of the former Vice-President. Burr was seized and brought to Richmond for trial on a charge of treason.

Fortunately for Burr, the man who presided at the trial was Chief Justice John Marshall, and it was almost a foregone conclusion what the verdict would be. It was sufficient for the Chief Justice to know that Jefferson desired a conviction to do everything—within technical legal limits—in favor of Burr. The Chief Justice showed marked friendliness to Burr, and he actually sat at the same table with one who was arraigned as a traitor. The whole trial was turned into a joke at Jefferson's expense, and Burr was acquitted because Chief Justice Marshall's calculated definition of treason was such that it could not apply to the defendant.

Although the Chief Justice acquitted Burr, and although the upper-class ladies of Richmond treated the former Vice-President like a conquering hero, the people still considered Burr a traitor. So deep was the popular aversion for him that in some places he was almost lynched, and finally he had to flee the country—"there is not a man in the U.S.," Jefferson wrote, "who is not satisfied of the depth of his guilt."

11

The President's real difficulties originated not with traitors at home but with enemies abroad. Two empires, the British and the French (under Napoleon), were locked in a mortal struggle for world supremacy. They were trying to strangle each other by blockade and counterblockade, both being naval Powers.

Facing the belligerent empires across the ocean was the

United States. It too was a marine Power, although not a significant naval one. It too was an Atlantic country depending upon the salt water for most of its exports and imports. Of the approximately 6,000,000 people in the United States, about 80 per cent lived in States that fronted the Atlantic. When the two leviathans, as Jefferson called them, churned the ocean with their powerful tails, they threw up waves high enough to affect the lives of the great majority of the American people.

The situation that confronted Jefferson was how to defend American shipping and American rights from the Anglo-French predators. The United States had no navy to speak of. The British, having crippled Napoleon's navy at Trafalgar, ruled the waves and, on the seas, waived the rules.

One of the rules the British suspended, and the one that most infuriated and humiliated Americans, was that against impressment of American sailors on the high seas. Being engaged in a life-and-death fight with the conqueror of Europe, a war in which naval power played a preponderant role, the British were frequently shorthanded as to sailors. To recruit their navy, the British therefore resorted to impressment, which is a polite word for abduction.

The theory behind the abductions was that the sailors thus seized—"impressed" into service—were British citizens. There was some truth in the claim. Many British subjects actually served in the American merchant marine, for the simple reason that they earned higher wages under the Stars and Stripes than under the Union Jack. A number of them were naturalized American citizens—only a little over half of the *Constitution's* crew of 419, however, were United States citizens in 1807—but on the high seas this was difficult to prove. Any sailor with a British accent was liable to be taken off an American ship, and many were, even just outside New York Harbor. And all that American captains could do about it was to protest to Washington; Washington protested to London, and London sometimes ordered the release of the unfortunates who had been abducted. This was one of the country's earliest lessons in the folly of being unarmed in a world at war. It also caused Jefferson to suffer a succession of severe headaches—sure sign of strain and tension.[5]

The most scandalous case of impressment occurred in the summer of 1807 when the American frigate *Chesapeake* (38 guns) was hailed by the British man-of-war *Leopard* (50 guns) outside Chesapeake Bay. The *Leopard* demanded permission to "search for deserters" on the American frigate. Commodore

[5] Madison to Monroe, Mar. 10, 1806: "The President is just taken with one of his afflicting periodical headaches. We hope . . . that it will be less severe than his former ones."

Barron refused, and the British frigate opened fire, killing three men and wounding eighteen. The *Chesapeake*, her decks cluttered and her guns unprepared for action, struck her flag.

The news of the attack on the *Chesapeake* caused a burst of anger throughout the land. Commodore Barron and a number of his officers were court-martialed for negligence, but this did not lessen the tension, or diminish the gravity of the outrage. If Jefferson had wanted to declare war on Britain he would have had a united country behind him. But the President kept his head, knowing that the United States was in no position to wage war against a powerful enemy. He protested to London and demanded both apology and reparation. He promptly ordered British warships out of American waters.[6] At the same time he asked Congress for money to build 188 gunboats to add to the existing miniature fleet of 69 of them.

Jefferson's gunboats, which he built upon the advice of naval experts, were a contemporary joke, and the Federalists never tired of making jests about them. These gunboats, like Ford's Tin Lizzies of a later date, easily lent themselves to humor. They were so small and light that a high wind could lift them and deposit them on land—a high wind once did with one. Each vessel carried two guns, and their weight was such that the whole works capsized in foul weather. The best that can be said for this pathetic ersatz fleet is that it did no one any harm.

12

The British ignored Jefferson's protests and actually intensified their hostile acts (Royal Proclamation of October 17, 1807). And the French, although not in a position to do the same amount of damage as the British, were no more friendly. Napoleon sneeringly referred to the American flag as "only a piece of striped bunting."

Between the British blockade of France and the French counterblockade of Britain, American commerce was caught in the jaws of an iron pincers. Napoleon sealed the European ports against England. In retaliation, the British issued Order in Council (November 11, 1807) declaring that all European ports that excluded the British should henceforth be "subject to the same restrictions."

Napoleon countered with a declaration that his navy would capture any ship that had permitted itself to be searched by British warships or that sailed from a British port. This was a

[6] Even Jefferson's bitterest critics approved of his prompt action. He was so surprised at their praise that he exclaimed with the Psalmist "Lord, what have I done that the wicked should praise me."

blow to neutral shipping in general and American shipping in particular. American vessels were now caught in a crushing dilemma. They could obey the British Orders in Council and thereby run the risk of capture by Napoleon's privateers; or they could adhere to Napoleon's decrees and expose themselves to seizure by the British.

To protect American rights and interests against repeated outrages and contemptuous violations was beyond the physical resources of the Government. A nation of 6,000,000 people, most of them making their living from agriculture, could not wage war against the two greatest empires in the world, or even against one of them. Yet to ignore the violations was to invite more of the same.

Lacking a strong fleet and an effective fighting force, the country could not go to war, even assuming that Jefferson believed in war as an instrument for settling international disputes, which he did not. Once, to be sure, Jefferson had used force to settle a difficulty. The action took place in the Mediterranean where Moroccan, Algerian and Tripolitanian pirates levied tribute and ransom on Occidental merchants. The Moslem marauders had collected about $2,000,000 from Americans in ten years, and the economizing Jefferson thought that the money could be used to better advantage at home. He sent a naval squadron to the Mediterranean, and after a series of gallant actions on the part of the American sailors, the Barbary corsairs agreed to respect the American flag. It was one thing, however, to teach a lesson to a handful of barbarians, and another to make two world empires at war obey the rules of civilized behavior.

But was there no substitute for war? Jefferson was convinced that there was. His substitute was known as the Embargo.

Behind the policy of the Embargo lay a theoretically sound idea. Since the object of war was to defeat an opponent, or to make him respect your rights, it followed that any method that achieved this aim was good. Guns were the conventional mode of waging war. But suppose another weapon were used—an economic weapon? A weapon that would withhold vital supplies from, and cut off the trade with, the enemy. Would it not beat the opponent as effectively as a gun? Jefferson, the philosopher and apostle of peace, thought it was worth trying. He was perhaps the first important statesman in the world to carry out the experiment of waging a nonmilitary war.

The success of an economic Embargo depended upon two factors, and Jefferson miscalculated both. One of them was the assumption that Britain's trade with the United States was of such importance that its lack would gravely damage her economy and impair her military position. This turned out to be far from the case. The other miscalculation was that the Embargo could be enforced. Jefferson assumed that the merchants of New York and New England would forego profits and co-operate with the Government.

On December 22, 1807, the Congress, after receiving a brief message from the President, passed the Embargo Act by an overwhelming vote. Immediately thereafter Secretary of the Treasury Gallatin dispatched messengers to New York and Boston and Norfolk and New Orleans and all other ports that had been doing a thriving business despite British provocations —to tie up all American ships until further notice.

The shipowners and merchants met the Embargo Act (and the supplementary Non-Importation Act of April 16, 1808) with contempt and derision. Profits in illegal trading soared, and systematic smuggling became a big business. Goods from Britain were smuggled in by way of Canada, Florida, and the West Indies. And soon the anti-British blockade—for that is what the Embargo amounted to—was shot so full of holes that it became worse than futile.

Smuggling, however, was no compensation for lawful trade, and the Embargo boomeranged on the American people, preventing them from exporting their cotton, tobacco, and wheat. The pity of it was that the chief sufferers were the people Jefferson most wanted to help and protect—the little folk, the farmers, traders, and mechanics. The big companies weathered the crisis very well.

Except for smuggling, business, which in America of Jefferson's day meant small business, was hit severely. Ports were idle, ships dismantled. Exports dropped from $110,000,000 to $20,000,000 in the first year of the Embargo. In five months there were one hundred and twenty-five bankruptcies in New York City.

The distress in the country was not only visible but vocal. Even the British heard of it. George Canning, the British Foreign Secretary, remarked with devastating wit that England was willing to help Jefferson do away with the Embargo Act because it was a "measure of inconvenient restriction upon the American people."

The hardships caused by the Embargo, as well as the President's patience under provocation, brought down a stream of vituperation upon his head. For the third time in less than two decades Jefferson found himself the main target of hatred.

Most of the verbal violence came from New England, a region that, owing to its commercial economy, suffered most under the Embargo. A typical letter from New England read:

"You Infernal Villain, How much longer are you going to keep this damned Embargo on to starve us poor people."

Long before the Embargo policies brought a hailstorm of hatred upon the President, he was determined to retire from public life at the end of his second term.

To the legislatures of Vermont and North Carolina, which asked him to run for a third term, Jefferson replied (December 10, 1807, and January 10, 1808) that he did not wish to violate the two-term precedent set by President Washington, his "illustrious predecessor."

The "no-third-term" precedent was only one of a variety of reasons that led Jefferson to reject the idea of remaining in Washington for an additional four years. One of the motives for his eagerness to leave office was, he said, declining physical vigor. Although he enjoyed good health, Jefferson was nevertheless in his middle sixties, and the burdens of the Presidency were beginning to be felt. Another reason was that, like George Washington before him, he began to be weary of the Presidency. To John Dickinson he wrote early in 1807: ". . . yet two years to endure. I am tired of an office where I can do no more good than many others. . . . To myself, personally, it brings nothing but unceasing drudgery & daily loss of friends. Every office becoming vacant, every appointment made, me donne un ingrat, et cent ennemis." A year later he wrote to Monroe: "My longings for retirement are so strong, that I with difficulty encounter the daily drudgeries of my duty."

The world, too, had changed for the worse. Bitter criticism, personal abuse, and an international situation riven by violence made Jefferson more eager than ever to hand over the reins to a younger man. At sixty-five it was particularly painful to be exposed to the "flagitiousness" of the press that was full of "atrocious lies," or to feel comfortable in a world trampled by Napoleon. So dark was the world outlook that Jefferson, usually buoyant and sanguine, sometimes despaired of the outcome.

It was time, he felt, to let a younger man take over. The country was on the verge of revolt against the Embargo; New England definitely threatened secession. Jefferson's own party was split. But he was still powerful enough to select James Madison as his successor. In the election of 1808 Madison won by a comfortable majority, but only after a promise that the Embargo would be repealed.

Three days before his term expired, on March 1, 1809, Jefferson approved the bill repealing the Embargo. He had carried on a bold experiment and had failed. He had tried to save the

country from losses, but the Embargo had ruined at lea
$50,000,000 worth of business. He had tried to spare the pe
ple humiliation, but he had only brought national wrath upo
himself. But he was not convinced that the Embargo polic
was wrong. He left the presidential office under a cloud murk
with disapprobation—but there was a surplus in the nation:
treasury and the finances were sounder than ever before. O
March 2 he wrote du Pont de Nemours:

> Within a few days I retire to my family, my books and farm:
> and having gained the harbor myself, shall look on my friend
> still buffeting the storm, with anxiety indeed, but not with envy
> Never did a prisoner, released from his chains, feel such relie
> as I shall on shaking off the shackles of power.

A crowd of ten thousand flocked to Washington to atten
Madison's inauguration. Jefferson accompanied his protég
and successor to the inaugural, this time in a carriage, an
escorted by cavalry. Times had changed. Another sign of th
times was an inaugural ball. It was held that evening at Long
Hotel in Georgetown and was attended by a brilliant assembl
of four hundred guests. The center of attraction was not th
black-garbed new President, nor his "portly, buxom" wif
Dolly, bright in yellow velvet and a turban, but the lanky Jef
ferson. The outgoing President sparkled with joy and enchant
ed the guests with his jests and laughter. At the same tim
President Madison flitted about like a wraith, weary and wor
ried. He knew that he had nothing to be gay about.

Jefferson rode out of Washington under a bleak sky. Slowl
he made his way through the muddy hills to Monticello, en
countering a severe snowstorm. Along the road the solitar
traveler expected to be received with hostility. To his surprise
Virginia farmers thronged to meet and cheer "Old Tom." The
drank his health and vigorously toasted "Thomas Jefferson—
the Statesman, the Patriot and the Sage."

He got to Monticello in the middle of March and his neigh
bors in Albemarle County flocked to give him a rousing wel
come. The gray ex-President had tears in his eyes as he ad
dressed them:

> Of you, then, my neighbors, I may ask, in the face of th
> world, "whose ox have I taken, or whom have I defrauded
> Whom have I oppressed, or of whose hand have I received
> bribe to blind mine eyes therewith?" On your verdict I res

CHAPTER FOURTEEN

SAGE

(1809-July 4, 1826)

At last Jefferson could look forward to years of unbroken serenity on his farm in the midst of his family. "I am supremely happy in being withdrawn from these turmoils," he said. Forty years ago he had begun to build his brick eyrie on top of the hill, but only now, at the age of sixty-six, did he have any prospect of inhabiting it without interruption. This time, come what might, he would remain in his beautiful home until his earthly days were over.

His life had been full and fruitful. He had experienced some defeats and many triumphs, and his name, he knew, was imperishably linked with the story of his country. He had doubled the territory of the United States, and had welded, from loose and scattered materials, a powerful political party. His ideals of liberty were graven into the law of the land, and his measures—the coinage, for example—were among the permanent institutions of the country. He had achieved all this by means of peace and persuasion. No one in all the land could say that Thomas Jefferson had shed blood or had inflicted injury upon his fellow men. "I have the consolation to reflect," Jefferson told Count Dugnani, the Papal Nuncio, in 1818, "that during the period of my administration not a drop of the blood of a single fellow citizen was shed by the sword of war or of the law."

The years of struggle and turmoil had given him an immense reservoir of moral strength. Time, like fire, having purified whatever weaknesses lurked in his character, he could face the opinion of his contemporaries and the judgment of history with equal serenity. Well past middle age, he was now that most rare of human species, a balanced and harmonious man capable of viewing the world with detached compassion and serene wisdom. Few men in history ever achieved such philosophical balance and spiritual harmony as did Jefferson in his later—his postpolitical—years. One of the few individuals who can compare with him in this respect was his contemporary, the German poet Goethe. "My temperament," Jefferson said at the age of sixty-seven, "is sanguine. I steer my bark with Hope at the head, leaving Fear astern."

159

And so, upon his retirement, he became what men called sage—the Sage of Monticello. At that period, the period o Napoleonic wars and international reaction, the country neede just such a figure to act, or rather to live, as an example c spiritual elevation and mellow wisdom. If there was still som lingering bitterness against him as the founder and leader of victorious political party, the country remembered him for th great role he had played. To a younger generation of Ameri cans the still hale and vigorous Virginian was a piece fron the tapestry of history—the author of the Declaration of Inde pendence and the friend and associate of the now revere George Washington.

2

Margaret Bayard Smith, wife of the editor of the *Nationa Intelligencer and Washington Adviser*, an ardent Jefferson ian triweekly, visited Monticello about four months after Jef ferson's retirement and left a record of her visit. She wrote.

> There is a tranquillity about him, which an inward peac alone could bestow. . . . His tall and slender figure is no impaired by age. . . . His white locks announce an age hi activity, strength, health, enthusiasm, ardor and gayety contra dict. His face owes all its charm to its expression and intelli gence; his features are not good and his complexion bad, bu his countenance is so full of soul and beams with muc benignity. . . . His low and mild voice harmonizes with hi countenance rather than his figure. But his manners—ho gentle, how humble, how kind. . . . To a disposition arden affectionate and communicative, he joins manners timid eve to bashfulness, and reserved even to coldness.

One evening Mrs. Smith had an interesting conversatio with the former President. Stimulated by an intelligent an sympathetic feminine listener, Jefferson spoke about himsel He admitted frankly what is, in perspective, clear to his biog rapher—that his whole life was a conflict between privat inclination and public duty:

> The whole of my life has been a war with my natural tast feelings and wishes; domestic life and literary pursuits were m first and my latest inclinations—circumstances and not my d sires led me to the path I have trod, and like a bow though lon bent, which when unstrung flies back to its natural state, resume with delight the character and pursuits for which natur designed me. The circumstances of our country, at my entranc into life, were such that every honest man felt himself con pelled to take part, and to act up to the best of his abilities.

Now that he no longer had to worry about politics, Jefferson could devote himself to the art of living. He kept himself in perfect physical shape, and his daily regimen was worthy of a young athlete. Every day the old gentleman rose at dawn and made his own fire from dry wood which he kept in a box near the fireplace. He bathed his feet in ice-cold water and then dressed with neatness and simplicity. Ordinarily he wore short breeches, but in later years he substituted pantaloons. When preparing to ride he donned overalls.

After dressing he would write and read until breakfast. Then he would mount his favorite horse and ride for several hours, six or eight miles daily, but sometimes as many as forty miles. Before mounting the horse he would wipe its mouth and flanks with a white handkerchief to see whether the animal was clean. "From breakfast, or noon at latest, to dinner," he told his good friend Dr. Benjamin Rush, "I am mostly on horseback, attending to my farm . . . which I find healthful to my body, mind and affairs."

After a hard ride he would dine, at about three, on some meat and vegetables. He drank water at least once a day and ate sparingly, though heartily, because he believed that one should always rise from the table a little bit hungry. He never smoked or played games of chance. After dinner he worked in his study, reading sometimes and writing often. He was, he said, "devoured by correspondences." At nine he retired to his room and read for about an hour, using spectacles at night but rarely during the day. Usually he went to bed at about ten and slept from five to eight hours.

He never wasted time and did not understand the meaning of idleness. Always he was doing something, and happy in what he was doing. His activities, he said, kept him "busy as a bee in a molasses barrel." He was often either drawing or designing or sketching or outlining. Now it was a plow, now a carriage, now a building, now a fence, now a garden. A lover of flowers, he laid out a garden and planted rare specimens. An architect, he drew blueprints for many buildings, some of which still stand as monuments to the many-sided genius of their creator.[1] An inveterate inventor, he experimented with innumerable gadgets and improvements. He invented polygraphs, pantographs, and newfangled plows. He designed a cunning dumb-waiter. He built himself a handy weathervane. He experimented with a hundred and one gimcracks.

Since his farms and those of his neighbors were located far

---

[1] Apart from Monticello, the best examples of Jeffersonian architecture are the Capitol in Richmond and the University of Virginia in Charlottesville. These are worth a special trip to the Old Dominion to see.

from cities, Jefferson built a number of industrial establishments to make himself and his friends reasonably self-sufficient. His most ambitious undertakings in this respect were a flour mill and a nail factory.

The nail factory, begun before Jefferson's retirement from politics, was profitable. It employed ten workers who earned $2 a day, a high wage for those days. Jefferson's nailery supplied the near-by stores as well as his neighbors, including James Monroe, with nails. It closed in 1812, when it was unable to obtain rods. There was also a small cotton mill which manufactured homespun from cotton obtained in Richmond. Three spinnning machines wove cloth for all of Jefferson's slaves. Wagonloads of homespun were also sold to merchants. The plantation had a smithy and a furniture shop.

But Jefferson's primary activity was farming, for agriculture was his sole means of support. It was also the only way he could hope to pay his debts, especially those he had accumulated as President. "In a couple of years more," he wrote early in 1810, "I shall be able to clear out all the difficulties I brought on myself in Washington."

As a farmer, Jefferson was fortunate in possessing a scientific son-in-law. Thomas Mann Randolph, the brilliant and high-tempered husband of Martha Jefferson, was of immense help to his father-in-law. It was Randolph, according to Jefferson, who pioneered in plowing horizontally around hills to save soil and water from runoffs. "For this improvement," Jefferson said, "we are indebted to my son-in-law, Mr. Randolph, the best farmer, I believe, in the United States, and who has taught us to make more than two blades of corn to grow where only one grew before."

But growing two blades where one grew before did not spell prosperity. It was actually ruinous, as farmers have discovered from time to time in periods of crises. The world war then in progress, with its devastating blockades and counterblockades, knocked the bottom from agricultural prices, a development that had been further aggravated by Jefferson's Embargo policy; Jefferson thus was the victim of his own work. Neither wheat nor tobacco, the crops of which he increased by 50 per cent, brought enough cash to pay for articles that he had to buy. The market for such products was shot to pieces and, Jefferson said in discouragement, you might as well burn the stuff or feed it to the animals.

3

Early in 1812, when Jefferson was in his sixty-eighth year, he received from a man of seventy-six a letter that gladdened is heart. There was not, to be sure, much to the letter. The writer simply informed Jefferson that he was sending him specimens of homespun and that his family was fine. But the signature was what mattered. The letter was signed—"with sincere Esteem your Friend and Servant"—John Adams. Thus began a classic correspondence in American history.

For eleven years, ever since the campaign of 1800, the two men had not been on speaking terms. Their estrangement, however, had not altered the fundamental respect that each entertained for the other. Time had blunted the sharp edges of their political differences, and now that both were in retirement they could resume a friendship that was started way back when they were both comparatively young "rebels" against the British crown.

The conciliation of the two friends was the work of Dr. Benjamin Rush, the Philadelphia physician who was also one of the signers of the Declaration of Independence. Dr. Rush, who admired both Jefferson and Adams, wanted the two ex-Presidents, and the two greatest living American patriots, to pick up the threads of their friendship that had been broken under the stress of party politics. Jefferson said that he had forgotten all bitterness he had once felt and that his esteem for Adams was as high as ever. Adams, when approached by Rush, was also eager for the renewal of the friendship. He told Rush, surely there had been differences between Jefferson and him on political matters, but they were "miserable frivolities." Jefferson, Adams said with characteristic humor, believed in "liberty and straight hair. I thought curled hair was as republican as straight." Anyhow, why worry about all that? "His administration and mine are passed away into the dark backwards." And he added, "I have always loved him [Jefferson] as a friend."

After this admission, Adams wrote to Jefferson the letter about the homespun. Jefferson was moved. The voice of Adams, coming from faraway Quincy, Massachusetts, was a voice from Jefferson's youth, bringing back the great and crucial days of the Revolution. His reply to the older man was therefore full of eagerness and warmth. It was a rambling letter, covering many points which, Jefferson knew, Adams would be eager to take up.

I have given up newspapers in exchange for Tacitus and Thucydides, for Newton and Euclid, and I find myself much happier. Sometimes, indeed, I look back to former occurrences. . . . Of the signers of the Declaration of Independence, I see now living not more than half a dozen on your side of the Po-

tomac, and on this side, myself alone.[2] You and I have been
wonderfully spared, and myself with remarkable health. . . .
I am on horseback three or four hours of every day. . . . I
walk little, however, a single mile being too much for me, and
I live in the midst of my grandchildren. . . . I salute you
with unchanged affection and respect.

This letter inaugurated a series of communications that are
remarkable for brilliance and bold adventuring in the realm of
ideas. The two old gentlemen, both men of massive learning
and vast intellectual curiosity, poured out their ideas with the
zeal and zest of youngsters. To the intimacy of their letters
they entrusted their innermost hopes and fears and prejudices
and convictions and indignations. No one who is interested in
the history of America should miss this record of two noble
minds.

They continued writing to each other until the end of their
days. At least one hundred and fifty bulging envelopes marked
"President Adams" and "President Jefferson" passed to and
from Monticello and Quincy. Jefferson wrote fewer letters
than Adams, but the latter did not care. He was so eager to
share his thoughts with Jefferson and to hear from him that
even an occasional letter was an event. "Never mind," Adams
told Jefferson, "if I write four letters to your one, your one is
worth more than four of mine."

4

Letters came unceasingly. In an average year Jefferson received about a thousand, and in some years the number
reached nearly thirteen hundred. At Jefferson's death, his
grandson Thomas Jefferson Randolph found twenty-six thousand letters and sixteen thousand answers on file.

To answer these letters was a stupendous task. Jefferson
conscientiously replied to as many as he could, but it was
crushing drudgery. "Is this life?" he groaned as he looked at
the stacks of communications awaiting a reply. "At best it is
but the life of a mill-horse, who sees no end to his circle but
in death. To such a life, that of a cabbage is paradise."

Laborsaving devices and timesaving methods helped some.
Jefferson invented a polygraph, an ingenious multiwriting machine that was useful in producing stereotyped letters. For job-
seekers, particularly those who wanted him to intercede with

[2] In January, 1812, when Jefferson wrote this letter, only ten of the
fifty-six signers of the Declaration of Independence were still alive. These
were besides Jefferson and Adams: Charles Carroll (Maryland), George
Clymer (Pennsylvania), William Ellery (Rhode Island), William Floyd
(New York), Elbridge Gerry (Massachusetts), Thomas McKean (Delaware), Robert Treat Paine (Massachusetts), and Benjamin Rush (Pennsylvania). Of the seventeen Southern signers, only Jefferson and Carroll
were alive.

the Administration in Washington, he had circulars printed stating that he was sorry but must decline "to exercise his influence with the President concerning appointments to office."

Visitors were a more difficult problem to solve and a considerably greater burden. Poor and rich alike flocked to Monticello. Some came to ask favors, others to request advice, still others to enjoy comfortable board and room. To all Jefferson gave unstintingly of his time, his money, and his resources.

Many came to Monticello simply to look at the great man. Often strangers would plant themselves in the passageway near the study to see the Sage of Monticello as he came out to eat dinner. Once a woman broke a windowpane with her parasol in order to get a better view of him. Curious men and women would pass near the house to catch a view of Jefferson as he sat in the shade of the portico.

Those who came out of curiosity were a compliment at best and a nuisance at worst. But the visitors who stayed there were a problem. Guests were so numerous and so frequent that Monticello sometimes looked like a big resort hotel at the height of the summer season. There were fifty beds for guests on the premises. At one time as many as seventy people were put up overnight. When the invasion became too great, Jefferson would travel a hundred miles to escape it—to Poplar Forest, a farm he owned near Lynchburg.

One of Jefferson's guests, in 1815, was Julius Melbourn, a mulatto who had been born a slave. When Melbourn entered the room, Jefferson rose with pleasure and evident curiosity. He had heard of Melbourn as a learned man and he was eager to see in the flesh the proof of what he always suspected —that colored folk were not inherently inferior to whites.

According to Melbourn, the two men had a long and sympathetic talk on many learned topics. Jefferson told his mulatto guest that he was thinking of establishing a university in Virginia where there would be no bar to any sect or color. He spoke warmly of "our colored brethren." He discussed the political philosophy of Montesquieu, whose principles he did not admire, and the British constitution, which he liked even less. He also talked of David Hume, the influential English philosopher, who was Jefferson's bête noire in the realm of ideas.

Another guest who left a record of his visit to Monticello was the French Baron de Montlezun. The Baron was struck by the youthful appearance of his host who, at seventy-three, "looks like sixty-three," and by his scientific interests. The products of Jefferson's paleontological and anthropological curiosity were stored in a small museum where the Baron ad-

mired such "excessively rare" objects as the head of a gigantic
ram, an Indian painting on five square feet of buffalo hide, and
an upper jawbone of a mammoth.

To the Baron we are also indebted for a description of
Jefferson's art collection. Of prints that hung on the walls at
Monticello, de Montlezun observed portraits of Washington,
Lafayette, John Adams, Sir Walter Raleigh, Franklin, Vespu-
cius, Columbus, Francis Bacon, Locke, and Newton. Of busts,
there were those of Cleopatra, Voltaire, Turgot, Czar Alexander I, Napoleon, Washington, Franklin, Lafayette, and John
Paul Jones. There were also a number of indifferent paintings
and at least three valuable ones. The latter included Poussin's
"Ascension," Raphael's "Holy Family," and Rubens's "Flagel-
lation of Christ."

Everywhere there were books, thousands of them. But guests
did not leave Jefferson much time for reading, "my greatest
of all amusements." He said: "Dr. Franklin used to say that
when he was young and had time to read he had not books;
and now when he had become old and had books, he had no
time."

5

In October, 1823, when Jefferson was well past his eightieth
birthday, he received a startling letter from President Monroe.
The President asked his advice on a matter of grave international importance, that of co-operating with Great Britain to
keep European Powers out of the Americas. The United States
and Britain, it must be remembered, had been on terms of
virtually uninterrupted hostility for half a century. Now Britain's Foreign Minister, George Canning, actually proposed
friendly co-operation. Canning was motivated by the news that
the reactionary Holy Alliance (Russia, Prussia, Austria, Spain,
and Bourbon France) was planning to reconquer South America for the greater glory of monarchy and the benefit of bigotry.
He quickly got in touch with Monroe. Monroe communicated
with Jefferson, and the latter, amazed at and pleased with the
offer from Britain, urged immediate acceptance of Canning's
proposition:

> The question . . . is the most momentous which has ever
> been offered to my contemplation since that of Independence.
> . . . Our first and fundamental maxim should be, never to en-
> tangle ourselves in the broils of Europe. Our second, never to
> suffer Europe to intermeddle with cis-Atlantic affairs.

Monroe accepted Jefferson's advice, and even his line of
reasoning. Jefferson's letter was written on October 24. On
December 2, President Monroe sent a message to Congress in

which he announced that the United States should declare any attempt of European Powers "to extend their system to any portion of this hemisphere as dangerous to our peace and safety."

Thus, fathered by Jefferson, was born the Monroe Doctrine.

6

Jefferson, although no churchgoer, was a sincere Christian, "a *real Christian*," as he called himself. He did not oppose the church but certain churchmen. He fully accepted the moral principles of Jesus, whom he regarded as one of the greatest figures in all history. What Jefferson rejected was sectarianism:

> An eloquent preacher . . . is said to have exclaimed aloud to his congregation, that he did not believe there was a Quaker, Presbyterian, Methodist, or Baptist in heaven. . . . He added, that in heaven, God knew no distinctions, but considered all good men as his children, and as brethren of the same family. I believe, with the Quaker preacher, that he who steadily observes those moral precepts in which all religions concur, will never be questioned at the gates of heaven, as to the dogmas in which they all differ.

He cut out the words of Jesus and pasted them, on blank pages, in chronological and subject order. The result was extremely impressive. "A more beautiful or precious morsel of ethics I have never seen," he told Charles Thomson; "it is a document in proof that *I* am a *real Christian*,[3] that is to say, a disciple of the doctrines of Jesus." And to another correspondent he wrote in the same vein:

> The sum of all religion as expressed by its best preacher, "fear God and love thy neighbor" contains no mystery, needs no explanation. But this won't do. It gives no scope to make dupes; priests could not live by it.

In his eightieth year, writing to Dr. Benjamin Waterhouse, the famous medical scientist of Boston, Jefferson thus summarized the doctrines of Jesus:

> The doctrines of Jesus are simple, and tend all to the happiness of man.
> 1. That there is only one God, and he all perfect.
> 2. That there is a future state of rewards and punishments.
> 3. That to love God with all thy heart and thy neighbor as thyself, is the sum of religion.

These pure principles, Jefferson added, have been corrupted and perverted by such men as Athanasius and Calvin, with their "*deliria* of crazy imaginations" which are "as foreign

[3] Italics Jefferson's.

from Christianity as is that of Mahomet." Jefferson hope
that Americans, who had surrendered their conscience "t
neither kings nor priests," would return to the unspoiled doc
trines of Jesus. This would make the United States a Unitaria
country.

Upon receipt of this blunt letter, Dr. Waterhouse asked Jef
ferson for permission to publish it, but the Sage, having mor
than once experienced the full fury of clerical rage, smiling]
declined. At eighty he did not feel like having his repose dis
turbed by thunderous fulminations from a thousand pulpits

> No, my dear Sir, not for the world. Into what a nest o
> hornets would it thrust my head! . . . Don Quixote undertool
> to redress the bodily wrongs of the world, but the redressment o
> mental vagaries would be an enterprise more than Quixotic
> I should as soon undertake to bring the crazy skulls of Bedlar
> to sound understanding, as inculcate realism into that of ar
> Athanasian. I am old, and tranquility is now my *summur*
> *bonum.* Keep me, therefore, from the fire and faggots of Calvi
> and his victim Servetus.

Jefferson's letters on religion, though they delighted thos
who received them, were never made public during his life
time. Many of his correspondents begged to be allowed to
publish some of his letters, but he was adamant in his refusal

He had a special contempt for certain kinds of clergymen
especially those who disfigured the "genuine and simple reli
gion of Jesus." He referred to the clergy as the *"genus irrita
bile vatum"* and as "mountebanks calling themselves the priest
of Jesus." Their business in life, Jefferson said, was to confuse
mankind with their "Abracadabra." He compared them to cut
tlefish, which have the "faculty of shedding darkness . . . thro
the element in which they move, and making it impenetrabl
to the eye of a pursuing enemy, and there they will skulk."

To dissipate clerical obscurantism and its accompanyin
disease of intolerance, Jefferson believed that it was vital to
practice religious freedom and to enlighten the people throug
universal education. "Religious freedom," he told Dr. De L
Motta, rabbi of the Jewish synagogue at Savannah, Georgia
"is the most effectual Anodyne against religious dissension."
To another man of the Jewish faith, Joseph Marx, Jefferso
expressed his regrets that the Jewish sect, "parent and basis o
all those of Christendom," should have been, in the past, sin
gled out by Christians "for a persecution and oppression whic
proved they have profited nothing from the benevolen
doctrines of him whom they profess to make the model o
their principles and practice." The twin evils of bigotry an
persecution could be avoided in the United States by a vigor

us policy of enlightenment. "To penetrate and dissipate these clouds of darkness, the general mind must be strengthened by education," Jefferson concluded.

7

In his old age, Jefferson developed a plan for public education and gave the last years of his life to its realization. "I am now," he wrote at the age of seventy-four to George Ticknor, "entirely absorbed in endeavours to effect the establishment of a general system of education in my native state." For years he had been reading up on educational methods and techniques in other lands; he also consulted specialists.

By 1817 Jefferson had the last detail of his plan worked out. It was one of the most ambitious projects ever designed for education in a free republic. He divided his educational system into three parts—elementary school, high school, and university. The elementary schools were to provide instruction in reading, writing, arithmetic, and geography. They were to be free to all children, for Jefferson insisted that it was the duty of government "to provide that every citizen . . . should receive an education proportioned to the condition and pursuits of his life."

In this connection it is noteworthy that Jefferson, ever the lover of liberty, hesitated to make attendance in elementary schools compulsory. Coercion of any kind was so distasteful to him that he would not see it applied even in so vital a matter as public education:

> It is better to tolerate the rare instances of a parent refusing to let his child be educated, than to shock the common feelings and ideas by the forcible asportation and education of the infant against the will of the father.

The high schools were to teach sciences and languages, and to provide, at public expense, preparation for the professions. These high schools were to be established throughout the State, within one day's ride of every inhabitant.

The crown of the whole system was to be the university. It was to be composed of a number of professional schools, giving instruction in what Jefferson called "useful" branches of science. These professional schools were to train architects, musicians, sculptors, gardeners, economists, military and naval scientists, horticulturists, agronomists, physicians, historians, clergymen, and lawyers.

People thought Jefferson's educational plan visionary, and when it was introduced in the State legislature, it was, as Jefferson expected, rejected. Legislators, commented the Sage of

Monticello drily, "do not generally possess information enoug to perceive the important truths, that knoledge is power, an knoledge is safety, and that knoledge is happiness."

But Jefferson was too seasoned a political maneuverer an too patient a philosopher to be discouraged by a first failur He knew that it was a tough task to persuade many simpl people, farmers and artisans, that a good system of educatio in a democracy was not a luxury, as some thought, but a neec Realization of the difficulties involved in "selling" his idea t the legislature only spurred the seventy-five-year-old Sage t greater efforts.

Early in 1818, the Virginia legislature appropriated the mu nificent sum of $45,000 for elementary education for the poor and the generous sum of $15,000 for the endowment an support of a university. This was the first crack in the wall o indifference. And Jefferson was an expert at widening suci fissures.

The legislature provided that twenty-four Commissioner be appointed to discuss the organization and location of th university. Among these Commissioners were former Presi dent Jefferson, former President Madison, and President Mon roe. The three men met at Monticello and quietly made plan for the founding of the university at near-by Charlottesville

In August, 1818, when Jefferson was in his seventy-fifth year, he rode to the lush-green Blue Ridge Mountains to mee the other Commissioners and decide upon the plans for a State university. The meeting took place at Rockfish Gap, in a mod est inn but in a scenic setting of incomparable beauty. Amon the twenty-one eminent Virginians who were present in the low-ceilinged, whitewashed, rustic room, Jefferson was easily the most impressive figure. Not only was his appearance dis tinguished, but his prestige was overpowering. "It was re marked by the lookers on," comments a contemporary, "that Mr. Jefferson was the principal object of regard, both to the members and spectators; that he seemed to be the chief mover of the body—the soul that animated it."

The Commissioners' primary problem was where to place the university. Each section of the State had its advocates. Jefferson had come prepared to make an astute defense of Charlottesville. His arguments were unexpected and unortho dox. He told the gentlemen present that the university should be at Charlottesville because the climate in that region was very salubrious. To prove the salubrity, Jefferson calmly pro duced a list of octogenarians who lived in Albemarle County, where Charlottesville was located.

Then he surprised the Commissioners with a cardboard shaped in the form of a map of Virginia. This showed that

Charlottesville was in the geographical center of the commonwealth. Then he brought forth another cardboard map listing
the inhabitants in every county. This revealed that Albemarle
County was also the population center of the State. Finally,
he pointed out that Charlottesville already had, in its so-called
Central College (to which Jefferson had contributed $1,000),
the nucleus of a higher institution around which the State university could be built. The Commissioners, overwhelmed by
such a wealth of shrewdly piled up data, agreed unanimously
that Central College at Charlottesville should become the University of Virginia. Half a year later the State legislature approved the choice.

For the next six years Jefferson lived only for the University
of Virginia. The institution was to be the crowning glory of
his life, and upon it he lavished all his energies, his talents,
his hopes. He turned himself into a one-man construction
plant, a one-man architectural firm, a one-man apprentice
school, and a one-man planning board. He did everything himself. He raised money. He drew up the architectural plans. He
procured the workmen, including the importation of sculptors
from Italy. He prepared all the details of construction. Since
there was a shortage of skilled labor, he also taught brick-
layers how to work and carpenters how to measure.

One visitor, D. P. Thompson, tells that in 1822 he was on
the university grounds and saw Jefferson take a chisel from
an Italian sculptor and show him how to turn a volute on a
pillar. Then the old gentleman approached the visitor with "an
elastic step and serene countenance" and greeted him with a
"sweet, winning smile." After inviting Thompson to Monticello, Jefferson mounted his blooded horse "with the agility of
a boy."

Daily the white-haired gentleman rode down the mountain
to Charlottesville to supervise the construction of his pet pro-
ject. These rides, four or five miles each way, were becoming
hazardous as Jefferson reached his eighties.

His favorite horse, a thoroughbred named Eagle, was usually
tied to a staple outside of Jefferson's study and could hardly
contain itself until its master appeared. When Eagle heard
Jefferson's footsteps it stopped pawing, turned its arched neck
in his direction, and neighed in greeting. In his eighties, Jefferson could no longer rise from stirrup. He mounted Eagle from
a low terrace; all the while the intelligent horse stood still,
knowing that its master was old and a little helpless. Despite
his swollen wrists (the result of a fall from Eagle), Jefferson
rode to Charlottesville alone. When his family pleaded with
him to take a servant, he said that if they insisted he would
give up riding altogether.

The sight of the thin old man and his old horse carefully picking their way through slippery mud and fording a treacherous river was unforgettable. Rider and horse were recognized by everybody and were constantly stopped. Friends and neighbors greeted them all along the way. They inquired after his health and asked how things were getting along. Some stopped the rider to ask his advice, and he always responded cheerfully.

Jefferson's greatest difficulty in building the university was financial. He designed his institution on a scale so ambitious that to some of the legislators he appeared like a Kubla Khan with his Xanadu. The legislature had appropriated an original sum of $15,000. That amount of money was, of course, a joke. Jefferson proceeded as if he could extract ten or even twenty times as much from the reluctant legislators. At every session he asked for more money. Bit by bit the money was voted, under protest. It was like pulling teeth. On more than one occasion the legislature, shocked at the realization that they had already sunk a fortune in the Charlottesville institution, refused appropriations altogether. But the legislature was no match for Jefferson's cajolery. He argued patiently and outmaneuvered strategically. He appealed to patriotism and pride —how would it look to the world if Virginia permitted a dozen fine public buildings to stand without roofs and without doors? Unless the buildings were finished, the whole investment would be a dead loss. With the resigned air of those throwing good money after bad, the legislature grudgingly voted Jefferson his money, piecemeal.

When friends asked him why he demanded only small appropriations, he replied, with a twinkle, that no one likes to have more than one hot potato at a time crammed down his throat. The "hot potato" crack caused some resentment in Richmond, but Jefferson's prestige in the State was so great that he could get away with any number of indiscreet remarks. By the time he finished constructing the principal buildings, he had spent $300,000—a tremendous sum for those days.

But the university was a sight worth seeing. Built entirely according to Jefferson's architectural plans and specifications, the red-brick University of Virginia rose from the red soil against the green mountain backdrop as one of the most beautiful institutions in the land. It made a powerful impression even upon those who, like George Ticknor, had studied at Harvard and at Göttingen.

But Jefferson well knew that what makes a university is teachers, and not structures. The problem of assembling a faculty was difficult. There were not many universities in the United States, and few of those trained scholars in sufficient numbers, or of sufficiently high caliber, to supply the domestic need. Jefferson wanted only the best men in their fields, and the best were available mainly abroad, particularly in England, "the land of our own language, morals, manners, and habits." He sent an American scholar, Francis Walker Gilmer, to Britain to ransack the universities of Oxford, Cambridge, and Edinburgh in search of first-rate scholars who would be willing to undertake the arduous journey to America. He also set in motion his powerful connections in England to help him get the professors he wanted.

To Samuel Parr, the eminent Oxford classicist, he wrote: "We are anxious to place in it none but professors of the first grade of science in their respective lines." And he asked him to assist Gilmer to find the men. To Dugald Stewart, the famous Scottish metaphysician, Jefferson made the same request in almost identical words—"anxious to receive [sic] none but of the highest grade of science in their respective lines."

After many troubles, Jefferson succeeded in assembling an excellent faculty of seven professors, only one of whom was a native American. This was John Tayloe Lomax of Virginia, who was given the chair of law. The others included George Tucker, a native of Bermuda, professor of moral philosophy; George Long of Cambridge, England, professor of ancient languages; George Blätterman, a German, professor of modern languages. Apart from these Georges, there were Thomas Hewitt Key, an Englishman, professor of mathematics; Charles Bonnycastle, also an Englishman, professor of natural Philosophy; and Robley Dunglison, likewise an Englishman, professor of anatomy and medicine. The salary of the professors was $1,500 a year, plus a rent-free house, plus a fee of $20 from each student.

One appointment only caused trouble. It was that of Thomas Cooper, a liberal-minded scientist. The clergy promptly raised what Jefferson called a "Hue and cry" against Cooper, and forced the Board of Visitors to cancel the appointment. Jefferson, furious at the "Holy Inquisition," as he called it, of the Virginia Presbyterians, was nevertheless unable to save Cooper, since the university was a tax-supported institution.

The university was scheduled to open on the first day of February, 1825, six years after it was begun. It was an exciting moment for Jefferson, who at the age of eighty-two was to see the last great dream of his life realized. But to his dismay three of the European professors did not arrive. He was so much upset that he exclaimed that he was "dreadfully nonplused"—a vigorous colloquialism that shows the depth of his agitation. The opening had to be postponed until March, by which time the professors had arrived, after a hazardous crossing. Jefferson received them warmly.

The old gentleman continued his keen interest in the university until the end. Two or three times weekly he invited the professors to dine at Monticello, and not only fed them good meals but also stimulated them with his rich and subtle conversation. Students were also invited to Monticello, especially on Sundays. They were awe-struck by the lively, thin, white haired gentleman, so tactful and so wise. When the students were at the table, Jefferson would eat by himself in a small recess in the dining-room, because, being a little deaf, he did not want to spoil the enjoyment of the young men while they were talking among themselves. There was nothing he would not do for these students, for they were the new generation that would carry on the things he believed in and the ideals he had labored for.

They did. Not only did the university students remember the founder with reverence, but they also went out into the world equipped to play their part. Jefferson sowed wisely, and the country reaped a rich harvest. From the red-brick class rooms of Jefferson's university there came, in the course of time, poets such as Edgar Allan Poe, scientists such as Walter Reed, and statesmen such as Woodrow Wilson. The founder would have been proud of this "multitude of fine young men."

8

Students and professors were not the only guests at Monticello. There were many others. The number of visitors was so constant and so great that in the end they practically ate Jefferson out of house and home. The specter of poverty began to haunt his remaining years. As early as 1814 he said to his grandson Thomas Jefferson Randolph, according to the latter, that "if he lived long enough he would beggar his family, that the number of persons he was compelled to entertain would devour his estate; many bringing letters from his ancient friends, and all coming with respectful feelings—he could not shut his door in their faces."

To maintain what amounted to a virtual hotel and to support his large family of grandchildren, cousins, in-laws, and all manner of kinsfolk, Jefferson had to resort to borrowing. There was little else that he could do. His farms brought in just about enough cash to pay taxes and interest. "Our means," he complained, "are ever absorbed as soon as received."

Debt and poverty began to weigh upon his old shoulders like an incubus. Despite the magnificent appearance of Monticello and the generous hospitality practiced there, evidences of poverty were visible all over the place. There were silver drinking cups on the table (marked "G.W.[4] to T.J."), but the chairs

---

[4] George Wythe, who had made Jefferson his heir.

had holes in them. "The first thing which attracted our attention," writes Francis Calley Gray, who visited Monticello in the winter of 1814, "was the state of the chairs. They had leather bottoms stuffed with hair, but the bottoms were completely worn through and the hair sticking out in all directions."

To raise money, Jefferson was ultimately driven to deprive himself of the things he cherished most—his books. After the British had burned Washington, including the books that belonged to the Government, in 1814, Jefferson offered to sell to the Congress his own private library. He had a magnificent collection of about ten thousand volumes, the fruit of fifty years of collecting in the book marts of Europe. Most of the books were bound, and many were rare items dealing with America. Jefferson offered his collection to Congress at any price that the latter thought fair. Fortunately for the country, Congress accepted, and paid Jefferson $25,000.[5] The money was a godsend, although the former President was able to keep only about one-third of it. More than $15,000 went to his creditors in Philadelphia and Georgetown.

Gradually he sank deeper into the morass of debt, and his chances of extricating himself from the financial swamp dimmed with the years. In 1819 a severe financial blow struck him. He had, with his customary generosity, endorsed a $21,200 debt of Wilson Cary Nicholas, one of his distant kinsmen. Nicholas failed, and Jefferson had no means whatever of paying that debt.

9

The future of Jefferson's large family of grandchildren was a constant worry. A few days before his eightieth birthday he drew up an account of his debts and his income. It was a discouraging birthday present. The balance sheet showed that Jefferson owed a total debt of $40,262.44 (including $5,250 to the Bank of the United States). The interest alone amounted to $2,121.90 in 1823. Since his farms brought him only $10,400 in that year, the interest alone consumed well over one-fifth of his income.

And all the while there was a growing family to support. Jefferson's daughter Martha, wife of Thomas Mann Randolph,

[5] Jefferson's collection formed the nucleus of the Library of Congress in Washington, which is today probably the greatest library in the world. Among the books were volumes on history, zoology, anatomy, surgery, medicine, technics, agriculture, botany, mineralogy, chemistry, physics, geography, geology, astronomy, mathematics, geometry, ethics, religion, law, politics, design, epics, romances, drama, rhetoric, oratory, criticism, philosophy, bibliography, and polygraphy. See the Jefferson Catalogue in the Library of Congress.

had eleven living children.[6] These children had children in turn. Anne Bankhead, one of Jefferson's grandchildren, had three sons and one daughter who lived near Monticello. Another grandchild, Thomas Jefferson Randolph, had seven offspring. The whole big family of grandchildren and great-grandchildren was centered around the adored figure of Jefferson. "Among these," he said at the age of seventy-seven, "I live like a patriarch of old."

Martha Jefferson Randolph, Jefferson's sole surviving child and matriarch of the whole family, was a remarkable woman; she resembled her father in many ways. She was blue-eyed, stately, cheerful, and nearly as tall as Jefferson. Like her father she was in the habit of humming a tune while working. From her father she acquired the habit of being constantly occupied. She had her father's happy disposition, his winning smile, and his imperturbability.

Jefferson's favorite was his namesake, Thomas Jefferson, Martha's oldest son. Upon that grandson, Jefferson (whose only son died in infancy) lavished all his affections. "Yourself particularly, dear Jefferson," the grandfather said to him, "I consider as the greatest of the Godsends which heaven has granted me." It was this same grandson who, after Jefferson's death, loyally assumed his grandfather's whole debt and in the course of time paid it off.

Grandson Thomas Jefferson was a colossus of a man, the delight not only of his grandfather but of all who beheld him. He was taller than his grandfather and physically as powerful as Jefferson's father, Colonel Peter. They certainly bred them big and strong in the mountains of Virginia. When the gigantic Thomas Jefferson Randolph visited Boston in the spring of 1826 and went to see his grandfather's old friend John Adams, little John Adams, a man of ninety-one, was greatly impressed with the size of the young Virginian. "How happens it," he wrote to Jefferson, "that you Virginians are all sons of Anak? We New Englanders are but pygmies by the side of Mr. Randolph."

Jefferson imbued his grandchildren with his own high moral standards. Once when he and grandson Thomas Jefferson were out riding, a colored man took off his hat and bowed. Jefferson returned the salute with the same grave courtesy, but his grandson ignored the colored man. Jefferson rebuked the boy: "Do you permit a Negro to be more of a gentleman than yourself?"

The grandchildren idolized him. They followed him around the grounds and garden, talking and playing. The old gentle-

[6] Jefferson himself named four of his male grandchildren after his friends—James Madison, Benjamin Franklin, Meriwether Lewis, and George Wythe. The oldest grandson was named Thomas Jefferson. The girls' names were Anne, Ellen, Cornelia, Virginia, Mary, and Septimia.

man directed their games and picked fruit for them with a stick to which was attached a hook and bag. He supervised the children's games and races. His favorite was the "stealing goods" game. The children would lay down their personal belongings —coats, hats, pocketknives—and then divide into two parties. The idea was for one group to try to steal from the other, and those who got caught were made prisoners. The old patriarch loved to watch that game, laughing heartily. He also liked to see the children run races around the lawn. He arranged the tots according to size and age, the youngest and smallest being given a head start. Jefferson held up a white handkerchief for a signal, and upon the count of three, they ran. The winner got fruit as a reward.

The children thought Grandfather adorable. And no wonder. He seemed to divine the secret longings of the little girls and the hidden ambitions of the boys, and lo, at the proper moment he fulfilled them. One little girl would suddenly receive from Grandfather a much-hoped-for silk dress, another an ardently desired guitar. According to the recollections of Virginia, one of the granddaughters:

> On winter evenings when it grew too dark to read, in the half hour which passed before candles came in, as we all sat round the fire, he taught us several childish games, and would play them with us. . . . When the candles were brought, all was quiet immediately, for he took up his book to read; and we would not speak out of a whisper, lest we should disturb him, and generally we followed his example and took a book; and I have seen him raise his eye from his own book, and look round on the little circle of readers and smile, and make some remark to mama about it.

10

Gradually the energies of the old philosopher slowed down, but only one of his senses, hearing, lost its strength. He concerned himself much with the state of his health, observing its slow, barely perceptible decline with the curiosity of a scientist. Although he dwelt frequently upon small attacks of illness, he was constantly surprised that his physical machinery was as good as it was. To the end of his days he had every tooth in his mouth.

When he was seventy-five, he gave, in a letter to Dr. Vine Utley, a curiously detached and full account of his physical condition and habits.

> I have lived temperately, eating little animal food, and that not as an aliment, so much as a condiment for the vegetables, which constitute my principal diet. I double, however, the Doctor's glass and a half of wine, and even treble it with a

friend; but halve its effects by drinking the weak wines only. The ardent wines I cannot drink, nor do I use ardent spirits in any form.[7] Malt liquors and cider are my table drinks, and my breakfast . . . is of tea and coffee. I have been blest with organs of digestion which accept and concoct, without ever murmuring, whatever the palate chooses to consign to them, and I have not yet lost a tooth by age.

I was a hard student until I entered on the business of life . . . and now, retired, and at the age of seventy-six, I am again a hard student. Indeed, my fondness for reading and study revolts me from the drudgery of letter writing. And a stiff wrist, the consequence of an early dislocation, makes writing both slow and painful. I am not so regular in my sleep . . . devoting to it from five to eight hours, according as my company or the book I am reading interests me; and I never go to bed without an hour, or half hour's previous reading of something moral, whereon to ruminate in the intervals of sleep. But whether I retire to bed early or late, I rise with the sun. I use spectacles at night, but not necessarily in the day, unless in reading small print. My hearing is distinct in particular conversation, but confused when several voices cross each other, which unfits me for the society of the table.

I have been more fortunate than my friend [Dr. Rush] in the article of health. So free from catarrhs that I have not had one (in the breast, I mean) on an average of eight to ten years through life. I ascribe this exemption partly to the habit of bathing my feet in cold water every morning, for sixty years past. A fever of more than twenty-four hours I have not had above two or three times in my life. A periodical headache has afflicted me occasionally, once, perhaps, in six or eight years, for two or three weeks at a time, which seems now to have left me. . . . I enjoy good health; too feeble, indeed, to walk much, but riding without fatigue six or eight miles a day, and sometimes thirty or forty.

He faced the inevitable future with the same philosophic objectivity as he observed the gradual slowing up of his body. He wrote William Short:

My business is to beguile the wearisomeness of declining life, as I endeavor to do, by the delights of classical reading and of mathematical truths, and by the consolations of a sound philosophy, equally indifferent to hope and fear.

The fire in him gradually died down. At the age of seventy-two he received a letter from the dim, dead past—it was from Maria Cosway, whom he had loved in Paris. Whether from love for Jefferson or for some other causes, the unhappy

---

[7] Jefferson always opposed hard liquor, believing it to be an enemy of health and society. He wished that people would drink wine rather than whisky. "I have . . . seen the loathsome and fatal effects of whisky, destroying the fortunes, the bodies, the minds & morals of our citizens," he wrote to William H. Crawford in 1818.

woman had long ago sought refuge in a convent. Jefferson did not reply to her letter for more than a year and a half, and when he did, it was in the form of a philosophic consolation: the religion you so sincerely profess," he wrote to the woman he had loved thirty-four years back, "tells us we shall meet again; and we have all so lived as to be assured it will be in happiness."

Sentimental emotions were only cold embers now. Even poetry, once a great passion, no longer interested him. "I have no imagination," he said at the age of eighty. And when Samuel Judah, a New York poet, sent him his works, Jefferson acknowledged the receipt politely and added—"the chill of 80 winters has so completely extinguished his [Jefferson's] sensibility to the beauties of poetry, as to leave him no longer competent either to enjoy or judge them."

He made an attempt, at the age of seventy-seven, to recapture his memories by putting them down on paper. On January 6, 1821, he began an autobiography with the following sentence: "At the age of 77, I begin to make some memoranda, and state some recollections of dates and facts concerning myself, for my own more ready reference, and for the information of my family." After writing about forty thousand words of autobiography, he gave up. He had, he said, an "invincible repugnance" to talk about himself, especially about his public activities. To his son-in-law John Wayles Eppes, he gave a further explanation:

> I am too old to begin any serious work. It had always been my intention to commit to writing some notes and explanations of particular and leading transactions, which history should know, but in parting with my library to Congress, I parted with my whole collection of newspapers, journals, state papers, documents, etc., without the aid of which I have been afraid to trust my memory.

In 1824 George Ticknor revisited Monticello and he was amazed to see how little change time had wrought in Jefferson's appearance. Browere's life mask, taken when Jefferson was eighty-two, corroborates Ticknor's description by showing Jefferson's face without a wrinkle. Ticknor wrote to his fellow historian, William H. Prescott:

> He is now eighty-two years old, very little altered from what he was ten years ago, very active, lively, and happy, riding . . . every day, and talking without the least restraint, very pleasantly, upon all subjects. In politics, his interest seems nearly gone . . . but on all matters of literature, philosophy, and general interest, he is prompt, and even eager. He reads much Greek and Saxon. I saw his Greek Lexicon, printed in 1817; it was much worn with use. . . .

Mr. Jefferson seems to enjoy life highly, and very rationally; but he said well of himself the other evening, "When I can neither read nor ride, I shall desire very much to make my bow."

11

The year 1824, when Jefferson had passed his eighty-first birthday, was memorable because of a visit from an old and cherished friend. It was the year when Lafayette made his triumphant tour of the United States. Jefferson looked forward to the visit of his friend with keen excitement. They had not seen each other for about thirty-five years, during which time the world had been through many revolutions and many wars.

Lafayette arrived at Monticello accompanied by an escort of Virginia gentlemen with Revolutionary banners. There was a fanfare of martial trumpets. The cavalcade stopped on the lawn in front of the portico where the thin, white-haired man was standing. As Lafayette got out of the carriage, Jefferson descended the steps of the portico. Jefferson could barely walk. Lafayette was lame. "As they approached each other," Thomas Jefferson Randolph recalls, "their uncertain gait quickened itself into a shuffling run, and exclaiming, 'Ah Jefferson!' 'Ah Lafayette!' they burst into tears as they fell into each other's arms." Hundreds of people witnessed the scene; there was not a dry eye among them.

The friends spent two happy weeks together. They had been through much, had done much, and the things they had to say to each other—on slavery, on South America, on democracy in Europe, on life and on death—were well-nigh inexhaustible.

Before his departure, Lafayette was given a banquet at Charlottesville. It was a memorable occasion because, among other eminent guests, there were present Jefferson, Madison, and President Monroe. Toasts were drunk to Lafayette and to Jefferson, and the latter delivered a speech by proxy. "My friends, I am old, long in the disuse of making speeches, and without voice to utter them." The brief and rare address praised Lafayette for all that he had done for the cause of American liberty, especially for the splendid aid he had given Jefferson in Paris:

> . . . this friend . . . was my most powerful auxiliary and advocate. He made our cause his own. . . . His influence and connections there were great. All doors of all departments were open to him at all times. . . . I only held the nail, he drove it. Honor him then.

Lafayette thought that there never was anybody like his friend Jefferson. He told a friend that the "history of the human race tells us of no one who has ever had a broader mind, a loftier soul, a stronger republicanism" than the Sage of Monticello.

Another visitor to Monticello a few months after the Frenchman was a chesty, massive, immaculately clad New England politician and orator whose name was Daniel Webster. Webster enjoyed Jefferson's generous hospitality and his frank talk for five days.[8] Afterward he put everything down on paper in minute detail.

Like other short men, Webster was particularly impressed by Jefferson's size. He described him as long, "thin and spare," with an expression full of "contentment and benevolence."

> His limbs are uncommonly long; his hands and feet very large, and his wrists of an extraordinary size. His walk is not precise and military, but easy and swinging. He stoops a little. . . . When sitting, he appears short, partly from a rather lounging habit of sitting, and partly from the disproportionate length of his limbs. . . . His general appearance indicates an extraordinary degree of health, vivacity, and spirit.

12

Financial worries were poisoning his last days. He was near bankruptcy and in danger of losing his home and his fields.[9] At the age of eighty-three he faced the terrifying prospect, not only of being without a home, but also of leaving his daughter and grandchildren utterly without means.

In February, 1826, on the eve of his eighty-third birthday, Jefferson wrote to Madison a letter that was a cry of pain. To pay his pressing debts, he proposed the idea of selling some of his properties around Monticello at auction. This was a practice resorted to before the Revolution, but now needed the approval of the legislature. If he could not get such permission, he explained to Madison, "I must sell everything here, perhaps considerably in Bedford, move thither with my family, where I have not even a log hut to put my head into." He was not sure, he added bitterly, that he would have left any "ground for burial."

He begged his old friend's pardon for troubling him with

[8] It was to Webster that Jefferson expressed his unflattering opinion of Andrew Jackson as a man "most unfit" for the Presidency. General Jackson, Jefferson said to Webster, "is a dangerous man." This was four years before Jackson was elected President.

[9] In November, 1826, Madison, in a letter to Lafayette, thus explained Jefferson's financial difficulties: "The expenses of his numerous household, his extensive hospitalities, and a series of short crops and low markets, to which are to be added old debts contracted in public service abroad and new ones for which private friendship had made him responsible; all these causes together, had produced a situation of which he seems not to have been fully aware, till it was brought home to his reflections by the calls of creditors."

these dreadful details. But to whom could he turn? His only consolation in these dark days was the knowledge that he and Madison had fought together for fifty years to build a democracy in America. He hoped that posterity would not forget them in the days to come.

> But why afflict you with these details? Indeed, I cannot tell, unless pains are lessened by communication with a friend. The friendship which has subsisted between us, now half a century, and the harmony of our political principles and pursuits, have been sources of constant happiness to me through that long period. . . . It has also been a great solace to me, to believe that you are engaged in vindicating to posterity the course we have pursued for preserving to them, in all their purity, the blessings of self-government, which we had assisted too in acquiring for them. If ever the earth has beheld a system of administration conducted with a single and steadfast eye to the general interest and happiness of those committed to it, one which, protected by the truth, can never know reproach, it is that to which our lives have been devoted. To myself you have been a pillar of support through life. Take care of me when dead, and be assured that I shall leave with you my last affections.

It was a farewell letter. This was the last time Jefferson communicated with his old friend.

To sell his lands through a lottery—a method that would enable him to retain Monticello and one farm—was, he said "a question of life and death." But there were doubts whether the legislature would authorize such a method of sale, and Jefferson was almost frantic with fear at the prospect of being thrown out of his home and left without any means of support. He wrote to his grandson Thomas Jefferson Randolph:

> You kindly encourage me to keep up my spirits. But oppressed with disease, debility, age, and embarrassed affairs, this is difficult. For myself I should not regard a prostration of fortune, but I am overwhelmed at the prospect of the situation in which I may leave my family. My dear & beloved daughter, the cherished companion of my early life and nurse of my age, and her children, rendered as dear to me as if my own from having lived with me from their cradle, left in a comfortless situation, hold up to me nothing but future gloom, and I should not care were life to end with the line I am writing, were it not that in the unhappy state of mind which your father's misfortunes have brought upon him I may yet be of some avail to the family. . . .
>
> Without you what could I do under the difficulties now environing me. This has been produced in some degree by my own unskillful management and devoting my life to the service of my country, but much also by the unfortunate fluctuations in the value of our money and the long continued depression of the farming business. But for these last I am confident my debts might be paid leaving me Monticello and the Bedford estate.

But where there are no bidders property however great offers no resource for the payment of debts.

A few days later the lottery bill was passed, with few dissenting votes. But it was not necessary. When news reached the outside world that the Sage of Monticello was in dire straits, offers of help came from every part of the Union. The country was deeply moved at the plight of the author of the Declaration of Independence. Mass meetings were held everywhere, North and South.[10] All over the nation people cried that it was a national shame that the old patriot should be allowed to be thrown out of his home in his old age. New York City raised $8,500 in no time. Philadelphia promptly collected $5,000. Baltimore citizens donated $3,000. Other cities contributed their share.

These spontaneous gifts from all parts of the country overjoyed the ailing old patriot. He had refused a gift from the State, but this was different. It was, he said, "the pure and unsolicited offering of love." Which it was. It was also perhaps the greatest tribute he had ever received—a vindication of his lifelong belief in the goodness of the people and his devotion to their cause. "I have spent three times as much money and given my whole life to my countrymen," he said, "and now they nobly come forward, in the only way they can, to repay me and save an old servant from being turned like a dog out of doors."

13

In February, 1826, Jefferson had a severe attack of diarrhea, but he minimized his pain in order not to alarm his family. He could not overcome his reluctance to being nursed, and would not have any member of the family watch in his room while he was sleeping. To reassure the anxious family, he tried to be up and about, and even to ride for a short time, pretending heroically that he was not gravely ill.

But he knew that he was dying. In the middle of March he drew up his will, writing the whole document in his own hand, clear, precise, and steady. The will bequeathed most of the real property to two of his grandsons, Francis Eppes and Thomas Jefferson Randolph. The latter was also given all of Jefferson's papers. A codicil to the will made the following provisions:

A gold-mounted walking staff of animal horn, to "my friend James Madison . . . as a token of the cordial and affectionate

10 In New York City, Mayor Philip Hone held a large public meeting "to take measures of relief, from debt, of Mr. Jefferson's estate." Another big meeting was held at historic Faneuil Hall, at Boston, to raise funds for "the relief of Mr. Jefferson." A mass meeting was also held at Richmond. See *Niles Weekly Register*, May 6, 1826, p. 172, and June 17, p. 281.

friendship which for nearly now an half century, has united us in the same principles and pursuits of what we have deemed for the greatest good of our country." His library (which he collected after the one he sold to the Congress) to the University of Virginia. A gold watch to each grandchild, to be given to the girls at the age of sixteen and the boys at twenty-one. To his personal colored servants Jefferson was particularly generous:

> I give to my good, affectionate, and faithful servant Burwell, his freedom, and the sum of three hundred Dollars to buy necessaries to commence his trade of painter and glazier, or to use otherwise as he pleases. I give also to my good servants John Hemings and Joe Fossett their freedom at the end of one year after my death: and to each of them respectively all the tools of their respective shops or callings: and it is my will that a comfortable log-house be built for each of the three servants so emancipated on some part of my lands convenient to them with respect to the residence of their wives.

Although he could barely move about, his mind retained its vigor undimmed. He read a great deal, especially the Greek dramatists (in the original) and the Bible. His speech was as vivacious and animated as usual.

Toward the end of June Jefferson grew worse. He reverted often to the scenes of the Revolution. Death he faced calmly. "Do not imagine for a moment," he said to his grandson, "that I feel the smallest solicitude about the result; I am like an old watch, with a pinion worn out here, and a wheel there, until it can go no longer." To the physician he said, "A few hours more, Doctor, and it will be all over."

Awakened from sleep by a noise in the room, he thought that it was the Reverend Mr. Hatch, the clergyman of the parish, who entered. He said: "I have no objection to see him, as a kind and good neighbor." His meaning was quite clear; he had no obections to Mr. Hatch as a neighbor, but did not want his visit as a clergyman.

The last visitor was Henry Lee, the son of General Henry Lee. Martha Randolph told him that he could not see her father, but Jefferson overruled her. Lee was surprised at the sick man's energy and lively conversation. "He talked of the freshet which was then prevailing in the James river—of its extensive devastation. . . . He soon, however, passed to the university, expatiated on its future utility . . . commended the professors, and expressed satisfaction at the progress of the students."

The conversation shifted to the imminence of death. Jefferson referred to it calmly, "as a man would to the prospect of being caught in a shower—as an event not to be desired, but not to be feared." Always the host, he asked his visitor to stay for dinner. Lee was reluctant. "You *must* dine here," Jefferson said with a touch of impatience, "my sickness makes no difference."

On July 2 he called in his family for a final farewell. He spoke with calm composure, as if he were leaving on a short journey. Pursue virtue, be loyal, be true, were his parting admonitions. One of his little grandsons, a boy of eight, was seemingly bewildered at the solemn scene. The dying man turned to the boy's older brother with a smile: "George does not understand what all this means."

He took a private and deeply moving farewell of his beloved daughter Martha. This was in the form of a brief poem, which was in a little casket that he handed her:

A DEATH-BED ADIEU FROM TH. J. TO M.R.

Life's visions are vanished, its dreams are no more;
　　Dear friends of my bosom, why bathed in tears?
I go to my fathers: I welcome the shore
　　Which crowns all my hopes or which buries my cares.
Then farewell, my dear, my lov'd daughter, adieu!
The last pang of life is in parting from you!
Two seraphs await me long shrouded in death; [11]
I will bring them your love on my last parting breath.

He slept through the night, and when he awoke he remarked, "this is the Fourth of July." It was only the third. He was fighting with every ounce of his ebbing energy to live until the Fourth of July. When Dr. Robley Dunglison came in the morning to give him his medicine (laudanum), Jefferson said in a husky and indistinct voice, "Ah! Doctor, are you still there?" Then he asked, "Is this the Fourth?" Dr. Dunglison replied, "It soon will be."

The night of July 3-4 he was partly delirious. He went through the motions of writing, and muttered about the Committee of Public Safety and that it should be warned. At eleven o'clock in the morning of July 4 his lips moved, and his grandson Thomas Jefferson Randolph, who did not leave his bedside, applied a wet sponge to his mouth. Then the sick man lost consciousness.

Death came to him two hours later, fifty minutes past noon of the Fourth of July, 1826. It was fifty years, to the day, after the Declaration of Independence.

At that moment, throughout the length and breadth of the

[11] This refers to his wife and daughter Maria.

United States, the people were celebrating the fiftieth anniversary of independence. At that moment, hundreds of thousands of people were listening to thousands of Fourth of July orations. In every town bells were ringing and cannon were booming.

At that moment, in Quincy, Massachusetts, John Adams was dying. He did not know that his friend at Monticello had already gone. "Thomas Jefferson still survives," Adams exclaimed, and with these words on his lips he died.

It was a rainy day when they buried Thomas Jefferson in the family plot near his wife. He had written his own epitaph. It was found in a drawer in his desk. Visitors to Monticello can read the words engraved on the gray granite obelisk over his grave:

> Here was Buried
> THOMAS JEFFERSON
> Author of the
> Declaration
> of
> American Independence
> of the
> Statute of Virginia
> for
> Religious Freedom
> and Father of the
> University of Virginia

This is all that he wanted to be remembered for.

Of the thousands of tributes that were paid to the departed patriot, the following are perhaps characteristic:

Secretary of the Navy Samuel L. Southard ordered that every navy yard and ship pay funeral honors to the "venerable Patriarch of the Revolution" by firing twenty-one guns and by lowering the flag at half-mast for a week.

And the true words as to Thomas Jefferson were pronounced by James Madison:

> . . . he lives and will live in the memory and gratitude of the wise & good, as a luminary of Science, as a votary of liberty, as a model of patriotism, and as a benefactor of human kind.

INDEX